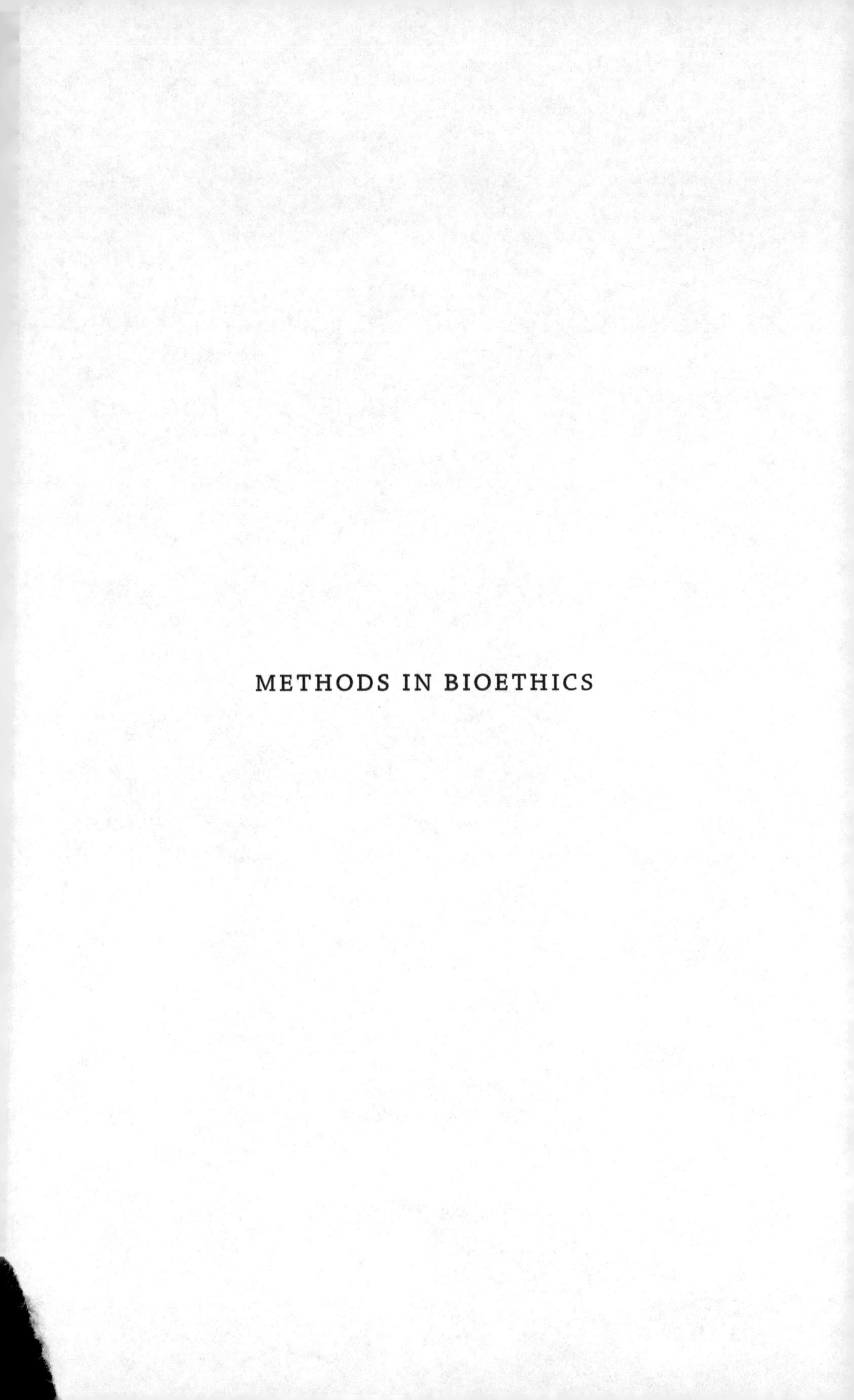

METHODS IN BIOETHICS

Methods in Bioethics

THE WAY WE REASON NOW

John D. Arras

Edited by
James Childress and Matthew Adams

Oxford University Press is a department of the University of Oxford. It furthers the University's objective of excellence in research, scholarship, and education by publishing worldwide. Oxford is a registered trade mark of Oxford University Press in the UK and certain other countries.

Published in the United States of America by Oxford University Press
198 Madison Avenue, New York, NY 10016, United States of America.

CIP data is on file at the Library of Congress
ISBN 978-0-19-066598-2

9 8 7 6 5 4 3 2 1
Printed by Sheridan Books, Inc., United States of America

To My Family:

My wife, Liz Emrey

My daughters, Melissa and Marina and their husbands, Mark and Jeff

My grandchildren, Luke, John, Grace, Gabriel and Alex

My brother, Dr. Ernest E. Arras, whose provocative and thoughtful discussions about bioethics sparked this book

"So I sat there and smoked my cigar until I fell into a reverie. Among others I recall these thoughts. You are getting on, I said to myself, and are becoming an old man without being anything, and without really taking on anything. Wherever you look about you on the other hand, in literature or in life, you see the names and figures of the celebrities, the prized and acclaimed making their appearances or being talked about, the many benefactors of the age who know how to do favours to mankind by making life more and more easy, some with railways, others with omnibuses and steamships, others with the telegraph ... then suddenly this thought flashed through my mind: You must do something, but since with your limited abilities it will be impossible to make anything easier than it has become, you must, with the same humanitarian enthusiasm as the others, take it upon yourself to make something more difficult. This notion pleased me immensely ..."

SOREN KIERKEGAARD, *trans.* Alastair Hannay, *Concluding Unscientific Postscript* (Cambridge: Cambridge University Press, 2009), 156–7.

Contents

Editorial Note

THE LATE JOHN D. ARRAS was a rigorous scholar, brilliant teacher, remarkable colleague, generous collaborator, eager and witty conversationalist, splendid human being, and a great friend to many. At the height of his powers, unbowed by an assortment of ailments, he died suddenly and unexpectedly on March 9, 2015, at age sixty-nine. At the time of his death, he was the William and Linda Porterfield Professor of Bioethics, Professor of Philosophy, Professor of Public Health Sciences, and a core faculty member of the Center for Biomedical Ethics and Humanities in the School of Medicine at the University of Virginia (UVA). He was also a long-time fellow of the Hastings Center, a major research center in bioethics.

A native Californian, John completed his undergraduate studies in philosophy and French at the University of San Francisco; his collegiate years included a year at the Institute of European Studies and University of Paris. He received his Ph.D. in philosophy from Northwestern University in 1972. While completing his doctorate, he and his wife, Liz Emrey, served as Peace Corps volunteers in Sierra Leone. After teaching philosophy at the University of Redlands for a decade, he taught bioethics at the Albert Einstein College of Medicine-Montefiore Medical Center in the Bronx for fourteen years.

In 1995, following a national search, John was appointed to the newly established Porterfield Chair in Bioethics at UVA. Given a mandate to develop an undergraduate program in bioethics, he did so with a flourish, involving faculty from several departments in building a model interdisciplinary program that earned the admiration of colleagues at UVA and elsewhere as well as the unstinting gratitude and devotion of legions of students.

John loved teaching and advising students, and he poured himself into these activities, which brought him wide recognition and many awards, but which, for him, were their own reward, a "kind of secular blessedness" and "as good as it gets." One student observed that "Professor Arras was willing to engage with students as if they have something important to say. More importantly, he would argue with you when he thought you were wrong." John cared deeply about students *and* their arguments, and they reciprocated.

This is also how he interacted with colleagues locally and beyond, in person, electronically, and in print. He thrived on vigorous and rigorous intellectual exchange, always tempered by his wry, self-deprecating humor, as well as by his genuine care and respect for fellow discussants.

John was a major contributor to public bioethics—that is, to the formulation of bioethical policies through public bodies; for instance, he was a long-time member of the New York State Task Force on Life and the Law. In 2010, President Obama appointed him to the newly formed Presidential Commission for the Study of Bioethical Issues. The chair of this commission, Amy Gutmann, a political philosopher and president of the University of Pennsylvania, offered a moving postmortem tribute:

> [John] brought out the very best in everyone who had the privilege and pleasure of working with and learning from him. For the past five years, we were honored to have John as a thoroughly engaged and beloved member of our [Commission]. . . .
>
> Even as he contended with more than his fair share of health challenges, John contributed far more than his share to our Commission's painstaking work. He had an unparalleled gift for bringing philosophical insight to thorny medical and scientific conundrums. Even that gift paled in comparison to John's wry, perfectly timed humor. Due in no small part to his flair for intellectual provocation—as feisty as it was friendly—our Commission rapidly became . . . something more than a commission. We became a fondly argumentative and loving extended family with John . . . "the lightning rod for many discussions."

Finally, John was a very productive and influential scholar. As the author of more than fifty journal articles and book chapters, he preferred, as his preface here indicates, "rumination over the adoption of hard and fast positions" and thus chose the essay as his preferred and "primary mode of expression," since it enabled him to keep "thinking . . . through new possibilities and foreseeing new problems." In addition, he edited or co-edited several books, including, most recently, *Emergency Ethics: Public Health Preparedness and Response*, which Oxford University Press published in 2016.

A few weeks before his death, John sent Peter Ohlin, his editor at Oxford University Press, the manuscript of his long-awaited *magnum opus*, at the time telling his wife, "I can die now—I finished my book." This is that book, a volume that collects and integrates his finely wrought critical essays—his ruminations—on methods in bioethics. While still at work on the book, he explored several different working titles, one being *The Way We Reason Now: Skeptical Reflections on Methods in Bioethics*. Although skeptical about methods and theories in bioethics—at least about those claiming to be definitive and final—John never doubted the importance of thinking about and actively pursuing social justice, a commitment he expressed in many different ways, including his stint in the Peace Corps.

After John's death, independent reviewers of his manuscript recommended its publication but, as is common, suggested a few revisions. After discussion with the editor and with Liz Emrey, John's widow, I agreed to take responsibility for making editorial changes in response to those suggestions. Happily, Matthew Adams, an outstanding graduate student in UVA's Department of Philosophy, who had been working with John on the manuscript when it was submitted, agreed to join me as co-editor. For both of us, this was a way to remember and honor John.

The reader may be curious about the editorial changes we have made. They include the reversing of John's latest title and subtitle in order to indicate more clearly the book's major focus; combining three original chapters on pragmatism and bioethics into two chapters (now chapters 5 and 6); reducing redundancy across chapters, which resulted from their origin as separate, discrete essays; inserting a few bridging and connecting devices among the chapters; revising the language in places in order to remove potentially distracting temporal identifiers (e.g., "five years ago," when the time elapsed has actually been much longer); completing footnotes and standardizing their form from chapter to chapter; and so forth. Throughout, our goal as editors has been to be as faithful as possible to John's work. This has meant addressing the reviewers' concerns, as well as any questions that emerged for us, as we believe John would have done had he lived to prepare the final manuscript for publication.

We made one major change that we had not anticipated: the deletion of two original chapters, entitled "Bioethics and Human Rights: Curb Your Enthusiasm" and "Philosophical Theory in Bioethics." As we worked through the book, we concluded that the volume would work better without these essays. The chapter on human rights less clearly addressed methodological matters than did the others, while the chapter on theory was less complete and helpful on the specific subject of method in bioethics. With omission of these chapters, John's book is more cohesive and more sharply focused on methods in bioethics. Interested readers are invited to read these essays elsewhere.*

John's individual chapters—and his overall argument—are impressive. This is his *magnum opus*, carefully and lovingly developed in his preferred form, the essay, over many years. Each essay, now a chapter (or combined into chapters), clearly, elegantly, precisely, and often wittily addresses some method or methods in bioethics. Individually, and even more so in this integrated collection, the essays contribute significantly to debates about methods in bioethics. No one seriously reflecting on methods in bioethics can fail to engage with John's analyses and critiques.

As the ellipses at the end suggest, John's preface was left incomplete. It lacked his acknowledgments because he expected to add these details later in the process of preparing the book for publication.

Because most of the book's essays are based on and incorporate previously published articles or chapters, we are greatly indebted to the journals and publishers, listed below, for permission to use these earlier writings in revised form.

Chapters 1 and 2 incorporate major sections from Arras, "The Hedgehog and the Borg: Common Morality in Bioethics," *Theoretical Medicine* 30, no. 1 (2009): 11–30, with permission from Springer.

Chapter 3 originally appeared as "Getting Down to Cases: The Revival of Casuistry in Bioethics," *Journal of Medicine and Philosophy* 16, no. 1 (1991): 29–51.

Chapter 4 reprints, with revisions, "Nice Story, But So What?: Narrative and Justification in Ethics," is from *Stories and Their Limits: Narrative Approaches to Bioethics*, ed. Hilde Nelson (New York: Routledge, 1997), 65–88, with the permission of the Taylor & Francis Group, LLC.

Chapter 5 combines major sections from two of Arras's previously published articles: "Rorty's Pragmatism and Bioethics," *Journal of Medicine and Philosophy* 28, nos. 5–8 (Fall 2003): 597–613; and "Pragmatism in Bioethics: Been There, Done That," *Journal of Social Philosophy & Policy* 19, no. 2 (2002): 29–58. Cambridge University Press has granted permission to republish materials from the latter.

Chapter 6 originated as "Freestanding Pragmatism in Law and Bioethics," *Theoretical Medicine* 22, no. 2 (2001): 69–85, and is reprinted here with some revisions by permission of Springer.

* We direct interested readers to Arras and Elizabeth Fenton, "Bioethics and Human Rights: Curb Your Enthusiasm," *Cambridge Quarterly of Healthcare Ethics* 19, no. 1 (2010): 127–133, 141–150; and to Arras, "Theory and Bioethics," in *Stanford Encyclopedia of Philosophy*, first published May 18, 2010; http://plato.stanford.edu/entries/theory-bioethics/.

Chapter 7 republishes "A Method in Search of a Purpose: The Internal Morality of Medicine," *Journal of Medicine and Philosophy* 26, no. 6 (2001): 643–662.

An earlier version of Chapter 8 was "Reflective Equilibrium in Bioethics," as it appeared in *Oxford Handbook of Bioethics*, ed. Bonnie Steinbock (New York: Oxford University Press, 2007), 46–71.

Chapter 9 is new for this book.

Besides these acknowledgments, Liz Emrey, John's widow, reported John's gratitude to the Bioethics Center at Otago University, in Dunedin, New Zealand, for giving him the resources and time to complete this book; to the Presidential Commission for the Study of Bioethical Issues, on which he served from 2010 until his death; to the bioethics community at UVA; and to William and Linda Porterfield, the donors of the funds for the UVA professorship he held for twenty years. Finally, John greatly appreciated the assistance of Matthew Adams in the preparation of his manuscript.

I too am grateful to Matthew Adams for joining me as co-editor on this book and particularly for his valuable suggestions and for implementing some revisions along lines he had previously discussed with John.

James F. Childress

June 20, 2016

Preface

I AM NOT a writer of books; I am, rather, a writer of longish, convoluted articles. That seems to be my natural milieu and métier. I have, however, harbored for quite some time now a desire to gather together between two covers all my far-flung papers on the theme of method in bioethics, both to make access to them easier for whatever misguided readers I might have and to provide me with an opportunity to reread, rethink, and partially rewrite many of them.

But since I'm not a book guy, this desire has not been particularly strong. At many moments during the past twenty years I have muttered to myself, "OK, it's time to do that book," but no sooner do I say this than I discern out of the corner of my eye some new and alluring methodological development in bioethics—e.g., pragmatism and reflective equilibrium—that commands my attention for a long time and abruptly shoves the book to the back burner.

I am happy to report here and now, however, that my procrastinating days are over. A delightful and productive sabbatical leave at the Bioethics Centre, University of Otago in New Zealand, provided me with the requisite leisure and stimulating company to kick-start the book project in earnest; and the progress that I made there inspired me to finish the job after my return to Charlottesville.

So, what's my take on method in bioethics? Since I've been writing about this issue for so long, people often ask for my settled view on method, for "my position." Am I a moral theorist? A principlist? Casuist? Narrativist? Pragmatist?

Reflective equilibrator? What? This is a good question, one for which I almost wish I had a ready and pithy answer. Unlike many of my academic colleagues who take an interest in such questions, I fancy myself to be more a ruminator than a committed defender of any given method. I tend to chew on various methodological approaches for a long time, attempting to appreciate both what's new, exciting, and fruitful, and what's potentially problematic or limiting in each of them. I think that just about any ethical theory or methodological approach worth its salt both expands and occludes our field of vision. The revival of casuistry by Jonsen and Toulmin in the 1980s, for example, proved to be a welcome antidote to tiresome and self-deluded top-down, deductivist modes of bioethical reasoning inspired by the dominant "principlist" paradigm of Beauchamp and Childress. But casuistry's exclusive focus on analogical precursors of the case at hand could render it insensitive or blind to possible bad policy consequences if deployed in the unjust world that we inhabit.

My preference for rumination over the adoption of hard-and-fast positions is echoed in my choice of the essay as my primary mode of expression. In this I follow Michel de Montaigne, one of my intellectual heroes, who modestly titled his monumental and deep reflections on the human condition *essais*. At the time Montaigne was composing this masterpiece during the French Renaissance, the word *essai* did not carry the established meaning that it has for us—i.e., any relatively short piece of writing on a non-fictional topic. For him, and for me, it means "an attempt," not some sort of closed, definitive statement or system. The essayist is trying something out. In my case, I'm trying out, or trying on for size, a wide variety of methods applicable to practical ethics. The spirit hovering over these essays is a kind of experimentalism, the tentative search for new and interesting possibilities of ethical insight. Dogmatism, the tenacious and single-minded defense of a way of interpreting the moral life, is the antithesis of my idea of the *essai*. For me, for better and for worse, this intricate process of "trying on" various modes of interpretation is where the real meat of this book lies. I am much less interested in where I end up, and even less interested in slapping some label on my tentative conclusions, than I am in the process of thinking itself, of working through new possibilities and foreseeing new problems.

Before we get going, a word might be in order addressing the limits or shortcomings of this project. "Methods of ethical thought" encompass a vast territory of normative and conceptual developments. As a finite human being with limited time, energy, competence, and interests, I have generally tried to cover as many bases as possible, but there are some salient lacunae. While I have always found much of interest and importance in the feminist literature, I have never, apart from a passing reference, felt compelled to contribute to it. Part of the problem might be that I have naturally looked to women scholars, such as Margaret Urban Walker, to blaze this particular trail, and they have done so admirably without needing any help from the likes of me. Although I count myself among the appreciators of much (but not all) of this literature, I have never felt that I had as much to add to it as I've had with the methods canvassed in this book.

Another gap in this account is the absence of commentary relating to the advent of empirical methods in bioethics. In the chapters on pragmatism, I note the importance of empirical studies to demonstrate the social relevance of bioethical theories and to generate new hypotheses. Do our labored theoretical findings on various issues actually make a difference in the real world? We won't know until we do empirical studies. Are there unidentified ethical problems embedded in the way we carry out various social policies—e.g., regarding the treatment of nursing home patients? We won't know until we do the empirical work. We need, in other words, something like a diffuse bioethical analogue of the General Accountability Office (GAO)[†] that assesses the performance of bioethics-related policies and practices. Unfortunately, as an inveterate armchair philosopher (albeit one who spent fourteen years deeply embedded in an academic medical context), I quite simply lack the skills to assess, let alone undertake, this emerging body of socially necessary research. So I leave this task to others with the appropriate background in the conduct of empirical research, trial design, and statistics. . . .

John D. Arras
February 2015

[†] Disclosure: My daughter, Melissa Emrey-Arras, is director of education, workforce, and income security at GAO.

1

Principlism

THE BORG OF BIOETHICS

HISTORICAL BACKGROUND

Though the field of bioethics is relatively young, it has generated and sustained, right from the start, an unusually self-conscious debate about its own methods. The focal point in this prolonged debate has been the "principlism" of Tom Beauchamp and James Childress, as articulated in their increasingly magisterial work, *The Principles of Biomedical Ethics* (henceforth *PBE*) (1979, 1983, 1989, 1994, 2001, 2009, 2013).[1] Eschewing both high-flying philosophical theory and low-lying particularist approaches, the principlism of Beauchamp and Childress situates itself in the middle of this spectrum, focusing on the mid-level normative principles of autonomy, beneficence, nonmaleficence, and justice. Whether one has been a proponent or a critic of this approach, there's no denying that it has profoundly shaped the field of bioethics and set the terms of the debate over methods.

In this chapter I'll provide a primer on the nature of principlism, its principal elements, and some of its transformational adaptations to criticism since the

[1] There are other influential "principlist" approaches to bioethics, most notably those of Robert Veatch and H. Tristram Engelhardt Jr. Although these authors have made major contributions to the field of bioethics in general, and to its methodological debates in particular, I shall mention them only in passing insofar as their approaches differ from the principlism of Beauchamp and Childress. See R. Veatch, "Resolving Conflicts Among Principles: Ranking, Balancing, and Specifying," *Kennedy Institute of Ethics Journal* 5 (1995): 199–218. See also T. Engelhardt, *Foundations of Bioethics*, 2nd ed. (New York: Oxford University Press, 1991).

first edition of *PBE*. These often fundamental transformations make it difficult to talk about *the* "nature of principlism," a method that presents the critic with a moving target.

Before getting down to business, we should acknowledge the intellectual virtues of principlism's avatars, Beauchamp and Childress. We're all familiar with a certain academic style of studied intransigence with regard to the defense of one's own pet theories. No matter how deafening or devastating the criticisms, the true believing scholars plunge ahead, ignoring their critics, forever embellishing their beloved pile of theoretical wreckage until death finally relieves them of this awesome responsibility.[2] Beauchamp and Childress, by contrast, have positively welcomed criticisms and have made strenuous efforts to acknowledge and accommodate them. To borrow a line from Hegel, ever since the first edition of *PBE*, its authors have been "educating themselves in public," providing their vast readership with an object lesson in the value of the free exchange of ideas. As J. S. Mill famously observed, criticism is vital to the intellectual enterprise.[3] It will reveal the falsehood or inadequacy of some of our ideas (we hope not all) while strengthening our true beliefs. Through vigorous and mutually respectful engagement with opposing voices, Beauchamp and Childress have maintained the intellectual vitality of their project unto to its seventh edition, even if they haven't convinced all their critics.

The open-mindedness and generosity of Beauchamp and Childress with regard to their many critics bring to mind the Borg in the science fiction series *Star Trek, The Next Generation*. A hive of cybernetically enhanced humanoids, the Borg explore the universe in search of interesting new cultures and technologies, which they promptly conquer and incorporate into their neural network en route to their goal of ultimate perfection.[4] Upon encountering an alien culture, the Borg ominously announce, "Resistance is futile, you will be assimilated." Many of Beauchamp and Childress's critics know the feeling. No sooner do they launch a seemingly crippling broadside against the juggernaut of *PBE* from a casuist, narrativist, feminist, or pragmatist perspective than their critique is promptly welcomed with open arms, trimmed of its perceived excesses, and incorporated into the ever-expanding synthesis of the next edition.

---

[2] One example of this intransigent academic style is the life and work of the libertarian psychiatrist Thomas Szasz (1920–2012), author of *The Manufacture of Madness* (New York: Syracuse University Press, 1997). For a devastating if unacknowledged book review, see H. Morris, *UCLA Law Review* 18 (1971): 1164–1172.

Another more poignant and disturbing example—for me, at least, since it relates to one of my intellectual heroes—is Hannah Arendt's refusal to acknowledge or address any criticisms of her highly controversial (and in my view brilliant but deeply flawed) book, *Eichmann in Jerusalem* (New York: Viking, 1963).

[3] J. S. Mill, *On Liberty*.

[4] See http://en.wikipedia.org/wiki/Borg_Queen#Borg_Queen. In making this comparison, I in no way mean to imply here that Beauchamp and Childress are humanoid cyborgs. They are friends; I would know. Well, maybe Beauchamp. . . .

In order to comprehend the enormous impact of *PBE* on the emerging world of bioethics, we need to go back to its origins in the 1970s, when moral theologians first staked out the emerging moral terrain of medicine in the modern era. Prior to the advent of *PBE*, what we would now call the field of bioethics was launched by two diametrically opposed moral theologians, Joseph Fletcher and Paul Ramsey. Fletcher was a "situation ethicist" who preached a doctrine of Christian love as applied to each moral action or policy. Closely allied to the act-utilitarian position in moral theory, Fletcher urged moral agents to perform that act or institute that policy that would maximize love in any given context. In Fletcher's hands, this approach provided a moral warrant for the vast expansion of biotechnology in partnership with God's creative works. For example, Fletcher was a zealous proponent of genetic engineering, calling for the "end of genetic roulette."[5] Ramsey, by contrast, was a rather stern but eloquent and rigorous defender of a Christian covenantal moral theology based upon strict adherence to moral rules derived from a biblical conception of our relationship with God. Whereas Fletcher could easily be translated into an act-utilitarian idiom, Ramsey could (with a bit more difficulty) be rendered in terms of Kantian deontological moral imperatives. And whereas Fletcher never met a technology he didn't like, Ramsey wrote like an Old Testament scourge against abortion, euthanasia, and assisted reproduction.[6]

But in spite of their manifest differences, both Fletcher and Ramsey based their respective positions on Christian moral theology, and here lay the rub. Having effectively launched this fledgling field, neither of these moral theologians could offer the citizens of a pluralistic, secular society a common moral framework through which each person, Christian or not, could advance arguments in the public square. This would prove to be a task for which principlism was ideally suited. Relatively insouciant regarding the ultimate provenance of their mid-level principles, Beauchamp and Childress were confident that most people could agree on a short list of norms that could provide a nonsectarian framework for moral discussion and debate. Indeed, in making this claim the authors underscored the significance of the fact that Beauchamp considered himself to be a rule-utilitarian, while Childress identified himself as a Christian deontologist.[7] In spite of this disagreement bearing on the source of our norms, they could agree, *inter alia*, upon the importance of the principle of autonomy for informed consent, the principle of nonmaleficence in the research context, and the principle of justice in debates over universal access to health care.

[5] J. Fletcher, *The Ethics of Genetic Control: Ending Reproductive Roulette* (New York: Prometheus, 1974).

[6] P. Ramsey, *Fabricated Man: The Ethics of Genetic Control* (New Haven, CT: Yale University Press, 1970).

[7] T. Beauchamp and J. F Childress, *Principles of Biomedical Ethics*, 1st ed. (Oxford: Oxford University Press, 1979), 40.

The method of principlism thus filled a big void. No-nonsense clinicians, inherently suspicious of loose talk about "values" and "ethics," valued this method's ability to lend structure and at least a patina of objectivity to moral discussions with and about their patients. Biomedical researchers and their regulators embraced principlism as articulated in their founding document, *The Belmont Report*,[8] on which Beauchamp and Childress had collaborated with members of the President's Commission in 1978.[9] To this day, *Belmont* remains the *vade mecum* of researchers, Institutional Review Board members, regulators, and policymakers everywhere. Even academics could put to one side their disagreements about deep theory and focus on making headway on the analysis of a broad range of front-burner moral problems in medicine.[10]

Looking back, the triumph of principlism turned out to be a good thing for the field of bioethics, although, as always, blessings tend to be mixed. Although it delivered, as promised, a serviceable moral framework for the civil and reasonable discussion of moral issues—no mean feat—this method did have a dark side. In addition to many legitimate philosophical problems, to be discussed in detail below, principlism often suffered from the excessive and untutored enthusiasm of its epigones. Although Beauchamp and Childress never promised anything more than a useful framework for justifying ethical judgments, and certainly not an algorithm for cranking out univocally correct answers to complex and vexing moral questions, their less morally literate followers often choked the medical literature with papers flatly declaring that this or that principle of bioethics provided the unique solution to this or that problem.[11] Exactly how it did this was often left unexplained and under-analyzed. As J. S. Mill astutely pointed out, however, any moral theory will work badly if we assume universal idiocy to be conjoined to it.[12]

---

[8] *Belmont Report: Ethical Principles and Guidelines for the Protection of Human Subjects of Research, Report of the National Commission for the Protection of Human Subjects of Biomedical and Behavioral Research* (1979). Available at www.hhs.gov/ohrp/humansubjects/guidance/belmont.html.

[9] For discussion, see A. R. Jonsen, "On the Origins and Future of the *Belmont Report*," and T. L. Beauchamp, "The Origins and Evolution of the *Belmont Report*," in *Belmont Revisited: Ethical Principles for Research with Human Subjects*, eds. J. F. Childress, et al. (Washington, DC: Georgetown University Press, 2005), 3–25.

[10] See J. H. Evans, "A Sociological Account of the Growth of Principlism," *Hastings Center Report* 30, no. 5 (2000): 31–38.

[11] This tendency toward a mechanistic and simplistic deployment of principlism inspired me—I believe I was the first—to coin the phrase "the Georgetown mantra of bioethics" in a lecture on method in bioethics at the University of Texas Medical Branch, Galveston, 1986. Georgetown University was for a short time the home of both Beauchamp and Childress during these formative years of bioethics. After spending four years at Georgetown University, Childress returned to the University of Virginia in 1979.

[12] J. S. Mill, *Utilitarianism*, ch 2.

THE ESSENTIALS OF PRINCIPLISM

What, then, *is* principlism of *PBE*? What are its core defining features, subject to our proviso about principlism being a moving target? First, there's the claim that the "spine of moral reasoning"[13] and our locus of moral certitude, such as we can ever obtain, reside in four normative principles.[14]

Inventory of Relevant Principles

(1) Autonomy—The value of self-direction with regard to the shape and direction of one's life and moral choices. Autonomy provides the moral core of the doctrine of informed consent in clinical medicine and biomedical research, as well as the moral foundation of many theories of reproductive ethics, medical privacy, access to health services, and many other areas of bioethical concern. It echoes Kant's categorical admonition against treating persons "merely as means" and grounds the Belmont Report's pivotal principle of "respect for persons."

(2) Beneficence—The value of advancing the welfare of other persons, enhancing their capabilities for fulfillment and alleviating their sufferings. Beneficence provides the moral foundation of the entire practice of medicine and the enterprise of biomedical research.

(3) Nonmaleficence—An unfortunately and excessively Latinate expression for the disvalue of harm and the derivative moral norm to avoid imposing harms on others. A better expression might have been, simply, "the harm principle."[15] This principle famously undergirds the venerable Hippocratic tradition in medicine via the maxim, "First do no harm" (*Primum non nocere*).

(4) Justice—At its most abstract, this principle bids us to "give each person his or her due," and treat like cases alike. More helpfully, especially in bioethics, it relates to fairness or equity in the distribution of goods, such as access to health care, and the fair sharing of the benefits and burdens of participation in biomedical research. Since there are actually several theories of social justice, many of them serving up contradictory

[13] T. Beauchamp, personal communication.

[14] The following account of Beauchamp and Childress's principles is, of course, grossly oversimplified. They devote entire chapters to each one.

[15] See J. Feinberg, *Harm to Others* (New York: Oxford University Press, 1987).

conclusions, talk of a single principle of justice has to be taken with a large grain of salt.[16]

Monism vs. Pluralism

The first thing to notice about this short list of moral principles is that it comprises a plurality of principles rather than a single, overarching master principle, such as J. S. Mill's principle of utility or Kant's categorical imperative. The authors thereby distance themselves from what Annette Baier calls "vaulting" moral theories that feature a capstone principle at the pinnacle of a theoretical structure, which then informs all moral judgments below it in deductive fashion.[17] The theoretical advantage of such an approach is that it could promise to resolve all conflicts among subsidiary and seemingly conflicting moral principles. Thus, when faced with apparently irresolvable conflicts between various maxims relating to just distributions emanating from our common morality—for example, to each according to his or her effort, or need, or moral desert, or contributions to society, etc.—Mill insisted that within his system all such principles were merely handy maxims that could usually point us in the direction of achieving maximal utility, and that conflicts among them could be neatly resolved by appealing to the ultimate principle of utility. The decisive downside of this approach, however, was that its promise of moral simplicity could not be redeemed. Such theories tended to obscure the inherent complexity and heterogeneity of values in our moral lives and the often tragic ways in which the things, people, and projects we value can conflict with one another.

The Moral Valence of Principles

Another salient feature of Beauchamp and Childress's principles is their moral valence or binding force. There are three possibilities here. First, moral principles might be regarded as mere rules of thumb—much like the "rule" to hit to your opponent's backhand in tennis—or as mere summaries of previous decisions regarding similar cases. Such principles lack genuinely normative force. Yes, one should generally hit to an opponent's backhand, but not if your opponent is Serena Williams. One doesn't say: "Darn, I realize I should have hit to Serena's backhand,

[16] In the words of Alasdair MacIntyre, one might well ask, "Whose Justice, Which Rationality?" See A. MacIntyre, *Whose Justice? Which Rationality?* (South Bend, IN: Notre Dame University Press, 1988).

[17] See A. Baier, "What Do Women Want in a Moral Theory?" *Nous* 19 (1985): 53–63.

and I really feel bad about going to her forehand instead, but I had no choice. My bad." Likewise, one doesn't say, "We have tended in the past to do *X* in situations of type *Y*, but this instance of *Y* called for us to do *Z*. We feel bad about that." Such "principles" lack normative force. A good example of their deployment in ethics is the "situation ethics" of Joseph Fletcher, who wrote:

> Whether we ought to follow a moral principle or not would always depend upon the situation. . . . In some situations unmarried love could be infinitely more moral than married unlove. Lying could be more Christian than telling the truth. . . . [S]tealing could be better than respecting private property. . . . [N]o action is good or right of itself. It depends on whether it hurts or helps people. . . . There are no normative moral principles whatsoever which are intrinsically valid or universally obliging. We may not absolutize the norms of human conduct. . . . Love is the highest good and the first-order value, the primary consideration to which in every act . . . we should be prepared to sidetrack or subordinate other value considerations of right and wrong.[18]

This approach to ethical norms bears a striking resemblance to the moral particularism of some contemporary ethical theorists, such as Jonathan Dancy.[19]

A second possibility is that moral principles should be viewed as being always and everywhere *absolutely* binding. In stark contrast to the particularist's claim that moral principles lack a constant moral valence or binding power, moral absolutists contend that at least some moral principles should always bind moral agents and that exceptions to such principles are not permitted. Kant and many religious ethicists hold that some sorts of actions are intrinsically wrong—e.g., because they violate the categorical imperative or god's law—and, in stark contrast to Fletcher's approach, they rule out making exceptions on consequentialist grounds. If lying is wrong, it's wrong to lie to Nazis; if stealing is wrong, it's wrong to steal a loaf of bread to nourish one's starving family. This account gives moral principles real binding force, but perhaps too much. Ruling out the violation of moral principles in these hypothetical cases will strike most people as a kind of pointless rule fetishism rather than a credible approach to ethics.

The third possibility, and the one adopted by Beauchamp and Childress, is to view moral principles as being binding *prima facie* (at first blush) or *pro tanto* (as far as they go). That is, moral principles are viewed as truly binding whenever they are relevant to a situation, unless and until one or more additional regulative principles

[18] J. Fletcher, *Situation Ethics: The New Morality* (Philadelphia: The Westminster Press, 1966).

[19] See, e.g., J. Dancy, *Ethics Without Principles* (New York: Oxford University Press, 2006).

enter our field of moral action, possibly thereby tipping the scales in another direction. To use a metaphor with which Beauchamp and Childress have become increasingly uncomfortable, we say in such cases that one principle "outweighs" another.

For example, psychiatrists have a solemn duty to respect and maintain the confidentiality of their patients. This duty is based on the principles of both autonomy and nonmaleficence. Patients should have the right to share or conceal personal information about themselves as they see fit, and revealing such sensitive information to others without permission can definitely be construed as a harm to the patient. The principles of autonomy and nonmaleficence thus have *prima facie* dominance within the psychiatrist–patient relationship. But now, what if a particular patient threatens to harm or even kill another person, as happened in the famous *Tarasoff* case?[20] As Beauchamp and Childress note in their discussion of this case, the *prima facie* bindingness of the principles of autonomy and nonmaleficence may well be eclipsed or outweighed by countervailing concerns about preventing serious and highly predictable harms to others.[21]

The Structure (or Lack Thereof) of Moral Principles

We noted above that the principlism of Beauchamp and Childress is pluralistic in the sense that they settle upon a plurality of moral norms rather than establishing any one Über-norm in the manner of Fletcher's appeal to Love, J. S. Mill's appeal to utility, or Kant's categorical imperative. There is another sense in which their approach is pluralistic: *viz*., their insistence that the four principles not be ranked in some *a priori* or serial fashion. In contrast to philosophers who yearn for a tidy listing of principles in the order of their relative priority—e.g., one principle to rule them all, subsidiary principles governing the norms immediately below them, and so on, all the way down[22]—Beauchamp and Childress stress the moral complexity of the situations we face, which makes it quite problematic to say that any given principle should *always* have priority over some others. While the authors of

[20] *Tarasoff v. Regents of the University of California*, 17 Cal. 3d 425, 551 P.2d 334, 131 Cal. Rptr. 14 (Cal. 1976).

[21] Beauchamp and Childress, *PBE*, 1st ed. (1979), 210–217.

[22] See, e.g., John Rawls rejection of so-called intuitionistic approaches to principles according to which the weight of competing principles must be determined *in medias res*, in favor of what he (idiosyncratically) refers to as a preferred "lexical" ordering of his principles of justice. Thus, the principle of equal liberty has *a priori* priority over principles determining the distribution of social and economic goods, and the principle of equal opportunity has lexical priority over the so-called difference principle. We should note here that Rawls favored this rigid lexical priority of his principles only in the design of a liberal society's "basic structure" or "constitutional essentials," whereas Beauchamp and Childress are

PBE do not agree with moral particularists that the *valence* of moral principles can vary from case to case[23]—i.e., that a particular norm can be a reason to do something in one case, but a reason not to do it in others—they do agree that the *weight* of moral principles will vary from case to case, depending on the particulars. Thus, the autonomy-driven principle of confidentiality ordinarily weighs quite heavily in our moral decision making, but in *Tarasoff* it was outranked by the harm principle. Cases like this one lead the principlists to conclude that the *a priori* ranking of principles should be rejected.

Other theorists of a principlist persuasion differ from Beauchamp and Childress on this issue. H. Tristram Engelhardt Jr., a self-styled postmodern libertarian, elevates the principle of autonomy over all others, including the principle of justice.[24] Robert Veatch gives pride of place to principles bearing on individual autonomy and justice over utilitarian concerns embedded in the principle of beneficence.[25]

Some critics of *PBE* have objected that this rejection of *a priori* ranking deprives principlism of "systematicity," a supposedly desirable characteristic of a philosophical theory.[26] Without a clear-cut prior ordering of principles, they claim, principlism leaves far too much room for squishy intuitive judgments in the vast majority of cases where principles conflict with one another, thus depriving it of the virtues of rigor, system, and predictability.

In response, Beauchamp and Childress reject, first, the idea that they are offering a philosophical theory rather than a practical guide for the perplexed using accessible mid-level principles. Second, they would challenge their critics to come up with a rigid priority ranking that will stand the test of time in myriad complex and unpredictable social circumstances. Beauchamp and Childress harbor serious doubts that the critics can ever successfully rise to this challenge.

---

concerned with the entire gamut of moral decision making at all levels of generality and specificity, at the lower levels of which a more flexible "intuitionistic" approach may well be more plausible. See J. Rawls, *A Theory of Justice* (Cambridge, MA: Harvard University Press, 1971); J. Rawls, *A Theory of Justice*, rev. ed. (Cambridge, MA: Harvard University Press, 1999).

23 See, e.g., Dancy, *Ethics Without Principles*.

24 Engelhardt, *The Foundations of Bioethics*, 2nd ed. I find the notion of a "postmodern libertarian" to be oxymoronic. As I understand it, postmodern theorists generally reject the notion of a unitary, autonomous "self," a notion that lies at the very heart of Engelhardt's manifestly Kantian, 18th-century style brief for autonomy.

25 R. Veatch, *A Theory of Medical Ethics* (New York: Basic Books, 1981).

26 B. Gert, C. M. Culver, and K. D. Clouser, *Bioethics: A Systematic Approach*, 2nd ed. (New York: Oxford University Press, 2006).

FROM PRINCIPLES TO CASES: DEDUCTION OR INDUCTION?

The relationship between these mid-level principles and cases within the methodology of principlism has been somewhat ambiguous and subject to historical fluctuation. During the early, heroic phase of bioethics, the principlists were partisans of an arguably "top down" orientation devoted to applying principles to the moral data of concrete cases. Evidence of this can be found in the very first edition of *PBE*, which featured a chart tracing the various stages of moral justification.[27] At the top of the chart, there are various ethical theories, which function as the ultimate sources of moral normativity. An arrow then connects these theories with the four principles that can be derived from them. Another arrow connects these moral principles to various moral rules derived from the principles. (For example, from the principle of autonomy flows the more specific rule to always obtain the informed consent of subjects in biomedical research.) Finally, the process of justification comes to rest with an arrow connecting the various moral rules with concrete moral judgments about particular cases—judgments based upon the rules at the previous level. Importantly, each level of judgments receives whatever justification or legitimacy it possesses from the levels above it. In other words, early on, the principlism of Beauchamp and Childress was decidedly deductivist.

A large part of the initial appeal of principlism lay in its promise of providing "principled" solutions to moral problems—solutions that could claim to be more than the "merely subjective" biases of practitioners or consultants. As one physician-graduate of the Georgetown University Kennedy Institute's week-long bioethics seminar explained to me, "This [method] is what our student-doctors need. It's really objective, based on principles, just like a science." This promise of objectivity appeared to be founded on the expectation that individual actions or social policies could be justified by "applying" the enumerated principles.

In some very simple moral situations consisting, for example, of a clear and uncontested moral rule and a fact pattern that contradicts it, this promise could be vindicated. Suppose, for example, that a physician decides to lie to her patient in order to improve his spirits and possibly facilitate his recovery. One could say that this doctor's act violates the principle of autonomy and the law of informed consent. Indeed, one could deploy reasoning in this case as a deductive syllogism: "It is wrong to lie to patients. Dr. Jones has told a lie. Therefore, Dr. Jones has done something wrong."

---

[27] Beauchamp and Childress, *Principles of Biomedical Ethics*, 1st ed. (1979), 5.

The problem, of course, is that even in a simple, straightforward case, this reasoning has suppressed a conflicting principle—the principle of beneficence. This is precisely the principle that Dr. Jones would appeal to should she try to defend her lie. ("I did it for his benefit. I was just following my Hippocratic impulses!") At first glance, this opposing principle may not be noticeable because the principle of autonomy has prevailed within the biomedical ethics community over the principle of beneficence in this type of case. One should remember, however, that the relative importance of the autonomy principle was not always this clear; that the debate between autonomy and paternalistic medicine rages on in other countries, such as Japan and China; and that the eventual victory of autonomy in the areas of truth-telling and informed consent, at least in theory, was won after a protracted ideological struggle.[28] As a result, the biomedical community now assigns much greater weight to respecting patients than to easing their psychological burdens.[29]

Principlism may provide the kind of moral justification sought in the easy cases, but what about the complicated cases in which battles between competing principles continue to rage—the cases in which clinicians and policymakers seek the advice of bioethicists? The " 'tough" cases will inevitably present not one clear-cut and uncontested principle but, rather, two or more conflicting values that require some sort of reconciliation. Precisely what kind of moral justification can principlism offer in the face of serious moral ambiguity and conflict? To what extent does the "application of principles" actually justify the moral choices that we make, both individually and collectively?

As we shall see in chapter 3, the partisans casuistry or case-based reasoning objected to the apparently unidirectional movement from principles to cases within principlism. A careful analysis of Beauchamp and Childress's early editions of *PBE* might suggest a more complicated and nuanced relationship between principles and cases in the process of moral justification, but the aforementioned (in) famous chart in that book gave the distinct impression that theory justified principles, that principles justified moral rules, and that rules justified moral judgments in particular cases. According to the critics, this unidirectional picture distorted

[28] See N. A. Christakis, "The Ethical Design of an AIDS Vaccine Trial in Africa," *Hastings Center Report*, June–July 1988, 31; A. Surbone, "Letter from Italy: Truth Telling to the Patient," *JAMA* 268 (1992): 1661. A television documentary provided a riveting portrayal of cultural differences regarding the practice of truth-telling. The physicians and nurses in a Japanese cancer ward were shown grappling with a cultural puzzle: a cancer patient who not only wanted to know the truth about her condition but also had the unbridled temerity to talk to other patients about their common plight. Their temporary solution was to send the woman on lots of long walks in the hospital gardens! See *The Art of Healing* (David Grubin Productions, and Public Affairs Television), reproduced in *Healing and the Mind: The Art of Healing* (Ambrose Video Publishing, 1993).

[29] J. Katz, *The Silent World of Doctor and Patient* (New York: Free Press, 1984).

or totally ignored the pivotal role of intuitive, case-based judgments of right and wrong. To be sure, the judgments in question were not to be confused with just any responses to cases, no matter how prejudiced, ill-considered, or subject to coercion they might be. Rather, the critics had something in mind more akin to John Rawls's notion of "considered" moral judgments[30]—the judgments about whose genesis and moral rectitude we feel most confident, such as our sense that slavery is wrong. It is precisely these judgments, they claimed, that give concrete meaning, definition, and scope to moral principles and that provide critical leverage in refining their articulation. Although in some simple instances the movement from principles to cases might be deductive, the casuistical critics claimed that we often move from clusters of similar cases to the inductive formulation of moral principles.

The critics were claiming, in effect, that principles and cases intertwine in a dialectical or reciprocal relationship. The principles provide normative guidance, and the considered judgments, in turn, help shape the principles that then provide more precise guidance for more complex or difficult cases. Following Rawls's terminology, principles and cases exist together in creative tension or "reflective equilibrium."[31]

The principlists responded to this line of criticism by simply embracing it, over time, with increasing forthrightness and enthusiasm.[32] Although they may have been slower than others to discern the formative and critical roles of case analysis with regard to principles and theories, Beauchamp and Childress now embrace reflective equilibrium as *the* methodology of principlism and emphatically denounce deductivism for precisely the same reasons given by their critics.[33] One can view principles as the primary substance of ethical analysis, they conclude, without being a deductivist.

FROM PRINCIPLES TO CASES: BALANCING, SPECIFICATION, INTERPRETATION

Another way to formulate these questions is to ask about the capacity of principlism to generate *determinate* answers to moral quandaries. Doubts about the

[30] Rawls, *A Theory of Justice*, (1971) 47, (1999) 42.

[31] Ibid., (1971) 48–51, (1999) 40–44. Rawls's notion of reflective equilibrium, somewhat sketchily drawn in *A Theory of Justice*, is clarified and defended in N. Daniels, "Wide Reflective Equilibrium and Theory Acceptance in Ethics," *Journal of Philosophy* 76 (1979): 256–282. (See chapter 8 in this volume.)

[32] T. Beauchamp, "Methods and Principles in Biomedical Ethics," *Journal of Medical Ethics* 29, no. 5 (2003): 269–274.

[33] Beauchamp and Childress, *Principles of Biomedical Ethics*, 1st ed. (1979), 23–28.

justificatory power of principlism's principles arise on several levels of moral reflection. Actually, these problems will appear for just about any method in practical ethics, so the following doubts are not intended as a knock-down argument against the project of *PBE*. They are, however, intended as a critique of anything resembling a mechanistic application of the bioethics mantra.

Interpreting the Principles

The principles themselves require a great deal of interpretation and ordering before they can begin to shape the conclusion of a moral argument. The bioethical literature abounds with superficial claims to the effect that "the principle of autonomy (or of beneficence, or of the 'best interest' of the patient) requires that we do such and such." The problem with this common formulation is that it ignores the difficulty (or the vacuousness) of passing immediately from very abstract statements of principle to very concrete conclusions about what to do, here and now. Quite apart from the vexing problem of rank-ordering competing principles in morally complex situations, a problem to which I shall return shortly, one first must determine exactly what these abstract formulations of principle actually mean. As Bernard Gert and colleagues derisively but pointedly observed, the unadorned principles of Beauchamp and Childress function more like mere "chapter headings"—i.e., abstract factors to consider in moral argument—than genuinely helpful action guides.

What does it mean, for example, to invoke the "best interests" principle in the case of a severely impaired newborn? What content can one give to this expression? How are the interests of such a child to be assessed and according to which conception of the good? Some might argue that a vitalist's conception of the good should shape our understanding of the child's interests; others might advocate a hedonistic conception of the good that would restrict the notion of interests to the qualia of pleasure and pain; while still others might advance a conception of the good based on conceptions of human flourishing and dignity, which might lead to nontreatment decisions even in the absence of pain and suffering.

Whatever the merit of these individual suggestions, the point is that unless one interprets "the principles of bioethics," they will indeed merely play the role of empty chapter headings, doing little if any actual work in moral analysis. Unless one furnishes principles with a definite shape and content, they will merely lend a patina of objectivity to bioethical debates while masking the need to make arguments and choices regarding the substance of those principles.

It is important to recall that the meaning of principles is shaped, not simply by explicit and constructive ethical theorizing, but also by the largely implicit influences of culture. The seemingly univocal "principle of autonomy" will mean different things and have different weights in different cultural settings. Compare, for example, the way in which the right of reproductive self-determination functions in the abortion debates of the United States and Germany. In the United States, longstanding legal traditions of rugged individualism have yielded, albeit after many years of bloody and ongoing conflict, a right that has been aptly characterized as nearly absolute but entirely asocial. So while a woman's claims to (nearly) absolute personal sovereignty have trumped the interests of husbands, parents, and the values of a large countervailing segment of the community, women remain largely isolated in their freedom, unsupported by the community's resources and concern.

In Germany, by contrast, the principle of autonomy exercises considerable force, to be sure, but its meaning and scope have been mediated by a public philosophy, traceable back to Rousseau, that stresses the complementary nature of individual freedom and social responsibility. Thus, Germans significantly curtail, by American standards, a woman's right to obtain an abortion, but German women who obtain abortions are given community services and abortion funding. Such differences in the presentation of various principles in diverse cultural settings have prompted Mary Ann Glendon to speak not of "rights talk" *tout court* but, rather, of different "rights dialects."[34]

Interpreting Conflicting Abstract Principles

In hard cases, principles conflict. That is why they are hard. Can principlism provide a means to justify resolutions to moral conflict? What help can principlism provide, for example, when the principle of autonomy is at odds with the "harm principle," as in cases involving maternal–fetal conflict or in cases involving decisions to reproduce in a context of genetic disease or AIDS? According to the principlists, one available remedy for such conflicts of principle is to judiciously weigh and balance the competing moral claims as they arise in different circumstances. If a woman is overwrought and her judgment skewed by excessive fear and anxiety, and if her choice would impose severe and irreparable harm on her offspring, then a principlist might find the harm principle to outweigh the claims of self-determination.

One problem with this notion of weighing and balancing competing principles is that it is highly metaphorical and intuitive. Some critics have contended,

---

[34] M. A. Glendon, *Rights Talk: The Impoverishment of Political Discourse* (New York: Free Press, 1993).

along with the guarded concurrence of Beauchamp and Childress themselves, that this kind of "balancing" runs the risk of being both highly subjective and unpredictable.[35] Suppose two observers—for example, an ardent feminist and a staunch "pro-lifer"—happen to disagree about the above outcome in the maternal–fetal conflict case? The latter approves, while the former sees it as a violation of the woman's integrity and as reducing her to the demeaning status of "fetal container." Can weighing and balancing help sort out, according to some canon of rational justification, the rival "intuitions" of the disputing parties?

According to Clouser and Gert, these kinds of intuitive conflicts can only be resolved on the higher plane of philosophical theory.[36] These critics contend that until the principlists develop a more robust ethical theory, a theory that would ultimately assign determinate weights to such competing values, the principlists' resolutions of hard cases must remain ad hoc, fundamentally unprincipled, and therefore unjustified. The principlists have rejected this solution owing to their belief that no *a priori* serial ordering of principles is possible.

Beauchamp and Childress, however, do take this problem of the rationality, or lack thereof, of balancing very seriously. They, too, worry about the "unprincipled" nature of intuitive balancing and the threat it poses to our ability to rationally explain our actions to one another. Given this conflict between intuitive balancing and the demands of intersubjective (or public) justification, Beauchamp and Childress have relegated this sort of move from principles to cases to a marginal corner in the toolbox of principlism. If one is going to engage in this sort of balancing, they contend, it should be undertaken as a last resort, and those deploying it would have to adhere to certain procedural safeguards.[37]

An alternative and more promising route from principles to cases has been developed by philosopher Henry Richardson,[38] and then applied to bioethics by David DeGrazia,[39] and finally by Beauchamp and Childress themselves in full Borg mode.[40] Richardson and DeGrazia contend that in many hard cases what is really going on is not the weighing and balancing of conflicting principles by

---

[35] D. Clouser and B. Gert, "A Critique of Principlism," *Journal of Medicine and Philosophy* 15, no. 2 (1990): 219–236.

[36] Ibid.

[37] Beauchamp and Childress, *PBE*, 4th ed. (1994), 34–37.

[38] H. S. Richardson, "Specifying Norms as a Way to Resolve Concrete Ethical Problems," *Philosophy & Public Affairs* 19 (1990): 279–310. See also Richardson, "Specifying, Balancing, and Interpreting Bioethical Principles," *Journal of Medicine and Philosophy* 25, no. 3 (2000): 285–307.

[39] D. Degrazia, "Moving Forward in Bioethical Theory: Theories, Cases, and Specified Principlism," *Journal of Medicine and Philosophy* 17 (1992): 511ff.

[40] Beauchamp and Childress, *PBE*, 4th ed. (1994), 28–32.

unsupported intuition but, rather, the progressive *specification* of more abstract norms. According to this view, a position ultimately warmly embraced in later editions of *PBE*, initial abstract formulations of principles will become increasingly concrete, specified, and delimited as one approaches the level of the particular case. Thus, what begins as a straightforward abstract principle—e.g., autonomy—might end up as a highly complex and richly nuanced principle with built-in exceptions for factors such as compromised rationality and severe and irreversible harm, as in the above example. As Richardson emphasizes, the more specified versions of the original principle are different norms from their original source, but they remain tethered to it by advancing the same value in ways that might be action-guiding in particular circumstances. Thus, the principle of autonomy might start out as a "mere chapter heading," but then it morphs into a less abstract principle—say, of reproductive autonomy—that itself becomes more concrete and more laden with clarifications and exception clauses as it approaches an actual hard case. Schematically, the final action-guiding principle would look something like: Women and men have a decisive right of reproductive liberty except when conditions *X*, *Y*, or *Z* obtain, where good reasons might be given within the ambit of the overarching principle for the enumerated exception clauses. While embracing specification as a more rationally justified method of getting from principles to cases than balancing, Beauchamp and Childress insist that truly robust justification will require both specification and coherence of the sort sought in reflective equilibrium.

In spite of the justificatory advantages of the method of specification, Beauchamp and Childress remain somewhat guarded in their embrace of it, and for good reason. In contrast with Richardson, who contends that a fully robust and reasoned specification can always be substituted for intuitively balancing conflicting principles, the authors of *PBE* are skeptical that specification can always be counted upon to fully resolve all such conflicts in a rationally satisfying manner. Indeed, in some cases a detailed specification may end up simply redescribing or relocating, rather than solving, the problem of indeterminacy among conflicting principles. If weighing and balancing competing principles in the reproductive case above falls short of ultimate rational justification for want of a hierarchy of values that is theoretically justified, then the specification of abstract principles through the process of specification and reflective equilibrium may also fall short. Just as the competing principles of reproductive autonomy and nonmaleficence appear to require ad hoc, context-specific, nuanced judgments unsupported by higher level, lexically ordered principles, so too may efforts to specify the principle of reproductive freedom down to the level of the particular case. Indeed, what motivates and guides the modification and specification of abstract principles, what compels one to lard them with qualifying clauses, if not precisely the sort of countervailing values and principles encountered by the balancer? Thus, whether one calls this balancing or specification, the respective weights of competing considerations must be sorted out. Unless they have a rationally defensible, higher level, lexical ordering principle at their disposal, "specifiers" may be in the same boat as the "weighers and balancers." Neither, in short, may be able to vindicate, all the way down, the claim to rational justification that gave principlism much of its initial appeal. At this point, Beauchamp and Childress might reasonably respond that, as Aristotle reminds us,[41] we should not seek from practical reasoning more than can reasonably be expected. Gaps in our chains of reasoning and ultimate conflicts between values and principles will remain. Prudent reasoning (*phronesis*) and muddling through will have to pick up the slack.

Interpreting Types of Cases

Apart from the sometimes ineliminable indeterminacies involved in balancing and specifying principles, the corresponding moral situation requires extensive, non-rule-bound interpretation as well. In some contexts, this might mean developing an appropriate moral vocabulary to describe what is happening in certain kinds of situations. It seems that moral progress often depends as much on finding (or fashioning) the right words as on applying the right principles.[42] This is especially the case in the areas of bioethical investigation defined by rapid technological change—such as genetic engineering, synthetic biology, neuroscience, prenatal interventions on the fetus, and the withholding of life-sustaining treatments. For example, the tentative search for compelling descriptions has created much of the perplexity over the withholding of artificial food and fluids. One wonders what is really going on in such cases. Is the withholding of artificial nutrition through a nasogastric tube an example of intentional "killing" or an example of a humble, merciful withdrawal of ineffective medical treatments? Those who breezily claim that bioethics is the application of principles to "the facts" forget that, apart from the indices of bioethics periodicals, the facts do not come neatly labeled. Cases and issues must be described, individuated, and labeled well before any principles can be applied.

---

[41] Aristotle, *Nicomachean Ethics*, Bk 1.

[42] See R. Rorty, *Contingency, Irony and Solidarity* (Cambridge: Cambridge University Press, 1989), 9. See also R. Rorty, "Feminism and Pragmatism," in *Feminist Interpretations of Richard Rorty*, ed. M. Janack (University Park: Pennsylvania State University Press, 2010), 19–46.

Interpreting the Particular Case

Even after developing a vocabulary to describe a particular moral situation, the application of moral principles must await the results of yet another layer of interpretation: the interpretation of actions, gestures, and relationships within the case. Even if one decides that a specific refusal of treatment does not necessarily amount to a form of suicide or intentional killing, one still must determine the meaning of that refusal in the context of its own setting and history. Indeed, some of the most illuminating and challenging writing in the field of bioethics has dealt precisely with this type of searching hermeneutic of the individual case.

Recall Robert Burt's brilliant and disturbing psychoanalytic interpretation of a now-famous burn patient's adamant refusal to be treated and his articulate request to die.[43] While Burt acknowledged the validity of the principle of autonomy, as well as the sincerity of the patient's request to die, he enlarged the understanding of this case by attempting to place the patient's treatment refusal in its emotional context. Perhaps, Burt suggested, the patient's refusal was less an unambiguous thrust of freedom than a plea for recognition, acceptance, and love from those surrounding him. Instead of being a statement, perhaps the refusal was a question in disguise: "Do you still care for me? Would you banish me from your sight?" Clearly, the relevance of the principle of autonomy for this case depends upon whether one interprets the patient's refusal as a statement or as a query. For example, if the patient is in fact testing the commitment of those around him, a mechanical application of the principle of autonomy to his expressed refusal could lead to a tragic result. Whether or not one agrees with Burt's controversial gloss on this case, his work shows that one can do creative and exciting work in bioethics while paying scant attention to the analysis or application of moral principles.

The search for moral justification through the application of principles thus proves to be a far more complicated matter than some followers of principlism might have initially assumed. While it still makes sense to talk about the "application" of principles to cases, this application is no simple matter of deduction, but actually involves multiple layers of interpretation and substantive moral reflection. The crucial point, however, is that each of these interpretative layers—of the principles, of their relative weights, of case description, and of the meaning of individual gestures—is a locus of interpretive conflict, a conclusion that Beauchamp

---

[43] The case is that of Dax Cowart. See R. Burt, *Taking Care of Strangers: The Rule of Law in Doctor-Patient Relations* (New York: Free Press, 1979).

and Childress now fully acknowledge.[44] Bioethics requires one to articulate and attempt to resolve the conflicts at all these levels. This is a difficult task. Reference to the "application" of principles to cases tends to mask these difficulties. It gives the impression that the task is "merely" one of intellectual procedure rather than substance.

THE SOURCE OF MORAL NORMS

A final significant feature of the method of principlism in this survey has to do with its conception of the ultimate source of the moral normativity of principles. We have already seen how Beauchamp and Childress hoped to simply bracket this question and instead focus their analytical energies on the mid-level principles and their application to cases. Their rationale for this foundational reticence is quite understandable. First, there's the problem of competing and irreconcilable philosophical foundations. If practical ethics must await the ultimate resolution of the age-old debate between, *inter alia*, utilitarians and Kantians, we will all have a very long wait indeed. Second, we may share the faith, exhibited by Beauchamp and Childress (and many others), in the convergence of different ethical theories in (roughly) the same mid-level moral principles. We have already seen how Beauchamp, a self-described rule-utilitarian, and Childress, a self-described Christian deontologist, could agree upon their list of normative principles. Why not focus, then, on those areas where agreement is possible and just bracket intractable and interminable debates among moral theorists at the foundational level?

This rationale held firm until the appearance of the third edition of *PBE* in 1989, when Beauchamp and Childress explicitly abandoned high-level moral theory as the ultimate source of justification for their four principles of bioethics, in favor of a conception of so-called common morality derived from our pre-reflective experience.[45] Two reasons might have played a role in this decision to relocate the ultimate source of moral normativity. On the one hand, it may have occurred to Beauchamp and Childress that the interpretation of principles may well be colored by one's ultimate theoretical allegiances. We imagine that we might be able to leave them at the doorstep of practical ethics—just bracket them—but they may well prove decisive in some problematic cases. For example, take the

[44] See Beauchamp and Childress, *PBE*, 4th ed. (1994).

[45] To be more precise, they have not denied that high theory might be able to provide a normative ground for the principles of bioethics, but they have decided to focus upon common morality as a more heuristically promising alternative in the face of seemingly interminable disagreement over moral theory.

recent case involving a proposed research study of anthrax vaccine on healthy children.[46] The utilitarian rationale for such a study is compelling: In case of an actual anthrax attack on the United States, the Centers for Disease Control and Prevention (CDC) have committed to providing anthrax vaccination to every child in the affected region—i.e., to thousands of children. But we currently have no data at all on the toxicity, safety, or effectiveness of this vaccine in the pediatric population. Hence, the need for a study involving only a couple hundred normal, healthy children that will ultimately enable emergency medical providers to administer safe and effective doses to thousands of exposed children in the event of an attack. True, the children enlisted in this study will be exposed to risks above the "minimal" level permitted by U.S. federal regulations, and exposing them to this higher level of risk will not benefit them in any way, but the number of children involved will be relatively small, the risks to which they are exposed will be minimized (we hope), and the results of such a study may well greatly benefit thousands of children. From the utilitarian point of view, this could be an easy call.

Not so from a Kantian or deontological point of view. Imagine someone like Paul Ramsey confronting such a case. He would no doubt argue, from his own Christian, Kantian, rule-governed perspective that placing children at any risk at all in research not undertaken for their benefit is simply morally prohibited, no matter how much good might be accomplished in the process for other children in the future. And even those deontologists who don't share Ramsey's rather monomaniacal adherence to principle in this area might still object to such a study on the ground that it doesn't provide sufficient protection for children. Theoretical commitments are not so easily bracketed.

A second rationale for the switch from high theory to common morality was a desire to unburden themselves of any remnants of deductivism in their approach to methodology. Locating the ultimate source of normativity in the decidedly pre-theoretical lived world of ordinary morality would allow Beauchamp and Childress to maintain, at least to their own satisfaction, their commitment to an objective, universal realm of moral principles without any need to justify them conclusively at the contentious bar of moral theory.[47] We now turn to a detailed examination of the notion of a common morality as articulated in the later editions of *PBE*.

---

[46] Presidential Commission for the Study of Bioethical Issues, *Safeguarding Children: Pediatric Medical Countermeasure Research*, March 2013. At http://bioethics.gov/node/833.

[47] See Beauchamp and Childress, *PBE*, 4th ed. (1994), 102.

DEEPER INTO COMMON MORALITY

Common Morality and Coherence

Beginning with the third edition of *PBE*, published in 1989, Beauchamp and Childress relocated the source of their bioethical principles from philosophical theory to what they have termed "the common morality." By insisting on the definite article here, Beauchamp and Childress mean to distinguish the wide variety of particular moralities found in different eras, cultures, and professions from their source in a morality that is common, as they put it, to all persons in all times and places who are committed to living a moral life. This morality encompasses both *rules of obligation* (e.g., do not kill or cause suffering for others, tell the truth, keep promises, do not steal, prevent evil or harm from occurring, rescue persons in danger, do not punish the innocent, obey the law, treat all persons with equal moral consideration, etc.) and *standards of moral character*, such as nonmalevolence, honesty, integrity, truthfulness, fidelity, lovingness, and kindness.

Beauchamp and Childress assert that the content of the common morality is dictated by the primary objectives of morality, which include the amelioration of human misery, the avoidance of premature death, and the predictable consequences of indifference, conflict, hostility, scarce resources, limited information, and so on. Adhering to the norms of the common morality is necessary, Beauchamp claims, "to counteract the tendency for the quality of people's lives to worsen or for social relationships to disintegrate."[48]

The moral authority of the common morality is thus established, according to Beauchamp and Childress, neither by means of ethical theory nor by means of *a priori* reasoning or reflection on the meaning of moral terms; rather, moral normativity is established historically or pragmatically through the success of these norms in all times and places in advancing the cause of human flourishing. Their account is thus historicist, but unlike most historicisms it does not embrace moral relativism. The norms of the common morality, they insist, are universally binding.

There are, however, two additional sources of moral justification in the later editions of *PBE*. In addition to the common morality, which provides us with universally binding but highly abstract norms, a complex process of specification and constrained balancing of principles provides some degree of justification for all subsequent moral reasoning in practical ethics. Responding to Gert and others' prior criticism that their principles of biomedical ethics were too abstract to function as anything more than mere "chapter headings" or reminders of issues that need to be considered—i.e., that they were insufficiently specific to serve as real

[48] T. Beauchamp, "A Defense of the Common Morality," *Kennedy Institute of Ethics Journal* 13 (2003): 261.

action guides in highly nuanced moral contexts—Beauchamp and Childress explain that the principles of common morality had to be specified more concretely and balanced against competing principles in specific situations. Normativity in practical ethics would thus be found in these specified norms that make more explicit the conditions under which our basic principles should hold sway—i.e., the when, where, why, how, by what means, to whom, or by whom the action is to be done or avoided.[49] For example, the principle of autonomy will have to be further specified in order to deal with the problem of presently incompetent patients who have signed an advance directive; and it will have to be balanced against other concerns, such as respect for life or slippery-slope worries about bad consequences, in the case of physician-assisted suicide.

Finally, Beauchamp and Childress seek further moral justification for the results of all this specifying and balancing in a process of reflective equilibrium, in which we seek coherence among all of our specifications and moral commitments at all levels.[50] Some lines of specification will survive this process, but others will not. When a line of specified moral reasoning contradicts other strongly held moral beliefs, we should adjust one or more of these action-guides to bring them all into harmony and coherence with one another.

Two features of this account deserve further elaboration. First, this procedure concedes that different, even contradictory, lines of specified moral reasoning can proceed from the same set of abstract moral principles in the common morality. This phenomenon explains the emergence of many different particular moralities that crop up in different times, places, and professional practices. Contrary to Gert's endlessly repeated (but false) complaint that Beauchamp and Childress fail to account for the fact that some highly contested moral problems lack a uniquely justified solution, an explanation is readily available among the raw materials of *PBE*.

Second, it should be emphasized that Beauchamp and Childress offer a hybrid approach to moral justification that differs in important ways from more standard accounts of reflective equilibrium in political theory and practical ethics. According to Norman Daniels, for example, moral justification is achieved by bringing all the various levels of our moral reflection—including our considered moral judgments, principles, moral theories, and background social theories—into "wide reflective equilibrium" with one another.[51] We thus zip back and forth between these different elements, none of which is accorded foundational status and all of which are

[49] Beauchamp and Childress, *PBE*, 6th ed. (2009), 17.
[50] Ibid., 381 ff. See also chapter 8 in this volume.
[51] See Daniels, "Wide Reflective Equilibrium and Theory Acceptance in Ethics."

liable to emendation in light of competing considerations at other levels of reflection. In contrast to this standard account, Beauchamp and Childress accord common morality a special place shielded from the jostling involved in the quest for coherence through wide reflective equilibrium. The norms of the common morality are justified pragmatically by meshing with the goals of morality, while the rest of the moral system envisioned in *PBE* proceeds by specification, balancing, and wide reflective equilibrium. Particular moral conclusions achieved through these procedures gain justification through both coherence and by being tethered ultimately to principles in the common morality.

Critique of Beauchamp and Childress on Common Morality and Justification

As we have seen, Beauchamp and Childress now endorse a hybrid account of moral justification. On the one hand, there is the common morality, which provides the source of our moral norms and is itself justified by its close fit with the goals of morality; and, on the other hand, there is the realm of moral specification, constrained balancing, and seeking coherence through wide reflective equilibrium. The project of *PBE* is thus foundationalist with regard to the common morality, and coherentist with regard to our actual reasoning in practical ethics. We reach our moral conclusions through specification, balancing, and adjusting norms for coherence, but these conclusions are ultimately justified through their long tether to the ultimate principles of the common morality.[52]

Since standard approaches to reflective equilibrium in contemporary moral theory are resolutely nonfoundationalist and unbifurcated in this way, since they regard all levels or sources of moral reasoning to be fair game for revision in light of more firmly held moral beliefs, it is reasonable to ask just how plausible such a hybrid approach is and what it actually accomplishes for reasoners in practical ethics. Another way of putting this question is to ask why Beauchamp and Childress find it necessary or helpful to sharply distinguish the norms of the common morality from what Rawls called our "considered moral judgments"—i.e., *revisable* fixed points in our initial process of reasoning. According to Rawls[53] and his most influential expositor on reflective equilibrium, Norman Daniels,[54] moral reflection begins with those moral judgments about particular issues or cases in which we have the most confidence. These will include those judgments that are formed under conditions favorable to sound judgment in which our moral capacities are

[52] See Beauchamp and Childress, *PBE*, 4th ed. (1994), 385.
[53] Rawls, *A Theory of Justice*, 1971) 17–18, (1999) 18–19.
[54] Daniels, "Wide Reflective Equilibrium and Theory Acceptance in Ethics."

displayed without distortion—for example, those judgments that we come to unhesitatingly and make in the absence of strong emotions or conflicts of interest. Rawls argues that the project of justifying ethical beliefs ideally involves the attempt to bring these most confidently held ethical judgments into a state of harmony or equilibrium with our ethical principles and our background social, psychological, and philosophical theories. Our most confident moral judgments or intuitions (e.g., "slavery is wrong") provide a touchstone for the adequacy of our principles; any moral principle that justified slavery would be either reformulated or rejected. Meanwhile, principles invested with a great deal of confidence could be used to reject some conflicting intuitions while extending our ability to judge confidently in less familiar moral settings. We thus go back and forth, nipping an intuitive judgment here, tucking a principle there, building up or reformulating a theory in the background, until all the disparate elements of our moral assessments are brought into a more or less steady state of harmonious equilibrium. According to this view, moral justification must be sought not in secure, incorrigible foundations outside of our processes of reflection but, rather, in the coherence of all the flotsam and jetsam of our moral life. Importantly, even our considered moral judgments are deemed to be only *provisionally* fixed points.

In response, Beauchamp and Childress might suggest that an extra and independent layer of moral justification is needed owing to the inability of coherence by itself to provide all the justification that we need. Citing the perfectly coherent "Pirates' Creed" (circa 1640),[55] which laid down norms for all well-behaved pirates—e.g., norms bearing on sharing the spoils of marauding, punishing prohibited acts (if any!), establishing "courts of honor," etc.—Beauchamp and Childress rightly conclude that more is required of a moral theory than coherence among all the disparate elements of one's moral vision. Although coherence can help justify our moral judgments—we certainly don't want our judgments to be in flagrant contradiction with one another—it cannot by itself secure their truth. Presumably, Beauchamp and Childress look to a separate realm of common morality to provide this extra foundational element of justification by anchoring our long chains of practical reasoning in our ultimate abstract norms.

If this is Beauchamp and Childress's primary rationale for excluding the common morality from the process of wide reflective equilibrium, then it is unclear how much additional justificatory advantage is actually gained by appealing to a hybrid account. True, coherence alone is not enough to guarantee moral truth, but we should recall that the process of reflective equilibrium is maximally inclusive.

[55] See Beauchamp and Childress, *PBE*, 4th ed. (1994), 384.

If you do not like the way the process of reflective equilibrium is going, if you think that it currently overlooks some crucial pieces of the moral picture—such as a different moral outlook or a background theory of social stability—then this method simply asks you to toss it into the mix alongside all our other beliefs. Although the initial moral data of reflective equilibrium—, i.e., our considered moral judgments—could conceivably be overturned (think, for example, of recent attitudes toward homosexuality), it is hard to imagine that most of them would or could be overturned in our lifetime; and if they are overturned, then it would no doubt be for the sort of good reasons that would lead Beauchamp and Childress to expand the scope of the norm of equal treatment within the common morality.[56]

Another reason to suspect that we would be getting less justificatory bang for the buck than Beauchamp and Childress might expect from their hybrid method comes into focus when we take a closer look at that tether that anchors our practical judgments to ultimate norms in common morality. As Beauchamp and Childress themselves admit, many different and conflicting lines of specification and balancing can originate in the same ultimate moral norms. Although some of these conflicts might be smoothed over through the process of seeking coherence, not all of them can be finessed in this way. We will, then, be stuck from time to time with two or more conflicting lines of moral specification, each of which will be traceable back to common sources in the common morality. Since, *pace* Gert's claims to the contrary, Beauchamp and Childress do not claim that there is a univocally correct way to specify and balance norms in particular moral contexts, their hybrid account will not necessarily allow us to choose between competing lines of specification and balancing that share the same ultimate anchor in the common morality.

Take, for example, our differing responses to the problem of active euthanasia. The operative moral principle here is "Do not kill," which can be plausibly further specified in both permissive and restrictive directions. Proponents can argue that one should not kill except when an explicit request is made by a competent dying patient suffering from great pain, etc. Opponents can argue that the prohibition against killing should be maintained when the bad consequences of a permissive social policy would predictably outweigh the good consequences, even if the proponents' autonomy-based argument works in theory. The fact that each of these opposing positions can be traced back to a common principle discoverable in the common morality provides little, if any, justificatory advantage to either side.

---

[56] Although Beauchamp and Childress seriously doubt that the principles and virtues of the common morality will ever change, they readily admit that the principles' scope of application has expanded to include coverage for women, minorities, etc.

In sum, then, the root problem underlying this critique is Beauchamp and Childress's decision to conceive of the common morality as a separate moral sphere immune to the perpetual dialectic of reflective equilibrium. I would suggest that this sort of bifurcation is neither necessary nor desirable. Our attempts at moral justification can most likely get along just fine without an appeal to ultimate, unrevisable foundations.

I hasten to add, however, that such problems in striving for the elusive goal of ultimate moral justification seem peripheral to the central project of *PBE*, which continues to be the skilled and artful deployment of mid-level norms (whatever their source) in the context of practical ethical problems. Because their account of common morality remains an afterthought within the overall system of *PBE*, albeit an important one, Beauchamp and Childress can acknowledge these problems and then get on with the business of debating cases and policies.

I believe that Beauchamp and Childress's shift from an emphasis on ethical theory as the source of moral norms to an emphasis on common morality was a salutary move. Ethical reflection, let alone theory, should grow out of our everyday, pre-theoretical moral experience. But it is another question whether rouging up common morality to make it look like some sort of ultimate and universal foundation for morality, untouched by the dialectics of time and reflective equilibrium, was an equally good move. The indisputable and lasting moral achievement of *PBE* lies in its masterful and wide-ranging reflection on vexing cases and complex issues that constitute the field of biomedical ethics. The attempt to ground such reflection in a foundation exempt from reflective equilibrium is, however, deeply problematic.

2

A Common Morality for Hedgehogs

BERNARD GERT'S METHOD

TWO HIGHLY INFLUENTIAL approaches to bioethics have stressed the importance of "common morality" for the justification of our moral judgments, yet they differ in their respective accounts of the content and functions of common morality in practical ethics. For the late Bernard Gert, a highly esteemed philosopher, an account of common morality has always occupied center stage, both in his descriptions of and in his theorizing about the moral life. Borrowing Isaiah Berlin's famous taxonomy,[1] we can say that Gert is definitely the hedgehog of contemporary bioethical reflection on method. Unlike the fox, who thinks many thoughts, Gert has had one big thought—which is one more than most of us have had—and his entire career might be faithfully construed as a prolonged meditation on and defense of his conception of common morality as the keystone of ethics.[2]

For Tom Beauchamp and James Childress, on the other hand, appeals to a common morality did not appear until well into the historical development of their

[1] I. Berlin, *The Hedgehog and the Fox: An Essay on Tolstoy's View of History* (London: Weidenfeld & Nicolson, 1953).

[2] B. Gert, C. M. Culver, and K. D. Clouser, *Bioethics: A Systematic Approach*, 2nd ed. (New York: Oxford University Press, 2006); B. Gert, *Common Morality: Deciding What to Do* (New York: Oxford University Press, 2004); Bernard Gert, *Morality: Its Nature and Justification* (New York: Oxford University Press, 1998 [2005 rev. ed.]); B. Gert, *The Moral Rules: A New Rational Foundation for Morality* (New York: Oxford University Press, 1970); B. Gert and C. M. Culver, *Philosophy in Medicine: Conceptual and Ethical Issues in Medicine and Psychiatry* (New York: Oxford University Press, 1982); B. Gert, C. M. Culver, and K. D. Clouser, *Bioethics: A Return to Fundamentals* (New York: Oxford University Press, 1997).

celebrated joint project, *Principles of Biomedical Ethics* (*PBE*). Whereas Gert views the norms and methodological resources of common morality as constituting the very warp and woof of all moral reflection, Beauchamp and Childress have adopted a narrower conception of common morality as providing ultimate justification for the account they give of the principles of bioethics, which earlier editions of *PBE* had located in philosophical theory. Eager to avoid early accusations of deductivism and top-down thinking, Beauchamp and Childress embraced a conception of common morality, embedded in ordinary pre-theoretical experience, as the source of the very principles whose implications they had so deftly explored in previous editions. For them, common morality now provides the warp, but not the woof, of bioethical reflection.

Gert and Beauchamp and Childress also differ in their respective responses to rival points of view. We have already noted in chapter 1 just how accommodating and responsive Beauchamp and Childress have been to often quite hostile criticisms. They are the Borg of Bioethics, eager to assimilate all rival methodological accounts into their neural network. By contrast, Gert's systematic apparatus—massive, powerful, and thorough—lumbers across the bioethical landscape like some great tank, turret whirling in every direction, guns blazing from every exposed angle, ready to fight for each square inch of territory. Nicked and battered from many skirmishes with opposing forces, this machine remains unbowed, reinforced, and fortified over the years with multiple layers of thick steel plating. Its driver has fretted over its appearance and performance down to the minutest rivet, including a new paint job just about every other year. Notwithstanding its many dents and patches, the tank still looms as a formidable presence on the bioethical horizon.[3]

In this chapter, I shall critically discuss Gert's take on the nature of "common morality" and its promise for enriching ethical reflection within the field of bioethics. To cover this ground thoroughly would, however, require more than one medium-size chapter, so I'll be restricting my scope to a few central problems and leaving it to other scholars to canvass a wider swath of other important issues regarding common morality as portrayed by the Hedgehog and the Borg. In delimiting my subject in this way, I will have to bracket several worthy contemporary conceptions of common morality, including those of W. D. Ross, Alan Donagan, Amartya Sen, and Martha Nussbaum, and those deployed by the human rights movement. I shall also have to bracket a very big swath of Gert's

[3] In my more wistful moments, I imagine Bernie Gert's last words: "Hey, you kids, get off my tank!"

more encompassing methodology, which actually has a lot in common with the principlism of Beauchamp and Childress.

GERT'S CONCEPTION OF COMMON MORALITY

Providing a mere thumbnail sketch of Gert's approach to common morality will prove to be a much more daunting task because, in contrast to Beauchamp and Childress, Gert's primary contribution to ethics and practical ethics *just is* his account of common morality. More specifically, Gert begins with a conception of the point and purpose of morality, which then yields the descriptive core of common morality, including lists of the various moral rules and moral ideals, and a decision procedure for determining when it is justified to violate any of the moral rules. This descriptive core is then shored up by Gert's *theory* of common morality, which attempts to provide a justification for the entire edifice. Although Gert concedes that his particular *theory* of common morality might well be problematic in various ways, although he doubts it, he insists that his account of the descriptive *content* of common morality is both true and universally embraced by all rational persons. For Gert, then, the point of "doing ethics" is not to come up with some nifty new theory of morality but, rather, to provide a faithful descriptive and interpretive rendering of the moral rules, ideals, and decision procedures that we all share. Borrowing a page from Wittgenstein, Gert declares that his account changes nothing in common morality, which does not alter over time, leaving its central precepts and decision procedures in place and intact.[4]

Gert begins his account with the claim that the whole point and purpose of morality is to lessen the amount of evil or harm suffered in the world,[5] a goal similar to that posited by Beauchamp and Childress. He then dips into an account of human nature, arguing that beings like us—i.e., vulnerable, mortal, rational, and fallible[6]—would favor adopting common morality as a public system that impartially applies to everyone. The content of common morality consists of moral rules and moral ideals. Given the point of morality, all ten of the rules (a Decalogue!) proscribe actions that either directly cause harm (e.g., killing, lying, causing pain, disabling, depriving of freedom or pleasure) or tend to produce harmful results (e.g., do not deceive, break promises, cheat, disobey the law, or fail to do your duty). Whereas the moral rules categorically prohibit violations (unless sufficient

---

[4] Gert, *Common Morality: Deciding What to Do*, 4.

[5] Ibid., 26.

[6] Ibid., 8.

reasons can be provided), the moral ideals merely encourage people to prevent or relieve the sorts of harms covered by the rules.[7] Gert thus asserts that it is more important for all people to obey the moral rules than to follow moral ideals. Citing Mill approvingly, he notes that "a person may possibly not need the benefits of others, but he always needs that they not do him hurt."[8] Accordingly, liability to punishment is always appropriate in cases of unjustified violations of moral rules, whereas failure to act in the spirit of the moral ideals on any given occasion usually need not be justified at all and is not a fit subject of punishment.[9]

With the rules and ideals of common morality in place, Gert next addresses the important question of when violations of the moral rules might be justified. To this end, he purports to discover a methodological procedure in common morality consisting of the following two steps. First, a person contemplating the violation of a moral rule must ascertain all the morally relevant facts or features of the case. What rule is in play? What kinds of good or bad effects might be anticipated? What are the desires and beliefs of the person who will be affected? Might the agent in question have a moral duty to violate the rule because of a particular relationship to the person affected (e.g., parent and child)? Are there any alternative actions that could achieve similar ends without violating the rule?[10]

The second required step in ascertaining the justifiability of any moral rule involves a hypothetical test estimating the consequences of everyone's knowing either that a kind of violation would be allowed or not allowed. Contrary to consequentialist theories that might approve of certain actions (e.g., lying) just so long as no one finds out about the deception, Gert insists that all justifications of rule violations must meet this test of publicity. Unsurprisingly, Gert acknowledges that often, especially when individual acts rather than public policies are at issue, the results of this second step will be somewhat indeterminate. He thus speaks of "estimating" rather than "determining" the outcome of this thought experiment, and concedes that in many cases there will be a spectrum of more or less acceptable estimates, each of which might suggest a different policy. Some cases, however, will be clear enough. For example, lying to potential research subjects in order to secure their consent could never be publicly endorsed, Gert plausibly suggests, because of predictable effects on the trustworthiness of the medical profession and the entire research endeavor.

---

[7] Note that Gert's inclusion of ideals and virtues here justifies his consternation at Beauchamp and Childress continuing to label his approach an "impartial rule theory." T. L. Beauchamp and J. F. Childress, *Principles of Biomedical Ethics*, 6th ed. (New York: Oxford University Press, 2009), 371.

[8] Gert, *Common Morality: Deciding What to Do*, 23.

[9] Ibid., 53.

[10] Ibid., 59–74.

In sum, Gert's moral system presents readers with a curious blend of intellectual humility and chutzpah. On the one hand, he claims that his moral system would be, and in fact is, approved by all rational beings not using any beliefs not universally shared, and that the moral rules are both universally applicable and unchanging. Sounding like a strict constructionist in constitutional theory, Gert argues that the moral rules do not change over time or "evolve" with changing social circumstances. Whereas Beauchamp and Childress insist on the unending specification and ramifying of moral norms outside the domain of common morality, Gert claims that such perpetual tinkering with the norms of morality would make it impossible for rational agents to know exactly what moral rules are binding with regard to any given case.

On the other hand, Gert modestly insists that his public system governing the conduct of all rational agents does not and cannot yield a single unique moral solution to every problem in practical ethics. In contrast to theories like utilitarianism, which posit the existence, if only in theory, of a single correct solution to every problem, Gert argues that practical ethics is littered with *aporiai* for which there is no unique solution to which all rational agents must assent. Instead of viewing people who differ with us on an issue like abortion as being irrational or mean-spirited, Gert proposes that we view them as having different notions of the class of beings deserving of impartial protection under the moral rules, as people who accord different weights to various harms or interpret the moral rules differently, as people who have different estimates of consequences of publicly allowing a disputed action, or as people who simply disagree on the facts at hand—i.e., differences that are ubiquitous yet often not amenable to rational resolution. Gert helpfully suggests that such a change in attitude could help us find mutually acceptable compromises and reconciliation within the sphere of politics.

Before moving on, I should mention two items whose absence from Gert's conception of common morality might make that conception somewhat controversial. First, notice that, according to Gert, morality exclusively concerns our behavior toward others. Unlike Kant[11] and contemporary Kantians,[12] he does not acknowledge the existence of moral duties to oneself. Thus, whether one is a servile housewife or slave—i.e., a person who is reconciled to her inferior social status and does not believe herself worthy of the human dignity accorded to her master—is a matter of moral indifference to Gert.

---

[11] I. Kant, *Lectures on Ethics*.

[12] T. E. Hill, "Servility and Self-Respect," in *Autonomy and Self-Respect*, ed. T. Hill (Cambridge: Cambridge University Press, 1991), 4–18; L. Denis, "Kant's Ethics and Duties to Oneself," *Pacific Philosophical Quarterly* 78 (2002): 321–348.

Second, and in my view much more problematically, Gert denies (with one notable proviso) the very notion of universal (i.e., non-role–based) moral *duties* to aid others or to prevent harm from befalling them. According to Gert, duties in the strict sense are always negative injunctions to avoid violating any of the moral rules (without sufficient justification); we are only encouraged, not required, to follow any given moral ideal.[13] This omission from common morality puts Gert at odds with Beauchamp and Childress, who claim to find in "the common morality" duties to prevent evil or harm from occurring and to rescue persons in danger.[14] With some vigorous prodding from Dan Brock and others,[15] Gert has come to accept one highly circumscribed moral duty to come to the assistance of others when (1) one is in a unique or close to unique position vis-à-vis the vulnerable party, (2) providing assistance would almost be "cost free," and (3) the evils or harms prevented would be very serious.[16] All other so-called moral duties to assist vulnerable parties are more properly construed, contends Gert, as duties stemming from one's role, such as that of a physician, parent, or public health worker, not as genuine moral duties *tout court* ascribable to all rational moral agents.

An important corollary to Gert's position here bears on the status of positive rights, such as those we find in many contemporary political theories and in the roster of human rights articulated in various declarations and covenants. According to Gert, all such rights are *political*, not moral; that is, they are correlated exclusively with the duties of governments, not of ordinary moral agents.[17]

Gert offers three reasons for drawing the important line between moral requirements and moral encouragements at precisely this point. He begins by drawing two conceptual connections, the first of which links the requirement of impartiality and our notion of moral duty. Moral duties must be observed impartially, without any favoritism toward one's family, clan, ethnic group, profession, social class, or nation. But since duties to aid would require positive actions requiring our time and resources, Gert observes that such "duties" could not be followed impartially, since we always have to decide whom to benefit or rescue, and we cannot benefit

---

[13] Gert, *Common Morality: Deciding What to Do*, 22.

[14] Beauchamp and Childress, *Principles of Biomedical Ethics*, 6th ed. (2009), 372, 374–375.

[15] D. W. Brock, "Gert on the Limits of Morality's Requirements," *Philosophy and Phenomenological Research* 62 (2001): 435–440.

[16] B. Gert, "Reply to Dan Brock," *Philosophy and Phenomenological Research* 62 (2001): 468.

[17] The curious reader might well wonder how it is that such duties can be ascribed exclusively to state governments if they are not also shared in some fashion by the citizens they represent. In addition, Gert's position here would rule out the very possibility that, should a given government fail to uphold its responsibilities to its citizens, those responsibilities might well shift not only to other states but also to other bodies, such as NGOs, international corporations, or, ultimately, to citizens of other countries. Although I believe that Gert is mistaken on this point, I will not pursue this issue further here. Gert, *Common Morality: Deciding What to Do*, 145.

or rescue everyone in need all the time. Furthermore, Gert holds that rules must be obeyed all the time, unless one has an adequate justification; but he regards time per se as irrelevant to one's obligation to obey the moral rules. Hence, he concludes, there cannot be a general duty to aid.

Second, Gert relies upon a conceptual connection between our notion of moral duty and punishment. Taking issue with philosophers and religious traditions that posit a moral requirement to help the needy, Gert insists that such talk of "requirements" is merely rhetorical because it fudges the important distinction between doing something morally wrong and not doing something that is morally good. This distinction, Gert believes, is properly demarcated by liability to punishment. Rational persons limited to rationally required beliefs, he claims, would not approve punishment for people who failed to live up to the moral ideal of assisting those in need, except in the one very restricted scenario mentioned above, but they would most definitely call for liability to punishment regarding a violation of a moral rule.

In addition to the above conceptual points, Gert asserts that establishing a genuine moral duty of assistance to the needy would be "worse than pointless"[18] insofar as it would bring the demands of morality into disrepute. Since we cannot impartially discharge such a duty, which would require all our time, effort, and resources in a futile quest to satisfy everyone's needs, rational impartial people would never agree to such a rule. In the manner of a libertarian political philosopher, Gert stresses what might be called the "supply side" of moral requirements in addition to the "demand side." Clearly, it would be a good thing if everyone in need could be assisted, but turning such assistance into a moral duty, enforced by a public system of punishments, would, Gert asserts, exact too high a price in terms of the freedom we prize to live our lives as we see fit.

CRITIQUE OF GERT'S CONCEPTION OF COMMON MORALITY

What Common Morality?

Gert asserts that, in contrast to most other philosophers before him, he is merely attempting to describe common morality as we all find it, not to modify or improve upon it, and then provide a justification for its strictures.[19] The purely descriptive part includes the moral rules and ideals, as well as the two-step procedure for justifying overriding a moral rule, which in turn includes a catalogue of morally

---

[18] Gert, *Morality: Its Nature and Justification*, 365.

[19] Although Gert implies otherwise, this was precisely the mission that both Kant and Mill set for themselves.

relevant reasons and a hypothetical decision procedure emphasizing impartiality, rationality, and publicity. Is there such a common morality? Does Gert present any evidence to the effect that such a thing or practice really exists? And how credible is Gert's claim that he is merely leaving everything as he finds it, and not merely stipulating or imagining what he would like common morality to be?

Although Gert is often pretty rough on most other philosophers, treating the likes of Kant and Mill as so many errant schoolboys, his claims for his conception of common morality often betray a typically philosophical insouciance with regard to empirical fact. If he were merely attempting, in large measure, to describe common morality as he finds it, then would not some anthropological evidence of this common morality be helpful, if not required? Instead, we are treated to typically "philosophical" refrains: "No rational person could think otherwise," "Everyone agrees that," "No one talks about." etc., as though the horizon of Gert's moral imagination constituted the boundaries of morality itself in all times and places. If there is indeed "overwhelming agreement" on the nature of common morality, as Gert alleges, then why have so many incredibly smart and morally sensitive people (Kant, Mill, Donagan, Beauchamp and Childress, et al.) missed, misunderstood, and mangled its true nature? For all I know, there could be a perfect fit between these two horizons, though I doubt it, but Gert at least owes us some empirical evidence for his descriptive conclusions.

So, is Gert merely describing or is he stipulating the nature and contours of common morality? I shall discuss just three problematic claims here, although many more could be flagged in a more complete account. First, there is his banishment of what we might call all self-regarding behavior from the ambit of common morality. According to Gert, morality only concerns behavior toward others,[20] which leads him to conclude, *inter alia*, that contraception is not, strictly speaking, a moral issue.[21] Although this sounds plausible—most people apart from the Catholic hierarchy would say that contraception is at the very least not a morally *serious* or *difficult* issue—other examples point toward what we might want to call moral duties to oneself, or to what Kant called duties to respect rational nature both in others and in ourselves. Consider the case of the servile housewife or servile slave, both of whom fully embrace their inferior position vis-à-vis their husband or master. Believing themselves totally unworthy of moral respect on account of their gender or lowly social status, such persons have forfeited their status as autonomous agents by finding pleasure in subordination and servitude. Contemporary Kantians might plausibly claim that this housewife and this slave

---

[20] Gert, *Common Morality: Deciding What to Do*, 21.

[21] Ibid., 74

have a moral duty to respect their own moral agency, their own rights to be self-determining beings.[22] These Kantians might be wrong, but Gert owes them an argument rather than dismissive stipulation.

Next, consider Gert's claim that common morality encompasses all the elements listed above. While Gert's observations regarding the content of the moral rules and ideals, and his catalogue of morally relevant factors, are more or less plausible candidates for any conception of a common morality, the second stage of his two-step procedure for determining justifiable rule violations—i.e., his hypothetical test— initially struck this reader as a classic case of sheer stipulation. Is this how rational people in all times and places would actually determine the rightness of their actions when called upon to do so? On second thought, however, it occurred to me that this test has all the earmarks of a standard move within a philosophical *theory* of right action. Indeed, it bears a striking resemblance to Kant's categorical imperative shorn of its implausible metaphysical trappings.

Third, there is the important issue of duties to assist others in need, which Gert, again with one highly restricted exception, relegates to the status of a mere moral ideal that we should be encouraged but not required to follow. Although Gert is, of course, correct to insist on drawing a line between behavior that is genuinely morally required and that which is merely encouraged, the question is whether he draws that line in the right place within the ambit of common morality. Here Gert is not merely stipulating; he gives plenty of colorable supporting arguments for his position. The question is whether those arguments fully support his denial of (almost all) moral requirements to assist. As we shall see in the next section, I have some serious doubts on this score.

Duties to Assist

Let us revisit Gert's arguments step by step, beginning with his two conceptual claims linking our notion of genuine moral duty with the requirements of impartiality and liability to punishment. Although it is true that we can indeed impartially follow the negative injunctions of the moral rules all the time and with regard to all persons, and although it is also true that, given the scarcity of time and resources, we always have to show some partiality or selectivity in rendering positive benefits to others, it is not at all clear that a complete and total failure to render any assistance to others over the course of a lifetime—again, except for

---

[22] Hill, "Servility and Self-Respect," 321–348.

Gert's single exception—would not violate what both Kant and Mill called "imperfect duties" to assist.[23]

Nor is it clear why a suitably hedged but expanded conception of a duty to aid would actually run afoul of the requirement of impartiality. Without conceding Peter Singer's extravagant claim that we should basically put our lives in hock in order to help bring about the best possible consequences overall, we can imagine a moral order in which we have some well-delimited moral duties to help others in need beyond Gert's exceptional case. For example, we can imagine altering just one of Gert's three conditions for justifying a duty to assist—i.e., his requirement that the proposed intervention be "virtually costless"—and conclude that we have a duty to alleviate great suffering or prevent great evils if (a) we are in the best position to do so, and (b) the cost will not be terribly or unfairly burdensome to us.

To me, such an alternative account is more plausible than Gert's treatment of this issue. Even assuming for the sake of argument that Gert, following Mill, may have been correct in asserting that we do not always need the help of others but we always need them not to harm us, I think that most rational agents (Mill included) would agree that if a great harm is pointed directly at one's head, and if another person is in a position to prevent that harm *without excessive or unfair cost to herself*, then it makes sense for morality to posit a duty to prevent such harm in such circumstances. Otherwise, the social practice of morality is in the incongruous position of existing to alleviate or prevent suffering but then just ignoring a major and (often) avoidable source of such suffering.

If we construe the duty of assistance in this broader but still suitably hedged fashion, moreover, we can see how it too, along with negative duties, could be deployed consistently with the norm of impartiality. Such a norm would apply to anyone who found himself or herself in the appropriate circumstances, including the prospect of great harm, being (nearly) uniquely situated to prevent it,[24] and being able to do so without incurring excessive or unfair risks or burdens to oneself. I do not see why rational and impartial people could not universally endorse such a principle.

As for the alleged conceptual link between violation of moral duty and liability to punishment, here too Gert is far too restrictive, presenting us with a view of common morality that many of us do not recognize. First, as Brock noted, some legal jurisdictions have passed so-called Good Samaritan laws that call for legal punishments for failure to assist in some circumstances.[25] So here is an instance

[23] J. S. Mill, *Utilitarianism*; I. Kant, *Groundwork of the Metaphysics of Morals*.

[24] Perhaps a more helpful gloss on this element would stress one's being in a position to prevent the harm while also incurring the least amount of risk or burden to oneself.

[25] Brock, "Gert on the Limits of Morality's Requirements."

where punishment is in fact deployed in response to a "mere" failure to render assistance. Conversely, there are many instances of clear-cut violations of moral rules that we do not believe warrant punishment. If I make a lying promise to someone that I'll return the favor if he will undertake a particularly unpleasant job for me, it is not at all clear that common morality would have me *punished* for it. Ditto for causing someone pain by embarrassing her in public just for fun. We would clearly say that such a person is a jerk, has a bad character, did something wrong, and even violated a moral duty, but we would not necessarily say that he should be liable to punishment.

In place of punishment, I think it enough to insist upon the appropriateness of serious *moral criticism*, levied either by our peers or by our own consciences, to demonstrate the existence of a moral duty. Such usage would be entirely compatible with J. S. Mill's assertion of a connection between moral duty and the penal sanction, from which Gert obviously draws inspiration (and some, but not all, exact wording) here. True, Mill held that we don't label anything as morally wrong unless the responsible person should be punished for it, but he immediately qualifies this with the important proviso, "in some way or other. . . . If not by law, by the opinion of his fellow creatures; if not by opinion, by the reproaches of his own conscience."[26] If this is what we are to mean by "punishment," a term that Gert never adequately defines,[27] then a much wider class of failures to prevent harm can be envisioned that rightly elicit the bad opinion of our fellow creatures and, hence, can rightly be viewed as violations of a moral duty.

It is interesting to note in passing that Gert concedes the appropriateness of criticizing some failures to provide assistance, but he resists the conclusion that such failures (usually) should be liable to punishment as violations of moral duty.[28] Notwithstanding Mill's eminently plausible assertion of a conceptual connection between violation of a moral duty and *some sort of sanction*, either through actual punishment or suffering the bad opinion of humankind, Gert nowhere provides a justification for completely ignoring the second half of Mill's formula. Moreover, it is unclear how Gert, who has already gone on record denying that a failure to follow a moral ideal *needs any kind of justification or excuse at all*,[29] can now say that failures to assist can be criticized but should not be punished. If such failures require no justification or excuse, on what ground could such criticism be warranted?

---

[26] Mill, *Utilitarianism*, 18, V, paragraph 14.

[27] The closest he comes is in his (inadequate) response to Dan Brock. Gert, "Reply to Dan Brock," 466–470.

[28] Gert, *Common Morality: Deciding What to Do*, 52–54.

[29] Gert et al., *Bioethics: A Systematic Approach*, 43.

I conclude, then, that both of Gert's structural or conceptual reasons for rejecting positive duties of assistance are inadequate and excessively restrictive.

Gert has one remaining (nonconceptual) argument at his disposal on behalf of his rejection of (most) positive duties, which I shall call "the burdens of morality" argument. As we have seen, Gert emphasizes the "supply side" of the moral equation, insisting that the burdens imposed by common morality not be viewed as excessive by impartial, rational agents. In this connection, Gert concedes that such agents would indeed approve of the imposition of a strict duty to assist, backed up by socially sanctioned punishments, but only in the narrowest of cases sketched above involving unique ability to help, virtually no cost, and a great evil to be averted. If someone fails to aid a vulnerable person in such a scenario, Gert opines that rational people would assent to punishment in such an extreme case, but only in such a case. (Interestingly, however, Gert does not call for carefully crafted Good Samaritan laws in such cases. Why not?) Piling on any additional duties to assist over and above this narrowest set of circumstances would, Gert suggests, strike such agents as an undue restriction upon their freedom to live their lives and deploy their resources as they see fit.[30] Here Gert's account of common morality appears to mesh perfectly with one prominent example of libertarian political philosophy, which also argues against a general duty of assistance except in this one sort of case.[31] I would argue that such a concession, while certainly correct for this very narrow range of cases, is entirely ad hoc if limited exclusively to such cases.

I suppose it depends upon exactly who these "rational, impartial people" are and what part of the world they inhabit. Let us then picture in our mind's eye the roughly billion people on earth who subsist on a dollar a day or less.[32] These are the people suffering from what Peter Singer calls "absolute poverty,"[33] whose lives (and the lives of their children) are currently wrecked by chronic malnutrition, disease, premature death, lack of education, the most rudimentary economic opportunities, and so on. It is interesting to speculate upon how such people might respond to Gert's question—i.e., what is more important to you as an impartial rational agent, being free from violations of your negative rights to person and property, or acquiring those positive goods such as food, medical care, and education that will allow you to forestall starvation and premature death? For these people, a duty to assist would most likely be construed as something much more important to their

---

[30] Gert, *Common Morality: Deciding What to Do*, 124.

[31] L. Lomasky, *Persons, Rights, and the Moral Community* (New York: Oxford University Press, 1987).

[32] P. Collier, *The Bottom Billion: Why the Poorest Countries are Failing and What Can be Done About It* (Oxford: Oxford University Press, 2008).

[33] P. Singer, *Practical Ethics*, 2nd ed. (Cambridge: Cambridge University Press, 1999).

basic interests than a mere duty to assist others in "advancing their ends," as Gert sometimes dismissively puts it.[34]

Suppose now that, notwithstanding the very real obstacles to international development and just for the sake of argument, the plight of the bottom billion could be substantially and permanently alleviated by the levy of a very modest tax on the most affluent members of the world's most affluent countries. Here we would have a case where a great and ongoing calamity involving a billion human beings could be avoided, but those in need of assistance exist halfway around the globe, not at all in close proximity, and the burdens imposed on the proposed taxpayers would be modest or "not unreasonable" but certainly not "virtually costless." So Gert would no doubt conclude that such a scenario failed his test for a true duty of assistance. It would be generous of us to assist, he would say, but no one has a genuine moral duty to help by paying such a tax.

This is not the place to join an important and lively debate currently raging in contemporary political philosophy,[35] so I shall merely note here that it is (or should be) at least an open and legitimate question whether the governments, citizens, corporations, and non-governmental organizations (NGOs) of the world's wealthiest nations have genuine moral requirements to assist the bottom billion and, if so, how far they extend. This is not a question that should be decided by moral fiat based upon the manner in which relatively well-off people would hypothetically balance their competing needs for security, subsistence, and liberty. It could well be the case that the practice described by Gert as our "common morality" might be better described as a common morality that developed over the centuries for relatively well-off people in well-off places.

This possibility has been thoughtfully explored by Samuel Scheffler.[36] Our commonsense conception of morality, Scheffler writes, exhibits a "restrictive" (i.e., narrow) notion of individual responsibility, one based upon some basic, seemingly commonsensical moral doctrines such as the following: (1) moral agents have a special responsibility for what they themselves do, not for what they merely fail to prevent (i.e., negative duties take priority over positive duties); (2) one has distinctive responsibilities or special obligations toward one's family and others in

---

[34] Gert or a libertarian might respond at this point that this judgment on the part of the bottom billion fails the test of impartiality. They are clearly just looking out for their own interests. But could not the same be said of well-off people in developed countries who refuse to assist? Our desire to maintain our current consumerist lifestyle might depend upon economic or political advantages that we may not deserve. To assume that we do deserve them may be to beg the question.

[35] T. Brooks, ed., *The Global Justice Reader* (Oxford: Blackwell Publishing, 2008).

[36] S. Scheffler, *Boundaries and Allegiances: Problems of Justice and Responsibility in Liberal Thought* (Oxford: Oxford University Press, 2001)

certain sorts of special relationships; (3) human social relations consist primarily in small-scale interactions among independent individual agents.

According to Scheffler, elements such as these have coalesced into a complex phenomenology of human agency, according to which acts have priority over omissions, proximate effects have priority over distant effects, and individual effects have primacy over group effects.[37] Scheffler shrewdly observes, however, that this seemingly commonsensical view of the moral landscape did not evolve in an historical vacuum, and that what we take for common sense (or common morality) could well undergo transformation in an emerging globalized environment. He notes that several salient features of the modern world—e.g., our burgeoning science and technology, the Internet, the ease of global travel, increased economic and political interdependency among nations, etc.—are presently conspiring to effect just such a transformation, putting great moral and psychological pressure upon our present conception of limited moral agency. All of us are increasingly enmeshed in various large-scale causal processes and practices, each making tiny contributions to cumulative social consequences of enormous import for others around the globe. We may well be entering a world in which we are both causally and morally bound to the people who grow our coffee and stitch our clothing in distant lands, even though, as individuals, we cannot control and often cannot fully comprehend our respective places in this vast global network.

Unlike Singer, Scheffler does not pretend that our commonsensical restrictive conception of human agency will soon easily be replaced by an alternative conception better attuned to a more robust sense of responsibility in a global age, but he does us a great service in highlighting how what we take to be commonsense morality is actually a historical artifact that could, and most likely will, change in the direction of a less narrow and more demanding conception of individual responsibility.

To sum up on the theme of duties of assistance, then, we have seen how neither of Gert's attempts at conceptual gerrymandering succeeds, and that serious moral duties to others are both compatible with impartiality and need not be screened for liability to punishment as defined by Gert. We have also seen that, given the goals that Gert has ascribed to morality and our vital needs for *both* liberty and subsistence, the "burdens of morality" argument also fails. Rational and impartial agents, realizing their own vulnerability in a complex and often indifferent world, would favor a moral system that included more demanding positive duties than Gert is willing to allow. Finally, we have seen with Scheffler's help that Gert's

[37] Ibid., 36–39.

conception of common morality does not exist in an historical vacuum, and that current developments on the global scene are already undermining our confidence in such a restrictive conception of individual responsibility. Which brings us to my final subject in this essay: *viz.*, Gert's claim that common morality does not change.

Does Common Morality Change?

Gert writes, "[M]orality does not change."[38] What can he possibly mean by this? Like Beauchamp and Childress, Gert recognizes the great diversity of specific moral codes in different places at different times; and, like them, he acknowledges that the particular moral culture of any given society can undergo profound changes over time, so what we view as morally acceptable behavior in the contemporary United States could easily have shocked the consciences of colonial Americans.[39] These differences can, Gert would suggest, be fully explained by differences in assigning weights to different harms and goods, different interpretations of the moral rules, different conceptions of what's morally relevant, and so on. But beneath all this diversity, Gert insists, lies the bedrock of common morality, which does not change, binding everyone at all times and all places to the same set of norms.

While many, perhaps most, people must find it comforting to be told that morality does not change, we need to look a bit more closely at this claim to see just how much solace it really offers to those who recoil at the specter of contingency in moral matters. Toward this end, I would first draw the reader's attention to passages where Gert appears to overestimate the degree of consensus among rational, impartial moral agents. Here is a typical example: "No one engages in a moral discussion of questions like 'Is it morally acceptable to deceive patients in order to get them to participate in an experimental treatment that has no hope of benefiting them but that one happens to be curious about' *because everyone knows that such deception is not justified.*[40]

Apparently, Dr. Chester Southam, the key protagonist in the famous Jewish Chronic Disease Hospital case, never got this news. As is well known, in the summer of 1963, Southam and colleagues injected twenty-two elderly, debilitated, and mentally compromised residents of a Jewish nursing home with live, cultured

[38] Gert et al., *Bioethics: A Systematic Approach*, 104.

[39] In the immortal words of Cole Porter: "In olden days, a glimpse of stocking / Was looked on as something shocking. / But now, God knows, / Anything goes." C. Porter, "Anything Goes," 1934.

[40] Gert et al., *Bioethics: A Systematic Approach*, 23, emphasis added.

cancer cells in order to confirm an hypothesis in the budding field of immunology.[41] What was truly remarkable, even shocking, at the time was not that Southam was a professor at a prestigious medical school, that he received NIH funding and the full-throated support of the medical profession of his day, or that leading journalists ridiculed his critics in the name of medical progress but, rather, that Southam was actually successfully brought up on charges of unprofessional conduct by the New York State Board of Regents. Here is a clear-cut example of wrenching moral change in a profession and a culture that Gert would brush aside, fully assured that rational, impartial agents would always and everywhere find such conduct morally unjustified.

Now Gert would no doubt respond to this story by noting that the differences in medical morality then and now have to do not with changes in the moral rules and ideals, the bedrock of his system, but, rather, *inter alia*, with what people from different eras took to be morally relevant (e.g., the wishes and rights of patients) and how they weighed the goods of medical research versus the protection of human freedom. This would allow Gert to acknowledge moral change at the periphery, as it were, while still maintaining that at its core morality does not change.

Although I follow Gert's reasoning here, I fail to see how it could provide moral comfort to those who want to be told that morality never changes. Dr. Southam, sitting in the dock before the New York Board of Regents, would most likely not have found much solace in Gert's explanation. His whole career was threatened by a momentous change in medical morality, which suddenly elevated patients' rights above the prerogatives of distinguished physicians.

In large measure, I suppose, this debate comes down to the question of what Gert means by "morality" when he says that morality does not change. If he means, as suggested above, that "morality" encompasses solely the moral rules and ideals, so that changes in the interpretation of moral rules or of what is morally relevant to the resolution of cases do not count, then his position seems plausible, even if not comforting to those uncomfortable with the prospect of moral change. It is not clear, though, that this move is actually open to Gert, who clearly includes in his conception of common morality not only the moral rules and ideas but also his two-step decision procedure involving the morally relevant factors and his hypothetical thought experiment featuring rational, impartial judges contemplating rules for a public moral system. If we broaden his notion of morality to include all these disparate elements, then it is hard to escape the conclusion that morality does indeed undergo significant change, even though the general rubrics

[41] John D. Arras, "The Jewish Chronic Disease Hospital Case," in *The Oxford Handbook of Clinical Research Ethics*, eds. E. J. Emanuel et al. (New York: Oxford University Press, 2008), 73–79.

through which we think about morality (e.g., "the morally relevant features") may not change.

The closer one reads Gert, the more his inventory of morally relevant factors looms as a decisive element in his moral system. Just as Beauchamp and Childress stress the need to specify moral norms stemming from the common morality in the presence of new factual contexts, so Gert stresses the need to get clear on all the factors that might be viewed as morally relevant to a particular case. Indeed, notwithstanding Gert's persistent (and in my view misguided) criticisms of specification in *PBE*, it appears that specification and attentiveness to morally relevant factors are roughly identical means of "keeping it real" in these rival systems—i.e., of making sure that the principles or rules of morality are properly deployed in concrete situations. But if our inventory of morally relevant factors can dramatically change over time, as it clearly did in the case of Dr. Southam and the medical establishment of his time, who obviously did not think that "his" research subjects' wishes and desires were at all morally relevant, then "morality" as even Gert defines it can indeed change in some very important and often disturbing ways. And if Scheffler's observations and speculations turn out to be harbingers of a significantly modified phenomenology of agency, if future generations in an entirely globalized world look back on our current commonsense conception of individual responsibility as being unthinkably narrow and parochial, then Gert's claim that morality does not change is likely to strike them as just so much philosophical posturing of a bygone era.

In sum, then, some aspects of Gert's approach to common morality are deeply problematic. He claims to be merely describing common morality as it is, but he often seems to be merely stipulating what he thinks common morality should be. He does not even seriously consider the Kantian conception of common morality that would include duties to self in the common morality; and his claim that, with one exceedingly narrow exception, there simply are no general duties to assist others in need has been shown to be woefully underargued and misguided. Finally, his claim that morality does not change has been shown to be false on the basis of Gert's own premises.

CONCLUSION

As we have seen, common morality figures prominently in the respective projects of Gert and Beauchamp and Childress, but their accounts differ so radically in motivation, content, and scope that one might well wonder whether they are talking about the same thing. For Beauchamp and Childress, an emphasis on common morality represents a repudiation of top-down, theory-laden, deductivist thinking and a basic starter kit of abstract moral norms meant to provide justificatory ballast to subsequent moral reflection. For Gert, by contrast, common morality is nothing less than a handy name for his entire system of ethics. So if we ask about the ultimate significance of common morality for bioethics, it should come as no great surprise that there is no univocal answer to this question. It all depends upon whose conception of common morality we have in mind.

To ask about Gertian common morality's contribution to bioethics is to ask a much broader and more daunting question than that posed by Beauchamp and Childress's conception of common morality—*viz.*, what is Gert's overall contribution to the field? This is far too large and important a question to tackle here, especially since even my analysis of Gert's conception of common morality has not pretended to be remotely comprehensive. To reach an all-things-considered assessment of Gert's contributions to bioethics, apart from his interesting early work in the philosophy of medicine, one would have to delve much deeper into other corners of his far-flung system, including his challenging theories of rationality and impartiality, the adequacy of his two-step decision procedure, and his underdeveloped thoughts about justice.

For now, then, I can only conclude that certain elements of Gert's magisterial conception of common morality are controversial at best and woefully inadequate at worst. He has a tendency to find in common morality what he himself put there, and his highly restricted conception of duties of assistance strikes this reader as ad hoc, inadequately defended, and unworthy of a project whose goal is to lessen the amount of misery in the world. For all that, Gert, who died in 2011, obviously was a giant in the fields of biomedical ethics and philosophy, whose far-reaching and impressively systematic approach to the subject has been an inspiration to many. For me, however, this longing for systematicity represents a heavy-handed and unpromising alternative to Montaigne's more modestly ironic *esprit de l'essai*.

3

Getting Down to Cases

THE REVIVAL OF CASUISTRY IN BIOETHICS

DEVELOPED IN THE early Middle Ages as a method of bringing abstract and universal ethico-religious precepts to bear on particular moral situations, casuistry has had a checkered history.[1] In the hands of expert practitioners during its salad days in the sixteenth and seventeenth centuries, casuistry generated a rich and morally sensitive literature devoted to numerous real-life ethical problems, such as truth-telling, usury, and the limits of revenge. By the late seventeenth century, however, casuistical reasoning had degenerated into a notoriously sordid form of logic-chopping in the service of personal expediency.[2] To this day, the very term "casuistry" conjures up pejorative images of disingenuous argument and moral laxity.

In spite of casuistry's tarnished reputation, some philosophers have claimed that casuistry, shorn of its unfortunate excesses, has much to teach us about the resolution of moral problems in medicine. Indeed, through the work of Albert Jonsen[3] and Stephen Toulmin[4] this "new casuistry" has emerged as a definite alternative

[1] A. R. Jonsen and S. Toulmin, *The Abuse of Casuistry: A History of Moral Reasoning* (Berkeley: University of California Press, 1988).

[2] B. Pascal, *Lettres écrites à un provincial*, ed. A. Adam (Paris: Flammarion, 1566/1981).

[3] A. R. Jonsen, "Can an Ethicist Be a Consultant?," in *Frontiers in Medical Ethics*, ed. V. Abernethy (Cambridge, MA: Ballinger Publishing, 1980), 157–171; A. R. Jonsen, "Casuistry and Clinical Ethics," *Theoretical Medicine* 7 (1986a): 65–74; A. R. Jonsen, "Casuistry," in *Westminster Dictionary of Christian Ethics*, eds. J. F. Childress and J. Macquarrie (Philadelphia, PA: Westminster Press, 1986b), 78–80; Jonsen and Toulmin, *The Abuse of Casuistry*.

[4] S. Toulmin, "The Tyranny of Principles," *Hastings Center Report* 11 (1981): 31–39; Jonsen and Toulmin, *The Abuse of Casuistry*.

to the hegemony of the so-called "applied ethics" method of moral analysis that has dominated most bioethical scholarship and teaching since the early 1970s.[5] In stark contrast to methods that begin from "on high" with the working out of a moral theory and culminate in the deductivistic application of norms to particular factual situations, this new casuistry works from the "bottom up," emphasizing practical problem-solving by means of nuanced interpretations of individual cases. This chapter will assess the promise of this reborn casuistry for bioethics.

Before we can exhibit the salient features of this rival bioethical methodology, we must first confront an initial ambiguity in the definition of casuistry. As Jonsen describes it, "casuistry" is the art or skill of applying abstract or general principles to particular cases.[6] In this context, Jonsen notes that the major monotheistic religions were likely sources for casuistic ethics, since they all combined a strong sense of duty with a definite set of moral precepts couched in universal terms. The preeminent task for devout Christians, Jews, and Muslims was thus to learn how to apply these universal precepts to particular situations, where their stringency or applicability might well be affected by particular factual conditions. Our morality may tell us, for example, that "killing is wrong," but we are then left with the difficult task of determining in concrete circumstances whether a particular act amounts to a form of killing and, if so, whether the killing might possibly be excused or justified. Although just about every moral viewpoint will condemn the killing of an innocent child for selfish motives, other more problematic cases challenge our understanding and deployment of this rule. Is disconnecting a patient from a ventilator a form of killing, or does it just amount to "letting die"? Is it permissible to kill an animal for food, a fetus for economic reasons, or a terminally ill cancer patient at her own request? In order to answer these more complicated questions, we need to develop a complex "casuistical" account of the rule and its application to particular cases.

Defined in this way as the art of applying abstract principles to particular cases, the new casuistry could appropriately be viewed not so much as a rival to the applied ethics model but, rather, as a necessary complement to any and all moral theories or religious ethics that would guide our conduct in specific situations. So long as we take some general principles or maxims to be ethically binding, no matter what their source, we must learn through the casuist's art to fit them to particular cases. But on this gloss of "casuistry," even the most hidebound adherent of the applied ethics model—someone who held that answers to particular moral

---

[5] T. L. Beauchamp and J. F. Childress, *Principles of Biomedical Ethics*, 3rd ed. (New York: Oxford University Press, 1989).

[6] Jonsen, "Casuistry."

dilemmas can be deduced from universal theories and principles—would have to count as a casuist. So defined, casuistry might appear to be little more than the handmaiden of applied ethics.

There is, however, another interpretation of casuistry in the writings of Jonsen and Toulmin that provides a distinct alternative to the applied ethics model. Instead of focusing on the need to fit principles to cases, this interpretation stresses the particular nature, derivation, and function of the principles deployed by the new casuists. Through this alternative theory of principles, we begin to discern a morality that develops not from the top down as in most interpretations of Roman law but, rather, from case to case (or from the bottom up) as in the common law. What differentiates the new casuistry from applied ethics, then, is not the mere recognition that principles must eventually be applied but, rather, a particular account of the logic and derivation of the principles that we use in moral discourse.

A "CASE-DRIVEN" METHOD

Contrary to "theory-driven" methodologies, which approach particular situations already equipped with a full complement of moral principles, the new casuistry insists that our moral knowledge must develop incrementally through the analysis of concrete cases. From this perspective, the very notion of "applied ethics" embodies a redundancy, while the correlative notion of "theoretical ethics" conveys an illusory and counterproductive ideal for ethical thought.

If ethics is done properly, the new casuists imply, it will already have been immersed in concrete cases from the very start. To be sure, one can always apply the results of previous ethical inquiries to fresh problems, but to the casuists good ethics is always "applied" in the sense that it grows out of the analysis of individual cases. It's not as though one could or should first develop a pristine ethical theory planing above the world of moral particulars, and then, having put the finishing touches on the theory, point it in the direction of particular cases. Rejecting the idea that there are such things as "essences" in the domain of ethics, Toulmin,[7] citing Aristotle and Dewey, argues that this pursuit of rigorous theory is unhinged from the realities of the moral life and animated by an illusory quest for moral certainty. Thus, whereas many academic philosophers scorn "applied ethics" as a pale shadow of the real thing (*viz.*, ethical theory), the new casuists insist that good

[7] Toulmin, "The Tyranny of Principles."

ethics is always immersed in the messy reality of cases, and that the philosophers' penchant for abstract and rigorous theory is a misleading fetish.

According to both Jonsen and Toulmin, the work of the National Commission for the Protection of Human Subjects of Biomedical and Behavioral Research provides an excellent example of this case-driven method in bioethics.[8] Although the various commissioners represented different academic, religious, and philosophical perspectives, Jonsen and Toulmin (who both served, respectively, as commissioner and consultant to the commission) attest that the commissioners could still reach consensus by discussing the issues "taxonomically." Bracketing their differences on "matters of principle," the commissioners would begin with an analysis of paradigmatic cases of harm, cruelty, fairness, and generosity, and then branch out to more complex and difficult cases posed by biomedical research. The commissioners thus "triangulate[d] their way across the complex terrain of moral life,"[9] gradually extending their analysis of relatively straightforward problems to issues requiring a much more delicate balancing of competing values.

Thus, instead of looking for ethical progress in the theoretical equivalent of the Second Coming—i.e., the establishment of *the* correct ethical theory—Jonsen and Toulmin contend that a more realistic and attainable idea of progress is afforded by this notion of moral "triangulation," an incremental approach to problems whose model can be found in the history of our common law. Just as English-speaking peoples have developed highly complex and sophisticated legal frameworks for thinking about tort liability and criminal guilt without the benefit of pre-established legal principles, so (Jonsen and Toulmin argue) ought we to develop a "common morality" or "morisprudence" on the basis of case analysis—without recourse to some pre-established moral theory or moral principles.[10]

CORE ELEMENTS OF CASUISTICAL ANALYSIS

In order to explicate the more salient features of contemporary casuistry in bioethics, we shall begin, appropriately, with a case drawn from the experience of a neonatal intensive care unit:

> Baby Boy Johnson was the "lucky" one. Ten months ago, he and his twin brother had been born prematurely at 28 weeks to their drug-addicted mother.

[8] Jonsen and Toulmin, *The Abuse of Casuistry*, 16–19, 264, 305, 338.

[9] Toulmin, "The Tyranny of Principles."

[10] For an interesting application of a casuistical method to law and policy, see Cass Sunstein, *Legal Reasoning and Political Conflict* (New York: Oxford University Press, 1998).

His brother had died shortly after birth, but Robert had survived, barely, languishing all this time in the pediatric intensive care unit (NICU). "Failure to thrive" is the generic medical description: Born at a mere 2.6 pounds, he now weighed only 6.6 pounds after months of intensive treatment.

Robert was a flaccid, immobile encyclopedia of pediatric ailments. Early on, he had developed a severe lung disorder requiring mechanical ventilation, followed by the usual litany of neonatal catastrophe: a serious intracranial bleed, damaging strokes, seizures, episodes of sepsis, and failure to absorb nutrients. To address the latter problem, a gastrostomy tube was surgically inserted but proved insufficient. Then the surgeon tried to bypass the failing gut with a catheter designed to deliver artificial nutrients directly into the bloodstream; but after two hours of pounding on Robert's skeletal frame, he gave up in frustration. A resident summed up the case: "No body mass, no lungs, no calories to the brain . . . no hope."

Given Robert's dismal prognosis, the doctors began to feel that they were torturing him for no good reason. A nurse told the group that she had to apologize to Robert each time she had to stick him with a needle, which was all-too-frequent. In spite of the caregivers' desire to release Robert from his suffering, his poor, unsophisticated mother and father continued to hope for a "miracle" in this temple of high-tech medicine. The father asks, "Will my son play football?" The mother, perhaps haunted by the likely possibility that her drug habit had damaged her son, asks, "When will my child get off the machine and come home?" Denying the inevitable, Robert's parents steadfastly demand of a horrified staff that "everything be done" for their devastated child.[11]

Paradigm, Analogy, Taxonomy

Rather than viewing such a case primarily as a site for the immediate deployment of various abstract bioethical principles, the modern casuist must first provide a robust and detailed description of the case, while fitting it under a certain rubric, such as "termination of treatment." This description will usually include an inventory of the likely moral reasons or "maxims" that might typically be invoked in such circumstances. Thus, the casuist would be attentive to what was going on in the case—that is, the interests and wishes of the various parties, the child's

---

[11] This case is quoted from J. D. Arras, "A Case Approach," in *A Companion to Bioethics*, eds., H. Khuse and P. Singer (Malden, MA: Blackwell Publishers, 1998), 107.

medical condition and prognosis, the distinct histories that brought each of the parties to this impasse—and the variety of maxims or middle-level principles triggered by situations of this type, such as "Parents should normally make medical decisions for their children" and "Medically futile treatment need not be offered."[12]

The next step is to fit the case as described into a taxonomy, a structured reservoir of responses to similar cases that contains various paradigm cases of conduct judged to be manifestly right or wrong, virtuous or shameful.[13] The casuist argues that if moral certitude is to be located anywhere, it resides in our responses to such cases. We know, for example, that it is wrong to kill people without their consent, a paradigmatically wrongful act. We know this, moreover, with greater certitude than we know exactly why killing is wrong or which moral theory best explains why it is. Indeed, were a seemingly attractive principle to call for a different response to one of these paradigm cases, that would usually be a good reason to jettison the proposed principle. Thus, casuists are fond of saying that whatever moral certainty we have is to be found at the level of the case, not at the level of abstract principles or theory.

The casuist then tries to locate the new and problematic case on a continuum of cases stretching from a paradigm of acceptable conduct at one end to one of unacceptable conduct at the other end. Thus, in our case, she might fix on the standard sort of case involving well-educated, well-meaning parents who are generally agreed to have a right of parental decision making. Or, she might conjure up the sort of case where the parents' putative right to make decisions might be effectively overridden. In this particular NICU, there was such a case. Several years before, a case involving a child with a fatal diagnosis (trisomy 18) and a horribly externalized gut (gastroischesis) had provided a defining moment for the unit's evolving moral taxonomy. The surgery to repair the gut would have involved significant and protracted pain and suffering for a child with an already fatal prognosis, but the child's parents had insisted on treatment, saying that surgery was "God's will." In this case, the entire medical team had reached consensus that they would not honor the usual maxim of deferring to parental wishes, because the treatment would have been painful, futile, and unaccompanied by compensating benefit.

The crucial task of the casuist, then, is to determine where along this spectrum of paradigmatic cases the present case falls. Indeed, for the casuist, to say that someone "knows bioethics" is in large measure to say that he or she is thoroughly familiar with all the "big" or paradigmatic cases and knows how to reason from them to a

[12] Jonsen, "Casuistry as Methodology in Clinical Ethics," *Theoretical Medicine* 12 (1991): 295–307.
[13] Jonsen and Toulmin, *The Abuse of Casuistry*; Jonsen, "Casuistry as Methodology."

suitable result in new and perplexing cases. This is done by means of *analogical* thinking.[14] The casuist must compare the case at hand with the paradigm cases in order to determine how they are alike and how they differ in morally relevant respects. In our ICU case, the casuist asks whether the situation involving the patient is closer to the paradigm cases in which parents' right of decision making is honored, or to the case of the child with trisomy 18. In spite of the evident differences between the Johnson case and the trisomy case, the medical team felt that the similarities were powerful and outweighed the differences. In both cases, treatment was deemed both "medically futile" and extremely burdensome for the child. In this way, casuistical reasoning gives a concrete significance to the abstract criterion of "excessive burden."

This process of reasoning has much in common with the common law. In contrast to normative systems founded on explicit codes and pre-established principles, both the common law and casuistry work from the bottom up, inductively and incrementally developing new principles to deal with problematic cases. Accordingly, casuistry is often referred to as a kind of "common law morality."

THE ROLE OF PRINCIPLES IN THE NEW CASUISTRY

Contrary to common interpretations of Roman law and to deductivist ethical theories, wherein principles are said to preexist the actual cases to which they apply, the new casuistry contends that ethical principles are "discovered" in the cases themselves, just as common law legal principles are developed in and through judicial decisions on particular legal cases.[15] To be sure, common law and "common law morality" (or "morisprudence") contain a body of principles, too; but the way these principles are derived, articulated, used, and taught is very different from the Roman law and deductivist ethical approach.[16]

Moral Principles: Derivation, Normative Status, Meaning, and Weight

Casuists disagree among themselves about the normative status and derivation of principles in moral reasoning. Some espouse a radically particularist position, claiming that moral principles are mere inductive generalizations based upon our intuitive responses to cases.[17] These principles, it is claimed, merely raise our

[14] Jonsen, "Casuistry as Methodology"; Sunstein, *Legal Reasoning and Political Conflict*.
[15] Jonsen, "Casuistry and Clinical Ethics."
[16] Hanna Pitkin, *Wittgenstein and Justice* (Berkeley: University of California Press, 1972).
[17] Toulmin, "The Tyranny of Principles," 31–39. See also B. Hooker and M. Little, *Moral Particularism* (Oxford: Oxford University Press, 2000).

intuitions about cases to a higher level of abstraction, and thus do not really tell us anything new. As such, principles have no independent normative force, and thus cannot be used to criticize our fundamental responses to paradigmatic cases. We shall refer to this as the "hard-core" conception of casuistry.

Other casuists, while acknowledging the dependence of principles on our history of moral experience, claim nevertheless that these principles can have an action-guiding or normative force that isn't reducible to our responses to paradigm cases.[18] For these more moderate or "soft-core" casuists, paradigm cases are precisely those that most clearly, powerfully, and unambiguously embody the truth of a given moral principle or maxim. They argue that casuistry, properly understood, is not so much an alternative as a necessary complement to the development and deployment of normative principles.[19]

In spite of this fundamental difference, both the radical, hard-core particularists and the moderate, soft-core casuists agree that whatever meaning a particular principle might have crucially depends upon the role it has played in the history of our previous interpretations. They agree that principles do not emerge from some celestial vault, fully articulated and ready for application to cases. Rather, their meaning is slowly developed and refined as we move from one set of important cases to another. Thus, the right to refuse medical treatment is not simply equivalent to an abstract right to liberty; its precise meaning is forged in the process of working through a large number of treatment refusal cases, each posing some new twist or nuance.[20]

Likewise, both hard- and soft-core casuistical factions agree that the weight of any given principle cannot be determined in the abstract. Like meaning, weight must be gauged in the context of the case. Casuists thus agree with the defenders of ethical "intuitionism" who reject the possibility of a pre-established hierarchy of values and principles. Eschewing any such "lexical ordering" of principles,[21] casuists insist that the details of each case determine the precise weight of all the relevant yet conflicting moral principles at stake. Thus, the principle of autonomy may prevail in one treatment refusal case where the patient's choice is deemed to be competent, well informed, and no threat to

---

[18] A. R. Jonsen, "Casuistry: An Alternative or Complement to Principles?," *Kennedy Institute of Ethics Journal* 5 (1995): 37–51.

[19] J. Arras, "Getting Down to Cases: The Revival of Casuistry in Bioethics," *Journal of Medicine and Philosophy* 16, no. 1 (1991): 29–51. See also Beauchamp and Childress, *Principles of Biomedical Ethics*, 4th ed. (New York: Oxford University Press 1994), 92–100; B. Brody, *Life and Death Decision Making* (New York: Oxford University Press, 1998).

[20] For an excellent example of a full-blown casuistical analysis of forgoing life-sustaining treatments in a wide variety of factual situations, see Brody, *Life and Death Decision Making*, chs. 5–7.

[21] J. Rawls, *A Theory of Justice* (Cambridge, MA: Harvard University Press, 1971), 42.

the welfare or resources of others; but it may be trumped in other cases where the claims of autonomy are weaker or the rival claims of others to scarce resources are stronger. Casuists caution that there is no rule that would allow us to determine, ahead of time, which value ought to prevail in any given case. Echoing a familiar Aristotelian theme, they insist that there is no substitute for good judgment (*phronesis*) based upon the particulars—the who, what, where, when, how much—of the case.[22]

The Priority of Practice

In the applied ethics model, principles not only "come before" our practices in the sense of being antecedently derived from theory before being applied to cases; they also have priority over practices in the sense that their function is to justify (or criticize) practices. Indeed, it is precisely through this logical priority of principles over practice that the applied ethics model derives its critical edge. It is just the reverse for the new casuists, who sometimes imply that ethical principles are nothing more than mere *summaries* of meanings already embedded in our actual practices.[23] Rather than serving as a justification for certain practices, principles within some versions of the new casuistry often merely seem to *report* in summary fashion what we have already decided.

This logical priority of practice to principles is clearly evident in Jonsen and Toulmin's ruminations on the experience of the National Commission for the Protection of Human Subjects. In attempting to carry out the mandate of Congress to develop principles for the ethical conduct of research on humans, the commissioners could have straightforwardly drafted a set of principles and then applied them to problematic cases. Instead, note Jonsen and Toulmin, the commissioners acted like good casuists, plunging immediately into nuanced discussions of cases. Progress in these discussions was achieved not by applying agreed-upon principles but, rather, by seeking agreement on responses to particular cases. Indeed, according to this account, the *Belmont Report* which articulated the commission's moral principles and serves to this day as a major source of the "applied ethics" approach to moral reasoning, was written at the end of the commission's deliberations, long after its members had already reached consensus on the issues.[24]

---

[22] Jonsen and Toulmin, *The Abuse of Casuistry*, 19, 58–74.

[23] Toulmin, "The Tyranny of Principles."

[24] Jonsen, "Casuistry and Clinical Ethics," 71.

The Open Texture of Principles

In contrast to the deductivist method, whose principles glide unsullied over the facts, the principles of the new casuistry are always subject to further revision and articulation in light of new cases. This is true not only because casuistical principles are inextricably enmeshed in their factual surroundings, but also because the determination of the decisive or morally relevant features of this factual web is often a highly uncertain and controversial business. By way of example, consider the question of withdrawing artificial feeding as presented in the case of Claire Conroy.[25] One of the crucial precedents for this case, both legally and morally, was the famous Quinlan[26] decision. What were the morally relevant features of Karen Quinlan's situation, and what might they teach us about our responsibilities to Claire Conroy? Was it crucial that Ms. Quinlan was described as being in a persistent vegetative state? Or that she was being maintained by a mechanical respirator? If so, then one might well conclude that Claire Conroy's situation—i.e., that of a patient with severe dementia being maintained by a plastic, nasogastric feeding tube—is sufficiently disanalogous to Quinlan's to compel continued treatment. On the other hand, a rereading of Quinlan might reveal other features of that case that tell in favor of withdrawing Conroy's feeding tube, such as the unlikelihood of Karen's ever recovering sapient life, the bleakness of her prognosis, and the questionable proportion of benefits to burdens derived from the treatment.

Although the Quinlan case may have begun by standing for the patient's right to refuse treatment, subsequent readings of that case in light of later cases have fastened onto other aspects of the case, thereby giving rise to modifications of the original principle, or perhaps even to the wholesale substitution of new principles for the old. The principles of casuistic analysis might thus be said to exhibit an "open texture."[27] Somewhat in the manner of Thomas Kuhn's "paradigms" of scientific research,[28] each significant case in bioethics stands as an object for further articulation and specification under new or more complex conditions. Viewed this way, casuistical analysis might be summarized as a form of reasoning by means of examples that always point beyond themselves. Both the examples and the principles derived from them are always subject to reinterpretation and gradual modification in light of subsequent examples.

---

[25] *Matter of Claire C. Conroy*, Supreme Court of New Jersey, 486 A.2d 1209 (1985).

[26] *Matter of Quinlan*, Supreme Court of New Jersey, 355 A. 2d 647 (1976).

[27] H. L. A. Hart, *The Concept of Law* (Oxford: Oxford University Press, 1961), 120ff.

[28] T. Kuhn, *The Structure of Scientific Revolutions*, 2nd ed. (Chicago: University of Chicago Press, 1970).

Casuistry as Rhetoric

In contrast, then, to methodological approaches that view ethics as a quasi-scientific enterprise bent on deductive demonstration of particular truths, casuistry emerges as a thoroughly *rhetorical* mode of inquiry.[29] Whereas the partisans of a geometric approach attempt to convince through long chains of reasoning finally punctuated by the claim, "You cannot think otherwise on pain of inconsistency!," casuists attempt to persuade by adducing numerous and often disparate considerations. Thus, instead of basing their argument for a right to health care on any single principle, such as utility, casuists typically invoke a cluster of complementary considerations including not just utility but also equal opportunity, communitarian themes, and the historical commitment of the medical profession to serve the poor.[30] Although this method lacks the theoretical simplicity and aesthetic allure of more monistic approaches, it is much more likely to convince a larger number of people, many of whom may not embrace a theorist's preferred foundational principle. This kind of multifaceted, rhetorical appeal typically yields moral conclusions that are admittedly only probable. Not apodictic; but the casuist argues, again following Aristotle, that this is the best we can hope for when arguing about particulars.

ADVANTAGES OF A CASUISTICAL APPROACH

Casuistry's close reliance on context gives it a distinct advantage over more theory-driven approaches in the practical worlds of policy formation and the medical clinic. It is a method of thinking especially well suited to busy physicians and nurses whose clinical outlook is already thoroughly case oriented and who have neither the time nor the inclination to bother with too much theory. Once exposed to casuistry as an explicit method, most health-care providers, even those weaned on the principlism of Beauchamp and Childress, discover to their astonishment that, in the manner of Molière's "bourgeois gentleman," they have all been "doing casuistry" all along.

---

[29] Jonsen and Toulmin, *The Abuse of Casuistry*, 326; Jonsen, "Casuistry: An Alternative or Complement to Principles?"

[30] For an example of such an approach as applied to the problem of access to health care, see President's Commission for the Study of Ethical Problems in Medicine and Biomedical Research, *Securing Access to Health Care: A Report on the Ethical Implications of Differences in the Availability of Health Services*, vol. I: *Report* (Washington, DC: U.S. Government Printing Office, March 1983). https://repository.library.georgetown.edu/bitstream/handle/10822/559375/securing_access.pdf?sequence=1.

Although casuists must clearly presuppose a fair measure of social agreement on which to base their proposed solutions, they stress that usually there is no need for agreement at the level of deep theory or principle. Consensus can often be reached at a relatively low level of analysis between the invocation of "middle-level" principles (e.g., the principle of informed consent) and the particulars of the case.[31] Thus, while the members of a bioethics commission might advance competing theories of why a certain practice, such as surrogate parenting, might be wrong, they might all be able to reason analogically to the conclusion that surrogate contracts constitute a form of "baby selling" and this might be all the agreement they need for the practical task at hand.[32]

Like the common law, which also eschews appeals to deep theory, casuistry thus appears particularly well suited to the resolution of conflicts within a pluralistic, democratic society.[33] In the absence of a single, state-sponsored vision of the good life, casuistry seeks an "overlapping consensus" between groups with disparate and often conflicting views. But whereas a theorist like John Rawls[34] seeks such consensus at the level of overarching, abstract principles, the casuist seeks it at the lower level of responses to paradigmatic cases—responses that might be explained or justified quite differently by different groups. (We thus might be tempted to call this kind of agreement an "underlapping consensus.")

Seeking consensus at this lower, less theoretical level has an additional benefit for life in a pluralistic society. Whether the competing voices in a public debate take the high road of elevated principle or the low road of analogical reasoning, there are bound to be winners and losers. But if an issue is resolved at the lower level, the losers are likely to feel far less offended and aggrieved than if they had lost on the higher plane of their most cherished principles. In the area of abortion, for example, the so-called pro-life faction might have reacted in a much more temperate and measured fashion had the Supreme Court decided *Roe v. Wade* in a way that did not completely nullify their deeply held belief that all human life is somehow sacred. An approach more closely tailored to the factual circumstances of that case might possibly have been less polarizing and thus more hospitable to future compromises.

---

[31] Jonsen and Toulmin, *The Abuse of Casuistry*; Sunstein, *Legal Reasoning and Political Conflict*.

[32] This was, in fact, the experience of the New York State Task Force on Life and the Law with regard to the question of surrogate parenting. See the Task Force's report, *Surrogate Parenting: Analysis and Recommendations for Public Policy*, May 1998. www.health.ny.gov/regulations/task_force/reports_publications/#surrogate_parent.

[33] Sunstein, *Legal Reasoning and Political Conflict*.

[34] Rawls, *Political Liberalism* (New York: Columbia University Press, 1993).

TEACHING AND LEARNING

In contrast to legal systems derived from Roman law, where jurors are governed by a systematic legal code, common law systems derive from the particular judicial decisions of particular judges. As a result of these radically differing approaches to the nature and derivation of law, common law and Roman law are taught and learned in correspondingly different ways. Students of Roman law need only refer to the code itself, and perhaps to the scholarly literature explicating the meaning of the code's various provisions, whereas students of the common law must refer directly to prior judicial opinions. Consequently, the case method of legal study is naturally suited to common law jurisdictions, for it is only through a study of the cases that one can learn the concrete meaning of legal principles and learn to apply them correctly to future cases.[35]

What is true of the common law is equally true of common law morality. According to the casuists, bioethical principles are best learned by the case method, not by appeals to abstract theoretical notions. Indeed, anyone at all experienced in teaching bioethics in clinical settings must know (often by means of painful experience) that physicians, nurses, and other health-care providers learn best by means of case discussions. (The best way to put them to sleep, in fact, is to begin one's session with a recitation of the "principles of bioethics"). This is explained not simply by the fact that case presentations are intrinsically more gripping than abstract discussions of the moral philosophies of Mill, Kant, and Rawls; they are, in addition, the best vehicle for conveying the concrete meaning and scope of whatever principles and maxims one wishes to teach. Contrary to ethical deductivism and Roman law, whose principles could conceivably be taught in a practical vacuum, casuistry demands a case-driven method of instruction. For casuists, cases are much more than mere illustrated rules or handy mnemonic devices for the "abstracting impaired." They are, as Jonsen and Toulmin argue, the very locus of moral meaning and moral certainty.

Although Jonsen and Toulmin have not considered the concrete pedagogical implications of their casuistical method, we can venture a few suggestions. First, it would appear that a casuistical approach would encourage the use, whenever possible, of real as opposed to hypothetical cases. This is because hypothetical cases, so beloved of academic philosophers, tend to be theory driven; that is, they are usually designed to advance some explicitly theoretical point. Real cases, on the other hand, are more likely to display the sort of moral complexity and untidiness

[35] E. W Patterson, "The Case Method in American Legal Education: Its Origins and Objectives," *Journal of Legal Education* 4 (1951): 1–24.

that demand the (nondeductive) weighing and balancing of competing moral considerations and the casuistical virtues of discernment and practical judgment (*phronesis*).[36]

Second, a casuistical pedagogy would call for lengthy and richly detailed case studies. If the purpose of moral education is to prepare one for action in the real world, the cases discussed should reflect the degree of complexity, uncertainty, and ambiguity encountered there. If for casuistry moral truth resides "in the details," if the meaning and scope of moral principles are determined contextually through an interpretation of factual situations in their relationship to paradigm cases, then cases must be presented in rich detail. It won't do, as is so often done in our textbooks and anthologies, to cram the rich moral fabric of cases into a couple of paragraphs.

Third, a casuistical pedagogy would encourage the use, not simply of the occasional isolated case study but, rather, of whole sequences of cases bearing on a related principle or theme. Thus, instead of simply "illustrating" the debate over the termination of life-sustaining treatments with, say, the single case of Terri Schiavo, teachers and students should read and interpret a sequence of cases (including, e.g., Quinlan, Saikewicz, Spring, Conroy, and Cruzan) in order to see just how reasoning by paradigm and analogy takes place and how the "principles of bioethics" are actually shaped in their effective meaning by the details of successive cases.

Fourth, a casuistically driven pedagogy will give much more emphasis than currently allotted to what might be called the problem of "moral diagnosis." Given any particular controversy, exactly what kind of issues does it raise? What, in other words, is the case really about? As opposed to the anthologies, where each case comes neatly labeled under a discrete rubric, real life does not announce the nature of problems in advance. It requires interpretation, imagination, and discernment to figure out what is going on, especially when (as is usually the case) a number of discussable issues are usually extractable from any given controversy.

PROBLEMS WITH THE CASUISTICAL METHOD

Since the new casuistry attempts to define itself by turning applied ethics on its head, working from cases to principles rather than vice versa, it should come as no surprise to find that its strengths correlate perfectly with the weaknesses of

---

[36] As Todd Chambers points out, however, even "real" cases are not entirely theory free. See Chambers, "Dax Redacted: The Economies of Truth in Bioethics," *Journal of Medicine and Philosophy* 3 (1996): 237–254.

applied ethics. Thus, whereas applied ethics, and especially deductivism, are often criticized for their remoteness from clinical realities and for their consequent irrelevance,[37] casuistry prides itself on its concreteness and on its ability to render useful advice to caregivers in the medical trenches. Likewise, if the applied ethics model appears rather narrow in its single-minded emphasis on the application of principles and in its corresponding neglect of moral interpretation and practical discernment, the new casuistry can be viewed as a defense of the Aristotelian virtue of *phronesis* (or sound, practical judgment).

Conversely, it should not be surprising to find certain problems with the casuistical method that correspond to strengths of the applied ethics model. I shall devote the second half of this essay to an inventory of some of these problems. It should be stressed, however, that not all of these problems are unique to casuistry, nor does applied ethics fare much better with regard to some of them.

What Is "a Case"?

For all their emphasis on the interpretation of particular cases, casuists have not said much, if anything, about how to select problems for moral interpretation. What, in other words, gets placed on the "moral agenda" in the first place, and why? This is a problem because it is quite possible that the current method of selecting agenda items, whatever that may be, systematically ignores genuine issues equally worthy of discussion and debate.[38]

I think it safe to say that problems currently make it onto the bioethical agenda largely because health practitioners and policymakers put them there. While there is usually nothing problematic in this, and while it always pays to be scrupulously attentive to the expressed concerns of people working in the trenches, practitioners may be bound to conventional ways of thinking and of conceiving problems that tend to filter out other, equally valid experiences and problems. As feminists have argued, for example, much of the current bioethics agenda reflects an excessively narrow, professionally driven, and male outlook on the nature of ethics.[39] As a result, a whole range of important ethical problems—including the unequal treatment of women in health-care settings, sexist occupational roles, personal

[37] R. C. Fox, and J. P. Swazey, "Medical Morality Is Not Bioethics—Medical Ethics in China and the United States," *Perspectives in Biology and Medicine* 27 (1984): 336–360; C. Noble, "Ethics and Experts," *Hastings Center Report* 12 (1982): 7–9.

[38] O. O'Neill, "How Can We Individuate Moral Problems?" in *Applied* Ethics *and Ethical Theory*, ed. D. M. Rosenthal and F. Shehadi (Salt Lake City: University of Utah Press, 1988), 84–99.

[39] A. L. Carse, "The 'Voice of Care': Implications for Bioethics Education," *Journal of Philosophy and Medicine* 16 (1991): 5–28.

relationships, and strategies of *avoiding* crisis situations—have been either downplayed or ignored completely.[40] It is not enough, then, for casuistry to tell us *how* to interpret cases. Rather than simply carrying out the agenda dictated by health professionals, all of us (casuists and applied ethicists alike) must begin to think more about the problem of *which* cases ought to be selected for moral scrutiny.

An additional problem, which I can only flag here, concerns not the identification of "a case"—i.e., what gets placed on the public agenda—but, rather, the specification of "the case," i.e., what description of a case shall count as an adequate and sufficiently complete account of the issues, the participants, and the context. One of the problems with many case presentations, especially in the clinical context, is their relative neglect of alternative perspectives on the case held by other participants. Quite often, we get the attending's (or the house officer's) point of view on what constitutes "the case," while missing out on the perspectives of nurses, social workers, and others. Since most cases are complicated and enriched by such alternative medical, psychological, and social interpretations, our casuistical analyses will remain incomplete without them. Thus, in addition to being long, the cases that we employ should reflect the usually complementary (but often conflicting) perspectives of all the involved participants.

Is Casuistry Really Theory Free?

Sometimes hard-core casuists claim that they make moral progress by moving from one class of cases to another without the benefit of any ethical principles or theoretical apparatus. Solutions generated for obvious or easy categories of cases adumbrate solutions for the more difficult cases. In a manner somewhat reminiscent of pre-Kuhnian philosophers of science clinging to the possibility of "theory-free" factual observations, to a belief in a kind of epistemological "immaculate perception," these casuists appear to be claiming that the cases simply speak for themselves.

As we have seen, one problem with this suggestion is that it does not acknowledge or account for the way in which different theoretical preconceptions help determine which cases and problems get selected for study in the first place. Another problem is that it does not explain what allows us to group different cases into distinct categories or to proceed from one category to another. In other words, the casuists' account of case analysis fails to supply us with principles of relevance that explain what binds the cases together and how the meaning of one

[40] V. Warren, "Feminist Directions in Medical Ethics," *Hypatia* 4 (1989): 77–82.

case points beyond itself toward the resolution of subsequent cases. The casuists obviously cannot do without such principles of relevance; they are a necessary condition of any kind of moral taxonomy. Without principles of relevance, the cases would fly apart in all directions, rendering coherent speech, thought, and action about them impossible.

But if the casuists rise to this challenge and convert their implicit principles of relevance into explicit principles, it is certainly reasonable to expect that these will be heavily "theory laden." Take, for example, the suggestion that anencephalic infants should be used as organ donors for children born with fatal heart defects. What is the relevant line of cases in our developed morisprudence for analyzing this problem? To the proponents of this suggestion, the brain-death debates provide the appropriate context of discussion. According to this line of argument, anencephalic infants most closely resemble the brain dead; and since we already harvest vital organs from the latter category, we have a moral warrant for harvesting organs from anencephalics.[41] But to some of those opposed to any change in the status quo, the most relevant line of cases is provided by the literature on fetal experimentation. Our treatment of the anencephalic newborn should, they claim, reflect our practices regarding nonviable fetuses. If we agree with the judgment of the National Commission that research which would shorten the already doomed child's life should not be permitted, then we should oppose the use of equally doomed anencephalic infants as heart donors.[42]

How ought the casuist to triangulate the moral problem of the anencephalic newborn as organ donor? What principles of relevance will lead her to opt for one line of cases instead of another? Whatever principles she might eventually articulate, they will undoubtedly have something definite to say about such matters as the concept of death, the moral status of fetuses, the meaning and scope of respect, the nature of personhood, and the relative importance of achieving good consequences in the world versus treating other human beings as ends in themselves. Although one's position on such issues perhaps need not implicate any full-blown ethical theory in the strictest sense of the term, they are sufficiently theory laden to cast grave doubt on the new casuists' ability to move from case to case without recourse to mediating ethical principles or other theoretical notions.

Although the early work of Jonsen and Toulmin can easily be read as advocating a theory-free methodology comprised of mere "summary principles," Jonsen's

[41] M. R. Harrison, "The Anencephalic Newborn as Organ Donor: Commentary," *Hastings Center Report* 16 (1986): 21–22.

[42] G. Meilaender, "The Anencephalic Newborn as Organ Donor: Commentary," *Hastings Center Report* 16 (1986): 22–23.

subsequent work appears to acknowledge the point of the above criticism. Indeed, it would be fair to say that they now seek to articulate a method that is, if not "theory free," then at least "theory modest." Drawing on the approach of the classical casuists, Jonsen now concedes an indisputably normative role for principles and maxims drawn from a variety of sources, including theology, common law, historical tradition, and ethical theories. Rather than viewing ethical theories as mutually exclusive, reductionistic attempts to provide an apodictic *foundation* for ethical thought, Jonsen and Toulmin now view theories as limited and complementary *perspectives* that might enrich a more pragmatic and pluralistic approach to the ethical life.[43] They thus appear reconciled to the usefulness, both in research and in education, of a severely chastened conception of moral principles and theories.

One lesson in all this for bioethics is that casuistry, for all its usefulness as a method, is nothing more (and nothing less) than an "engine of thought" that must receive *direction* from values, concepts, and theories outside itself. Given the important role such "external" sources of moral direction must play even in the most case-bound approaches, we all need to be self-conscious about which traditions and theories are in effect driving our casuistical interpretations. This means that we need to devote time and energy to studying and criticizing the values, concepts, and rank-orderings implicitly or explicitly conveyed by the various traditions and theories from which we derive our overall direction and tools of moral analysis. In short, it means that adopting the casuistical method will not absolve us from studying and evaluating either ethical theories or the history of ethics.

Indeterminacy and Consensus

One need not believe in the existence of uniquely correct answers to all moral questions to be concerned about the casuistical method's capacity to yield determinate answers to problematical moral questions. Indeed, anyone familiar with Alastair MacIntyre's[44] disturbing diagnosis of our contemporary moral culture might well tend to greet the casuists' announcement of moral consensus with a good deal of skepticism. According to MacIntyre, our moral culture is in a grave state of disorder: lacking any comprehensive and coherent understanding of morality and human nature, we subsist on scattered shards and remnants of past moral frameworks. It is no wonder, then, according to MacIntyre, that our moral debates and disagreements are often marked by the clash of incommensurable

[43] Jonsen and Toulmin, *The Abuse of Casuistry*, ch. 15; Jonsen, "Casuistry: An Alternative or Complement to Principles?"

[44] A. MacIntyre, *After Virtue* (Notre Dame, IN: University of Notre Dame Press, 1981).

premises derived from disparate moral cultures. Nor is it any wonder that our debates over highly controversial issues such as abortion and affirmative action take the form of a tedious, interminable cycle of assertion and counter-assertion. In this disordered and contentious moral setting, which Maclntyre claims is *our* moral predicament, the casuists' goal of consensus based upon intuitive responses to cases might well appear to be a Panglossian dream.

One need not endorse MacIntyre's pessimistic diagnosis in its entirety to notice that many of our moral practices and policies bear a multiplicity of meanings. They often embody a variety of different, and sometimes conflicting, values. An ethical methodology based exclusively on the casuistical analysis of these practices can reasonably be expected to express these different values in the form of conflicting ethical conclusions.

This second criticism thus alleges that casuistry might work well within cultures featuring pervasive agreement on fundamental values, but that it must founder in highly pluralistic or even "postmodern" cultures like our own.[45] Whether or not this criticism has merit, it does highlight the important fact that casuistry is more a method than a doctrine, more an engine of thought than a moral compass. The direction that this engine takes will invariably depend upon the value commitments of a community of inquirers.[46] Thus, it makes perfect sense to talk about an Orthodox Jewish casuistry embedded in Halakah (Jewish law), a Roman Catholic casuistry, or even the casuistry of a particular neonatal ICU or hospital ethics committee.

The objection, then, is that casuistical reasoning depends upon deep-seated agreement on fundamental values and will necessarily fail to reach determinate conclusions when deployed in modern, pluralistic societies where such agreement is lacking. In contrast to the similar methodology of common law, which enjoys the advantages of having clearly defined decision-making authorities (judges) and paradigm cases that legally bind all subsequent interpreters (legal precedents), casuistry as practiced in secular, pluralistic societies features no clearly authoritative "moral experts," and its precedents (paradigms) are always subject to revision and reinterpretation at the hands of rival commentators.

Political theorist Michael Walzer's remarks on health care in the United States provide an illuminating case in point. Although Walzer might not recognize himself as a modern-day casuist, his vigorous anti-theoretical stance and reliance on

[45] K. W Wildes, "The Priesthood of Bioethics and the Return of Casuistry," *Journal of Medicine and Philosophy* 18 (1993): 3–49.

[46] M. G. Kuczewski, *Fragmentation and Consensus: Communitarian and Casuist Bioethics* (Washington, DC: Georgetown University Press, 1997).

established social meanings and norms certainly make him an ally of the methodological approach espoused by Jonsen and Toulmin.[47] According to Walzer, if we look carefully at our current values and practices regarding health care and its distribution—if we look, in other words, at the choices we as a people have already made, at the programs we have already put into place, etc.—we will conclude that health-care services are a crucially important social good, that they should be allocated solely on the basis of need, and that they must be made equally available to all citizens, presumably through something like a national health service.[48]

One could argue, however, that current disparities—both in access to care and in quality of care—between the poor, the middle class, and the rich reflect equally "deep" (or even deeper) political choices that we have made regarding the relative importance of individual freedom, social security, and the health needs of the "nondeserving" poor. In this vein, one could claim that our collective decisions bearing on Medicaid, Medicare, and access to emergency rooms—the same decisions that Walzer uses to argue for a national health service—are more accurately interpreted as grudging aberrations from our free-market ideology. According to this opposing view, our stratified health-care system pretty well reflects our values and commitments in this area: *viz.*, a "decent minimum" (read "understaffed, ill-equipped, impersonal urban clinics") for the medically indigent; decent health insurance and HMOs for the working middle class; and first-cabin care for the well-to-do.[49]

Viewed in the light of Walzer's democratic socialist commitments, which I happen to share, this arrangement may indeed look like an "indefensible triage"; but placed in the context of American history and culture, it could just as easily be viewed as business as usual. Thus, on one reading our current practices point toward the establishment of a thoroughly egalitarian health-care system; viewed from a different angle, however, these same "choices we have already made" justify pervasive inequalities in access to care and quality of care. The problem for the casuistical method is that, barring any and all appeals to abstract principles of justice, it cannot decisively adjudicate between such competing interpretations of our common practices.[50] When these do not convey a univocal message, or when they carry conflicting messages of more or less equal plausibility, casuistry cannot help

[47] M. Walzer, *Spheres of Justice* (New York: Basic Books, 1983); M. Walzer, *Interpretation and Social Criticism* (Cambridge, MA: Harvard University Press, 1987).

[48] Walzer, *Spheres of Justice*, 86ff.

[49] R. Dworkin, "*Spheres of Justice:* An Exchange," *New York Review of Books* 30 (1983): 44; G. Warnke, "Social Interpretation and Political Theory: Walzer and His Critics," *The Philosophical Forum* 21 (1989/1990): 204–226.

[50] Dworkin, "*Spheres of Justice:* An Exchange."

us to develop a uniquely correct interpretation upon which a widespread social consensus might be based. Contrary to the assurances of Jonsen and Toulmin, the new casuistry is an unlikely instrument for generating consensus in a moral world fractured by conflicting values and intuitions. Interestingly, then, the same moral pluralism of contemporary democratic societies, which Cass Sunstein views as an ideal milieu for casuistical or analogical reasoning to seek low-level consensus, is seen by "postmodern" critics like Wildes as a decisive deficit of casuistry.[51]

In Jonsen and Toulmin's defense, it should be noted that abstract theories of justice divorced from the conventions of our society are equally unlikely sources of uniquely correct answers. If philosophers cannot agree among themselves on the true nature of abstract justice—indeed, if criticizing our foremost theoretician of justice, John Rawls, has become something of a philosophical national pastime[52]—it is unclear how their theorizing could decisively resolve the ongoing debate among competing interpretations of our common social practices. Even Rawls became increasingly loathe in his later writings to appeal to an abstract, timeless, and deracinated notion of justice as the ultimate court of appeal from conflicting social interpretations. Eschewing any pretense of having established a theory of justice *sub specie aeternitatis,* Rawls eventually settled on the view that his theory of "justice as fairness" is only applicable in modern democracies like our own.[53] He claims, moreover, that the justification of his theory is derived, not from neutral data, but from its "congruence with our deeper understanding of ourselves and our aspirations, and our realization that, given our history and the traditions embedded in our public life, it is the most reasonable doctrine for us".[54]

Notwithstanding the many differences that distinguish their respective views, it thus appears that Rawls, Walzer, and Jonsen and Toulmin could all agree that there is no escape from the task of interpreting the meanings embedded in our social practices, institutions, and history. Given the complexity and tensions that characterize this moral "data," the search for uniquely correct interpretations must be seen as misguided. The best we can do, it seems, is to argue for our own determinate but contestable interpretations of who we are as a people and who we want to become. Neither theory nor casuistry is a guarantor of consensus.

---

[51] Wildes, "The Priesthood of Bioethics and the Return of Casuistry."

[52] N. Daniels, *Reading Rawls*, 2nd ed. (Stanford, CA: Stanford University Press, 1989); R. J. Arneson, ed., "Symposium on Rawlsian Theory of Justice: Recent Developments," *Ethics* 99 (1989): 695–944.

[53] J. Rawls, "Kantian Constructivism in Moral Theory: The Dewey Lectures 1980," *Journal of Philosophy* 77 (1980): 515–572, 318.

[54] Rawls, "Kantian Constructivism in Moral Theory: The Dewey Lectures 1980," 519. See also J. Rawls, "Justice as Fairness: Political Not Metaphysical," *Philosophy & Public Affairs* 14 (1985): 228; and Rawls, *Political Liberalism*.

Having appropriately bitten this particular bullet, the casuist might nevertheless attempt to reclaim some lost ground in this debate by reasserting Sunstein's point made above, that casuistry may often be of some use to us in forging consensus at the shallow level of responses to cases even when consensus at the deeper level of principle or theory is unlikely. The casuist can, furthermore, resist the implication, pressed by MacIntyre and Wildes, that modern societies are hopelessly Balkanized into small, hermetically sealed interpretive communities. In spite of the differences between regions and groups, modern societies are becoming increasingly *cosmopolitan*, increasingly marked by the overlap and interpenetration of disparate cultural and linguistic subgroups. Finally, it might be noted that, in spite of our manifest differences, the various interlocking communities of hospital clinicians, academics, judges and juries, medical societies, policy centers, and grass-roots movements somehow manage to grope their collective way toward an overlapping consensus on a number of fronts in bioethics—even on the highly contested terrain of death and dying;[55] but not, of course, on the most highly divisive issues like abortion—largely with the aid of casuistical reasoning. While it would be overly sanguine to view casuistry as a kind of universal solvent for bioethical disputes, it would be overly pessimistic to ignore the ability of analogical reasoning at least to narrow the range of legitimate disagreement even when it cannot effect consensus.

Conventionalism and Critique

The hard-core version of casuistry and its "summary view" of ethical principles gives rise to worries about the nature of moral truth and justification. Eschewing any theoretical derivation of principles and insisting that the locus of moral certainty is the particular, the casuist asks "What principles best organize and account for what we have already decided?" Viewed from this angle, the casuistic project amounts to nothing more than an elaborate refinement of our intuitions regarding cases. As such, it begins to resemble the kind of relativistic conventionalism articulated by Richard Rorty.[56]

Obviously, one problem with this is that our intuitions have often been shown to be wildly wrong, if not downright prejudicial and superstitious. To the extent that this is true of *our own* intuitions about ethical matters, then casuistry will merely refine our prejudices. Any casuistry that modestly restricts itself to

---

[55] The *Schiavo* case reminds us, however, that even apparently solidly entrenched societal consensus is subject to challenge by heretofore marginalized groups.

[56] R. Rorty, *Contingency, Irony, and Solidarity* (Cambridge: Cambridge University Press, 1989).

interpreting and cataloguing the flickering shadows on the cave wall can easily be accused of lacking a critical edge. If applied ethics might rightly be said to have purchased critical leverage at the expense of the concrete moral situation, then casuistry, especially in its hard-core incarnation, might be charged with having purchased concreteness and relevance at the expense of philosophical criticism. It may well be that some of our most strongly felt convictions, far from being obviously right, are actually the fruit of profoundly unjust social practices and institutions. If we could just step back and gain some critical distance, the injustice might become visible; but because casuistry anchors itself in paradigm cases, which are themselves based upon deeply entrenched social practices and attitudes, it will often leave such systemic injustices undetected and unchallenged.

This charge might take either of two forms. First, one could claim that the casuist is a mere expositor of *established* social meanings and thus lacks the requisite critical distance to formulate telling critiques of regnant social understandings. Second, casuistry could be accused of ignoring the power relations that shape and inform the social meanings that its practitioners interpret.

In response to the issue of critical distance, the casuist can and should admit that this approach, which is essentially backward looking, may have some conservative tendencies. It remains true, however, that the overall direction of casuistical thought, whether conservative or progressive, will ultimately depend on who is judging and which principles and values animate their analogical reasoning. Progressive social critics using progressive social norms will reason analogically to progressive conclusions. In his eloquent dissent in the case of *Bowers v. Hardwick*,[57] Justice Blackmun came to the conclusion, subsequently affirmed seventeen years later by the Supreme Court in *Lawrence et al. v. Texas*,[58] that laws banning homosexual behavior were unconstitutional. Blackmun reached this prescient conclusion not only by means of a nuanced casuistical review of existing law bearing on such related "privacy" topics as contraception, abortion, and the use of pornography in the home, but also by means of a vigorously Millian principle of individual liberty.

The casuist could also observe in this connection that the social world of established meanings is by no means monolithic and usually harbors alternative values that offer plenty of critical leverage against the current social consensus. Even at those moments when the values of the philistines, the hypocrites, and the unjust majority seem unshakeable, untapped resources for potentially subversive cultural

---

[57] *Bowers v. Hardwick*, 478 US 186 (1986).

[58] 539 US 558 (2003).

criticism can often be identified.[59] As Michael Walzer has argued, even such thundering social critics as the prophet Amos and Martin Luther King Jr. have usually been fully committed to their societies, rather than "objective" and detached; and the values to which they appeal are often fundamental to the self-understanding of their people or society.[60] Rev. King spoke to white racists not as an outsider but, rather, as a fellow Christian, and he invoked values embedded in his culture's rich traditions and taxonomy to devastating effect. The lesson for casuists here is not to become so identified with the point of view of health-care professionals that they lose sight of other important values in our culture.

Finally, in response to the critical-distance problem, the casuist can respond that even if this method is susceptible to the lure of common opinion and ideology, other rival methodological approaches usually fare no better. Although principlists or theorists might think themselves better equipped than casuists to recognize and criticize lines of case judgments that deviate from the path of justice, they are often just as blind to the deeply entrenched prejudices of the day. Theorists and principlists have known for centuries, for example, about the importance of politically liberal principles bearing on "equal concern and respect," autonomy, and human dignity, but this did not prevent them from shunting women into the dark recesses of the so-called private sphere in which such principles were simply not recognized.

The second claim, relating to power relations, while not necessarily fatal to the casuistical enterprise, is harder to rebut. As Habermas has contended in his longstanding debate with Gadamer, interpretive approaches to ethics (such as casuistry) can articulate our shared social meanings but often ignore the economic and power relations that shape social consensus. His point is that the very conversation through which cases, social practices, and institutions are interpreted is itself subject to what he calls "systematically distorted communication."[61] In order to avoid merely legitimizing social understandings conditioned on power and domination—for example, our conception of the appropriate relationship between nurses and physicians—casuistry will have to supplement its interpretations with a critical theory of social relationships, or with what Paul Ricoeur has called a "hermeneutics of suspicion."[62]

---

[59] Walzer, *Interpretation and Social Criticism*; Kuczewski, *Fragmentation and Consensus: Communitarian and Casuist Bioethics*.

[60] Walzer, *Interpretation and Social Criticism*.

[61] J. Habermas, "The Hermeneutic Claim to Universality," in *Contemporary Hermeneutics*, ed. J. Bleicher (London: Routledge & Kegan Paul, 1980), 181–211.

[62] P. Ricoeur, "Hermeneutics and the Critique of Ideology," in *Hermeneutics and Modern Philosophy*, ed. B. R. Wachterhauser (New York: State University of New York Press, 1986), 300–339. I cannot let this opportunity pass by without posthumously thanking my beloved former professor, who put me on the right philosophical path.

Reinforcing the Individualism of Bioethics

Analytical philosophers working as applied ethicists have often been criticized for the ahistorical, reductionist, and excessively individualistic character of their work in bioethics.[63] While the casuistical method cannot thus be justly accused of importing a short-sighted individualism into the field of bioethics—that honor already belonging to analytical philosophy—it cannot be said either that casuistry offers anything like a promising remedy for this deficiency. On the contrary, it seems that the casuists' method of reasoning by analogy only promises to exacerbate the individualism and reductionism already characteristic of much bioethical scholarship.

Consider, for example, how a casuist might address the problem of heart transplants. He or she might reason like this: Our society is already deeply committed to paying for all kinds of "halfway technologies" for those in need. We already pay for renal dialysis and transplantation, chronic ventilatory support for children and adults, expensive open-heart surgery, and many other "high-tech" therapies, some of which might well be even more expensive than heart transplants. Therefore, so long as heart transplants qualify medically as a proven therapy, there is no reason why Medicaid and Medicare should not fund them.[64]

Notwithstanding the evident fruitfulness of such analogical reasoning in many contexts of bioethics, and notwithstanding the possibility that these particular examples of it might well prevail against the competing arguments on heart transplantation, it remains true that such contested practices raise troubling questions that tend not to be asked, let alone illuminated, by casuistical reasoning by analogy. The extent of our willingness to fund heart transplantation has great bearing on the kind of society in which we wish to live and on our priorities for spending within (and without) the health-care budget. Even if we already fund many high-technology procedures that cost as much or more than heart transplants, it is possible that this new round of transplantation could threaten other forms of care that provide greater benefits to more people; and we might therefore wish to draw the line here.[65]

The point is that, no matter where we stand on the particular issue of heart transplants, we *might* think it important to raise such "big questions," depending

[63] Fox and Swazey, "Medical Morality Is Not Bioethics"; Noble, "Ethics and Experts"; MacIntyre, *After Virtue*.

[64] D. Overcast et al., "Technology Aassessment, Public Policy and Transplantation," *Law, Medicine and Health Care* 13 (1985): 106–111.

[65] G. Annas, "Regulating Heart and Liver Transplants in Massachusetts," *Law, Medicine and Health Care* 13 (1985): 4–7.

on the nature of the problem at hand. We might want to ask, to borrow a title from Daniel Callahan, "What kind of life?"[66] But the kind of reasoning by analogy championed by the new casuists tends to reduce our field of ethical vision down to the proximate moral precedents, and thereby suppresses the important global questions bearing on who we are and what kind of society we want. The result is likely to be a method of moral reasoning that graciously accommodates us to any and all technological innovations, no matter what their potential long-term threat to fundamental and cherished institutions and values.

The Importance of Consequences in Social Policy Analysis

One common objection to the common law—which, as we have seen, is the legal analogue of casuistical moral reasoning—is that it is essentially backward looking, valuing conformity with past decisions much more than the cumulative weight of consequences. It was this feature that led Jeremy Bentham, one of the founders of utilitarianism, to declare that the common law was a mere hash of conflicting intuitions passed down from one generation to another. Society needed, Bentham declared, an approach to law based upon the hard-headed, scientific assessment of social consequences. In place of what he saw as the irrational patchwork of the common law and analogical reasoning, Bentham advocated a more forward-looking and highly codified approach to law.[67] Perhaps the best contemporary example of this Benthamite spirit is the pragmatist judge and legal thinker Richard Posner, who has criticized the judiciary for basing decisions exclusively on past legal decisions, which he regards as "an impoverished repository of fact and policy." Confronted with the question whether oil and gas can be owned even if they have not been "reduced to possession," judges should, argues Posner, go out and talk with natural resources economists, petroleum engineers, or ecologists rather than basing their decision on past cases dealing with rabbits and other fauna. Instead of viewing law as a hermetically sealed compendium of case-based reasoning, Posner contends that law is best regarded as a policy science.[68]

A prime example of the downgrading of social consequences within the common law and casuistical traditions is provided by recent legal reasoning with regard to physician-assisted suicide (PAS). In the important case, *Compassion in Dying v. Washington*,[69] the Court of Appeal for the Ninth Circuit—i.e., the level of

---

[66] D. Callahan, *What Kind of Life?* (New York: Simon and Schuster, 1990).

[67] G. J. Postema, *Bentham and the Common Law Tradition* (Oxford: Clarendon Press, 1986).

[68] R. Posner, *Overcoming Law* (Cambridge, MA: Harvard University Press, 1995).

[69] 79 F.3d 790, 838 (9th Cir. 1996).

federal review just below the Supreme Court—concluded that all citizens had a constitutionally guaranteed right to privacy that encompassed the decision to end one's life with the aid of a physician. Two features of the court's reasoning stand out for purposes of this essay. First, the court reasoned that if one took seriously the legal principles animating past legal precedents bearing on such issues as contraception, abortion, and the cessation of life-sustaining treatments, one would be logically compelled to include PAS within the reach of those same principles. Thus, if one believes in a right to privacy, a right to be free of governmental interference, when it comes to making crucially important decisions about whether or not to bear a child; if one believes that the individual, not the state or a religious majority, should have the right to decide whether or not to prolong life-sustaining medical treatments; if one believes that the imposition of majoritarian values bearing on the very meaning of life (and death) constitutes a kind of tyranny; then it is a very short step indeed to conclude that individuals should be free, in conjunction with their physician, to choose an earlier death rather than a longer, more protracted, and more painful death. Viewed exclusively through the lens of analogical reasoning, the case for PAS would appear to be logically, morally, and legally compelling.

The second important feature of the court's legal reasoning was its explicit repudiation of consequentialist or "slippery slope" considerations. In response to those who worried that legalizing PAS might, for example, inexorably lead to active euthanasia on the part of physicians, Judge Reinhardt curtly observed that "here we decide only the issue before us."[70] Borrowing a page from Richard Posner, one might urge instead that judges deciding upon such a momentous question as PAS would be well advised to go talk with geriatric psychiatrists, palliative care specialists, and hospice workers, but Judge Reinhardt forcefully precluded that option, declaring that a refusal to contemplate potential bad consequences was required by the judicial role itself![71] Although legislators might be free to ponder such social considerations, he opined, judges must restrict themselves to the logic of the preceding cases and the rights enunciated therein.

Critics of legalizing PAS have responded that coherence with past legal decisions should not be our sole focus, especially if we can expect bad social consequences to flow from a policy of retail PAS. They note that a policy that made PAS widely available would be likely to yield two distinct kinds of bad consequences. First, we could expect slippage from the narrow range of socially approved cases to a much more inclusive policy. Permitting physician-assisted death (e.g., writing a prescription for barbiturates) today only for currently competent patients in unbearable

[70] Posner, *Overcoming Law*, 832.

[71] Ibid., 831.

pain might inevitably morph into a policy of active killing by physicians based upon third-party substituted judgments after a mere diagnosis of a terminal illness. Second, critics worry about the likelihood of mistake, abuse, and slipshod medical care in applying whatever standards we might adopt. Noting, for example, that many patients who request PAS also happen to be clinically depressed or suffer from untreated pain, skeptics predict that many patients who don't fit properly rigorous criteria for PAS will end up dying prematurely. Opponents of PAS thus contend that although individual instances of PAS might be morally permissible, or even praiseworthy, a permissive legal policy might lead us down a very slippery slope to manifestly unpalatable social consequences. Policymakers should thus carefully attend not only to coherence with past decisions but also to predictable social consequences.[72]

It is important to note that the point of the PAS example here is not to endorse the empirical credibility of the slippery-slope argument in this particular setting. It may well be that the critics' fears are overblown and that we have little to fear from legalizing PAS. The point is, rather, that any responsible social policy will at least have to take such fears of bad consequences seriously. But since casuistry and the common law are predominantly backward-looking modes of moral and legal analysis, they must be supplemented with consequentialist, epidemiological, or statistical modes of reasoning. We will thus need to know not simply whether the principles embedded in past cases can be extended to cover the present case but also whether an otherwise consistent and coherent policy might nevertheless lead to unacceptable social consequences within certain social, economic, or medical contexts.

CONCLUSIONS

The revival of casuistry, both in practice and in Jonsen and Toulmin's 1988 defense, is a welcome development in the field of bioethics. Its account of moral reasoning (emphasizing the pivotal role of paradigms, analogical thinking, and the prudential weighing of competing factors) is far superior, both as a description of how we actually think and as a prescription of how we ought to think, to the tiresome invocation of the applied ethics mantra (i.e., the principles of respect for autonomy, beneficence, and justice). By insisting on *a modest* role for ethical theory in a pragmatic, nondeductivist approach to ethical interpretation, Jonsen

[72] Arras, "Physician-Assisted Suicide: A Tragic View," in *Physician Assisted Suicide: Expanding the Debate*, eds. M. P. Battin et al. (New York: Routlege, 1998), 279–300.

and Toulmin join an important chorus of contemporary thinkers troubled by the reductionism inherent in most analytical ethics.[73]

As for its role in bioethics education, no one needs to tell teachers about the importance of cases in the classroom. It's pretty obvious that discussing cases is fun, interesting, and certainly more memorable than any philosophical theory, which for the average student usually has a half-life of about two weeks. Moreover, a casuistical education gives students the methodological tools they are most likely to need when they later encounter bioethical problems in the real world, whether as health-care professionals, clergy, lawyers, journalists, or informed citizens. For all the obviousness of these points, however, it remains true that all of us teachers could profit from sound advice on how better to use cases, and some such advice can be extrapolated from the work of Jonsen and Toulmin.

For all its virtues vis-à-vis the sclerotic invocation of "bioethical principles," the casuistical method is not, however, without problems of its own. First, we found that the very principles of relevance that drive the casuistical method need to be made explicit; and we surmised that, once unveiled, these principles will turn out to be at least somewhat theory laden. Second, we showed that the casuistical method is an unlikely source of uniquely correct interpretations of social meanings and therefore an unlikely source of societal consensus. Third, we have seen that, because of the hard-core casuists' view of ethical principles as mere summaries of our intuitive responses to paradigmatic cases, their method might suffer from ideological distortions and lack a critical edge. Moreover, relying so heavily on the perceptions and agenda of health-care professionals, casuists might tend to ignore the existence of important issues that could be revealed by other theoretical perspectives, such as feminism. Finally, we saw that casuistry, focusing as it does on analogical resemblances, might tend to ignore or downplay unwelcome social consequences or certain difficult but inescapable "big questions" (e.g., "What kind of society do we want?"), and thereby reinforce the individualistic tendencies already at work in contemporary bioethics.

It remains to be seen whether casuistry, as a program in practical ethics, will be able to marshal sufficient internal resources to respond to these criticisms. Whatever the outcome of that attempt, however, an equally promising approach might be to incorporate the insights and tools of casuistry into the methodological approach known as "reflective equilibrium."[74] According to this method, the

---

[73] B. Williams, *Ethics and the Limits of Philosophy* (Cambridge, MA: Harvard University Press, 1985); S. Hampshire, *Morality and Conflict* (Cambridge, MA: Harvard University Press, 1983); C. Taylor, "The Diversity of Goods," in *Utilitarianism and Beyond*, ed. A. Sen and B. Williams (Cambridge: Cambridge University Press, 1982), 129–144.

[74] Rawls, *A Theory of* Justice; Daniels, "Wide Reflective Equilibrium and Theory Acceptance in Ethics," *Journal of Philosophy* 76 (1979): 256–282.

casuistical interpretation of cases on the one hand, and moral theories, principles, and maxims on the other, exist in a symbiotic relationship. Our intuitions on cases will thus be guided, and perhaps criticized, by theory; while our theories and moral principles will themselves be shaped, and perhaps reformulated, by our responses to paradigmatic moral situations. Whether we attempt to flesh out this method of reflective equilibrium or further develop the casuistical program, it should be clear by now that the methodological issue between theory and cases is not a dichotomous "either/or" but, rather, an encompassing "both/and."

4

Nice Story, but So What?

NARRATIVE AND JUSTIFICATION IN ETHICS

EVERYWHERE ONE LOOKS in the academy these days, theory is out and stories are in. On any number of different fronts—including anthropology, history, literary criticism, and even philosophy—we are currently witnessing a headlong retreat from theory and so-called master narratives such as Enlightenment rationalism, Freudian psychoanalysis, and Marxism. Many scholars in the social sciences and humanities seem particularly eager to jettison the last vestiges of the Enlightenment ideals of objectivity, rationality, truth, and universality as these pertain to matters both epistemological and axiological. The consensus seems to be that, just as our ability to know is profoundly circumscribed by the contingencies of time, place, and our own psychological makeup (all knowledge is thus "local"), so our values are said to reach no farther than the bounds of our community or nation. Furthermore, it is maintained that any attempt to extend the boundaries of either our knowledge or our values is not just wrong and ill-fated (because, given our finitude, it cannot be accomplished) but also dangerous (because it will inevitably amount to an imposition of our ways of knowing and valuing upon others). Thus, the belief in objectivity and universality that once drove the so-called "Enlightenment project"—a belief that such great but diverse thinkers as Voltaire, Rousseau, Kant, Locke, and Marx once viewed as profoundly liberatory—is now the object of a profound suspicion. Behind the search for universality must lie the will to dominate, to bend others to our ways of thinking and valuing. Objectivity and universality, once thought to be the key to our common deliverance from the narrowness and stupidity of local custom, have come to be seen as the seeds of tyranny.

In the place of the Western mind's traditional quest for the objective and universal laws undergirding nature, history, and morals, we now find the flourishing of narrative, storytelling, anecdote, and autobiography. Here, too, the argument is both epistemological and moral. All knowing is necessarily bound up with a narrative tradition of one kind or other, and all valuing grows out of and expresses the stories that constitute us as members of a particular family, community, or nation. Rather than lusting after the immutable laws of nature and humankind, historians, social scientists, philosophers, and legal scholars have begun to celebrate the particularity and localism inherent in the medium of the little story, the *petit récit*. In a litany that has by now become quite familiar, we see anthropologists like Clifford Geertz making the case for "local knowledge,"[1] literary critics like Jane Tompkins lauding the critic's own autobiography,[2] legal scholars like Paul Gewirtz probing the role of narrative and rhetoric in law,[3] and philosophers like Richard Rorty siding with the poets and novelists against the theoreticians.[4]

This flourishing of narrative has brought about what literary critic David Simpson has conceived as a major shift in the "balance of trade" among academic departments of universities.[5] Literature has emerged as the major exporter of methods and themes to other departments once dominated by more objectivist and scientific tendencies. Indeed, the traditional sharp boundaries between such academic subjects as history, anthropology, literature, and philosophy have recently yielded to make way for the triumph of a "literary culture" that now appears to dominate the academy. Simpson calls this refiguring or abolishing of boundaries between traditional disciplines "the academic postmodern." At my university, this development is strikingly illustrated by the spectacle of the famous (now sadly deceased) philosopher Richard Rorty using the philosophy department essentially as a mail drop while doing most of his teaching in the department of English literature; at the same time, our English professors write books on why literary criticism has to be more philosophical.

The field of bioethics has taken its own narrative turn. Long dominated by the aspirations to objectivity and universality as embodied in its dominant "principlist" paradigm, bioethics has witnessed an explosion of interest in narrative and

[1] C. Geertz, *Local Knowledge: Further Essays in Interpretive Anthropology* (New York: Basic Books, 1983).

[2] J. Tompkins, "Me and My Shadow," *Gender and Theory: Dialogues on Feminist Criticism* (New York and Oxford: Blackwell, 1989), 121–139.

[3] P. Brooks and P. Gewirtz, *Law's Stories: Narrative and Rhetoric in the Law* (New Haven: Yale University Press, 1996).

[4] R. Rorty, *Philosophy and the Mirror of Nature* (Princeton, NJ: Princeton University Press, 1979); R. Rorty, *Contingency, Irony and Solidarity* (Cambridge: Cambridge University Press, 1989).

[5] D. Simpson, *The Academic Post Modern and the Rule of Literature: A Report on Half Knowledge* (Chicago: University of Chicago Press, 1995).

storytelling as alternative ways of structuring and evaluating the experiences of patients, physicians, and other health-care professionals. To be sure, the universalist mantra of autonomy, beneficence, and justice still holds sway in many quarters, and its principal defenders have proved to be quite adept at ingesting or co-opting much recent criticism without giving up on their central claims regarding the pivotal role of principles in the moral life.[6] Still, one wonders whether the current plethora of conferences, journal issues, and articles devoted to narrative bioethics presages not merely an important shift away from "principle-driven" ethics—a movement that has been proceeding apace for some time now under the auspices of casuistry and feminism—but also the imminent triumph of the literary sensibility in a field that has traditionally wished to appear as a source of "hard knowledge" to its beneficiaries and funders in the medical and research establishments.

In spite of the enthusiasm for narrative and the plague of stories[7] it has engendered, we have not gained much clarity about the precise meaning of narrative ethics and how it relates, or should relate, to ethics in general. After dutifully plowing through much of the extant literature on this trend, I must confess to being at a loss as to what it all means. In particular, the connection between narrative and moral justification remains maddeningly obscure. What, one wants to ask, is the relationship between narrative and the achievement of moral justification, between the telling of a story and the establishment of a warrant for believing in the moral adequacy or excellence of a particular action, policy, or character? In order partially to dispel some of this murkiness, I shall attempt in the present chapter a modest typology of narrative ethics. There are several different conceptions of "narrative ethics," and each carries significantly different implications for the question of moral justification. As we shall see, some conceptions are relatively modest and unthreatening to the claims of principles and theory, while the more robust versions of narrative ethics threaten to replace the regnant paradigm.

MORAL JUSTIFICATION IN THE *ANCIEN* (MODERN) *RÉGIME*

At the risk of gross oversimplification, one might say that the model of moral justification at work in most "theory-driven" accounts of ethics,[8] including the first

[6] See my depiction of Beauchamp and Childress as "The Borg of Bioethics" in chapter 1 this volume.

[7] Simpson speaks of an "epidemic of storytelling" (see Simpson, *The Academic Post Modern and the Rule of Literature*, 25), and Daniel Callahan objects to the "tyranny of the story" in "Does Clinical Ethics Distort the Discipline?" *Hastings Center Report* 26, no. 6 (1996): 28.

[8] By "theory-driven" I mean here principally utilitarianism and Kantian deontology, including Rawlsian theories of justice. Excluded from this definition are all forms of Aristotelian ethics, virtue ethics, and coherentist models of ethical justification.

three editions of the principlism of Beauchamp and Childress, involved an effort to connect with a normative essence, idea, or norm beyond the vagaries of actual human behavior. Whether one purported to find this normative ideal in the principle of utility, the categorical imperative, or Rawls's two principles of justice, one sought to ground one's ethical judgments of right action and sound policy in a source beyond the contingencies of historical accident, beyond the narrow confines of one's community and tradition. Whether one owed ultimate theoretical allegiance to Mill, Kant, or Rawls, ethical rationality was conceived along the lines of a scientific (or at least quasi-scientific) model. From Plato's cave to Rawls's original position, the motivation behind the method remained unchanged: in order to attain truth and justify one's ethical judgments, it is first necessary to purify these judgments of any and all subjective elements involving the agent's "story"—that is, his or her inclinations stemming from a particular upbringing, social class, or networks of relationships. This model finds its most thoroughgoing adherent in Kant, whose preoccupation with human nature was limited to our "rational nature as such" rather than to the particularities of human anthropology. This position finds an unintentionally comic contemporary echo in Engelhardt's claim to have established a "transgalactic" foundation for morality.[9]

It was quite natural, then, that the more theory-driven approaches to ethics would have little, if any, use for narrative or storytelling in their quest for ethical justification. Kantians have been more concerned with our ability to universalize the maxims animating our behavior, while utilitarians, in their familiar role as cost-benefit analysts, have sought to achieve a kind of science of desire. In each case, stories play a decidedly limited role in the formulation of moral problems and no discernible role in the justification of their resolutions. This denigration of narrative is not accidental; it is, or so I would argue, a constituent part of the rationalistic, Enlightenment tradition. The spirit of this tradition is nicely illustrated in the figure of Auguste Comte, the nineteenth-century French social theorist who regarded religion as merely a collection of stories, a form of consciousness that had to be surpassed first by philosophy (metaphysics) and eventually by modern science, which occupied the highest rung in the hierarchy of rationality.[10] As Jean-Francois Lyotard aptly puts the matter, according to the

---

[9] H. T Engelhardt Jr., *The Foundations of Bioethics* (New York: Oxford University Press, 1986). Ironically, the moral tone of Engelhardt's transgalactic theory bears a striking resemblance to a kind of flinty individualism centered somewhere near Houston, Texas.

[10] I owe this account of Comte to David Burrell and Stanley Hauerwas, "From System to Story: An Alternative Pattern for Rationality in Ethics," in *Knowledge, Value and Belief*, ed. H. T. Engelhardt Jr. and D. Callahan (Hastings-on-Hudson, NY: Hastings Center, 1977), 125.

"man of science," narratives are mere "fables, myths, legends, fit only for women and children."[11]

The remainder of this essay will be devoted to an exposition and preliminary assessment of three distinct formulations of "narrative ethics" that each in its own way attempts to redress the balance in favor of narrative. We will first consider narrative as a supplement to (or ingredient of) principle-driven approaches to ethics. From this angle, narrative is seen as an indispensable and ubiquitous feature of the moral landscape. Here narrative not only allows us to delineate moral problems in a concrete fashion but also plays an important role in the formulation of moral principles and the depiction of character. Then we will briefly inspect the view, powerfully articulated by Alasdair MacIntyre and Stanley Hauerwas, that narrative functions principally as the very ground of all moral justification. Narrative functions here not merely as a supplement or handmaiden to principles and theory but also as the exclusive basis of ethical rationality itself. Finally, we shall canvass the place of narrative within a distinctly "postmodern" ethical stance, where narrative and the authenticity of the narrator appear to play the role of substitutes for ethical justification. As we shall see, each formulation of narrative ethics poses a progressively greater challenge to currently dominant ways of thinking about the role of stories in moral justification.

NARRATIVE AS SUPPLEMENT TO AN ETHIC OF PRINCIPLES

The most benign and least controversial version of "narrative ethics" asserts that an ethic of principles and theory cannot stand alone, that it must be supplemented by an understanding of the narrative structure of human action in order to achieve a more fully rounded and complete ethic. This assertion itself rests upon three distinct observations about the relationship between narrative and ethics: (1) that narrative elements are deeply embedded in all forms of moral reasoning; (2) that our responses to stories are the ground out of which principles and theories grow; and (3) that narrative is the only medium in which a concern for character and virtue can be intelligibly discussed.

---

[11] "The scientist questions the validity of narrative statements and concludes that they are never subject to argumentation or proof. He classifies them as belonging to a different mentality: savage, primitive, underdeveloped, backward, alienated, composed of opinions, customs, authority, prejudice, ignorance, ideology." J. F. Lyotard, *The Postmodern Condition: A Report on Knowledge* (Minneapolis: University of Minnesota Press, 1984), 27.

The Pervasiveness of Narrative in Ethical Reasoning

Contrary to the vision of the "man of science" quoted above, according to which there exists a sharp division between forms of reasoning driven by stories and those driven by principles and theories, some advocates of narrative ethics insist that stories and moral theorizing are mutually interpenetrating and interdependent. They point out that moral narratives often embody a kind of argument (a "moral"), while much ethical argument is pervaded by narrative elements; and they claim that a keener awareness of these narrative elements embedded in all moral reasoning will permit a more reflective and penetrating mode of moral analysis.

Rita Charon, a physician and literary scholar, highlights a number of ways in which a heightened literary consciousness can augment our reasoning skills in a field like clinical bioethics.[12] For the practicing physician, Charon notes, closer attention to the narrative elements in the situation—and in particular to the patient's own story—would permit the recognition of ethical issues that often go unnoticed. What's really troubling a particular patient—for example, the likely impact of scheduled surgery on her ability to maintain her roles as worker, wife, and mother—will often not find its way into the dominant form of medical narrative, the medical chart. Although the chart and other forms of medical discourse, such as the truncated language of clinical rounds, pretend to have achieved a high level of universality and scientific objectivity, they often screen out the very meanings that the disease or illness has for the patient.[13] In the absence of an understanding of the existential implications of the patient's condition and the meanings of various treatment alternatives, the physician is likely not even to recognize moral tensions or problems latent in the medical encounter.

Charon also usefully points out that the various skills and sensitivities of the literary critic are indispensable in coming to terms adequately with the whole gamut of medical narratives, including not only the chart but also all the stories that caregivers, patients, family members, and authors tell about their experiences surrounding a particular "case." In particular, she notes, closer attention to the way in which medical narratives are presented—including, for example, the way in which the various elements are framed, the content is selected, and the author's point of view is established—can help us read more deeply and critically. Quoting with approval the German literary theorist Walter Benjamin ("The traces of the

---

[12] R. Charon, "Narrative Contributions to Medical Ethics: Recognition, Formulation, Interpretation, and Validation in the Practice of the Ethicist," in *A Matter of Principles? Ferment in U.S. Bioethics*, ed. E. R. DuBose, R. Hamel, and L. O'Connell (Valley Forge, PA: Trinity Press International, 1994), 260–283.

[13] For a well-developed autobiographical account of how such a truncated medical vision can adversely affect the care (and lives) of patients, see Oliver Sacks, *A Leg to Stand On* (New York: Summit Books, 1984).

storyteller cling to the story the way the handprints of the potter cling to the clay vessel"), Charon argues that sensitivity to such questions as authorship and point of view constitute, along with several other important skills, a kind of "narrative competence" that is a prerequisite to doing good ethics.[14]

For Rita Charon, then, "narrative ethics" essentially means a mode of moral analysis that is attentive to and critically reflective about the narrative elements of our experience. It is important to note, however, that Charon's plea for a narrative ethics is not meant as a fundamental challenge to an ethic driven by principles and theories. On the contrary, she explicitly wishes to leave intact the basic structure of principle-driven ethics.[15] On this view, narrative competence is recommended as a supplement, as a way to improve our use of the existing methods of moral analysis by gearing their deployment to the rich particularity of patients' lives. Principles retain their normative force; narrative sensitivity just makes them work better. "Narrative ethics" on this gloss is thus not a newer, better kind of ethics; it simply allows us to apply principles with greater sensitivity and precision.[16]

Narrative as Ground and Object of Ethical Principles

A different conception of the relationship between narrative and moral justification, but a conception still faithful to the depiction of narrative ethics as a supplement to principles, might be sought in the notion of reflective equilibrium. This approach to moral methodology was first articulated in the early work of John Rawls,[17] and has since been the subject of much amplification and commentary at the hands of other ethical theorists.[18] Chapter 8 of this book is dedicated to an in-depth exploration of reflective equilibrium; I will, therefore, content myself here with a very brief sketch merely sufficient to make my point about the connection between narrative ethics and reflective equilibrium.

As Rawls and his followers depict it, reflective equilibrium offers an alternative picture of moral justification to the sort of "top-down" account favored by moral

---

[14] Charon, "Narrative Contributions to Medical Ethics," 266.

[15] "The principlist methods of ethical inquiry remain as the structure for clarifying and adjudicating conflicts among patients, health providers, and family members at the juncture of a quandary. The principles upon which bioethics decisions have been based . . . continue to guide ethical action within health care" (Charon, "Narrative Contributions to Medical Ethics," 277).

[16] See J. Childress, "Narrative(s) Versus Norm(s): A Misplaced Debate in Bioethics," in *Stories and Their Limits: Narrative Approaches to Bioethics*, ed. H. L. Nelson (New York: Routledge, 1997), 252–271.

[17] J. Rawls, *A Theory of Justice* (Cambridge, MA: Harvard University Press, 1971), 48–51.

[18] N. Daniels, "Wide Reflective Equilibrium and Theory Acceptance in Ethics," *Journal of Philosophy* 76 (1979): 256; N. Daniels, "Wide Reflective Equilibrium in Practice," in *Philosophical Perspectives on Bioethics*, ed. L. W. Sumner and J. Boyle (Toronto: University of Toronto Press, 1996), 96–114. See also D. Furrow, *Against Theory* (New York: Routledge, 1995), ch. 1.

"deductivists." Deductivists view the process of moral justification as involving a unidirectional movement from preexisting theories and principles to their "application" at the level of the case. To justify an action or policy on this account is simply to bring it under the relevant theory, principle, or moral rule. According to the partisans of reflective equilibrium, this unidirectional picture distorts or totally ignores the pivotal role of intuitive, case-based judgments of right and wrong. To be sure, the sort of judgments they have in mind are not to be confused with just any responses to cases, no matter how prejudiced, illconsidered, or subject to coercion they might be. Rather, they are referring to those intuitive responses in which we have the most confidence, like those embedded in the conclusions that slavery or the killing of innocent children are wrong. Rawls referred to this class of intuitive responses as our "considered judgments." It is precisely these judgments, it is claimed, that give concrete meaning, definition, and scope to moral principles and that provide critical leverage in refining their articulations.

The partisans of reflective equilibrium claim, in effect, that principles and cases have a dialectical or reciprocal relationship. The principles provide normative guidance, while the cases provide considered judgments. The considered judgments, in turn, help shape the principles that then provide more precise guidance for more complex or difficult cases. Principles and cases thus coexist in creative tension or "reflective equilibrium." Ethical justification is then sought not in any kind of correspondence between our ethical judgments and some sort of transcendent realm of ethical norms or kingdom of ends but, rather, in the overall meshing or coherence achieved among our intuitions about cases, our rules, principles, moral theories, and nonmoral theories about society, personhood, and so on.

Now, the reason for bringing up this business of reflective equilibrium in the context of the present essay is that the cases about which we have these considered judgments are themselves narratives. They tell stories about what's happening in and around people's bodies and about their social relationships—stories that prominently feature some sort of moral dilemma or conflict. So, rather than viewing stories as being essentially remote from the realms of principle and theory—or, in the "man of science's" words, as "savage, primitive, underdeveloped, backward"[19] and so on—the advocates of this coherentist approach to moral justification would have us view narrative and stories as intimately bound up with the most sophisticated renderings of principle and theory-driven moral reasoning. For no matter how far we progress toward the ethereal realms of principle and theory, we ought never to lose sight of the fact that all our abstract norms are in fact distillations (and, yes, refinements) of our most fundamental intuitive

[19] Lyotard, *The Postmodern Condition*, 27.

responses to stories about human behavior. Our moral vocabulary and the very contours of our moral universe are shaped by the stories that we hear at our parents' knees. Principles and theories do not emerge full-blown from some empyrean realm of moral truth; rather, they always bear the marks of their history, of their coming-to-be through the crucible of stories and cases. Thus, the defenders of a coherentist theory of moral justification, a theory aptly captured in the metaphor of reflective equilibrium, would claim, like Rita Charon, that narrative and moral theory are not alternatives but, rather, are inseparable elements in a perpetual to-and-fro movement from stories to principles and back again. According to both Charon and these moral coherentists, "narrative ethics" is not a new way of doing ethics; rather, it is a recognition and full appreciation of the debt that principle- and theory-driven modes of discourse owe to stories. Here too, then, narrative ethics works to supplement, rather than supplant, a principled approach to ethics.

Narrative and the Depiction of Character

While some partisans of narrative ethics advance very strong and controversial claims,[20] I think that all would agree that an appropriately complete story or history is a prerequisite to any responsible moral analysis.[21] Before we attempt to judge, we must understand, and the best way to achieve the requisite understanding is to tell a nuanced story.

Thus, when we debate the issue of assisted suicide, for example, we should do so not as some sort of abstract, asocial, and timeless proposition but, rather, in the context of a full-bodied case. Dr. Timothy Quill's well-known case study of Diane, a patient requesting assisted suicide, provides an excellent illustration of this narrative approach.[22] Instead of focusing on the derivation and specification of principles, Dr. Quill gives us a rich picture of the "players" and their characters. There was first and foremost his patient, Diane, a courageous but fearful cancer patient seeking control of her dying process, a woman who had already overcome a previous cancer threat and her own debilitating alcoholism; and there was Dr. Quill himself, who emerges as a competent and clearly compassionate physician torn between loyalties to his patient and the ethics of his

---

[20] Nussbaum, for example, argues that narrative is the only proper medium for some philosophical issues. See "Introduction: Form and Content, Philosophy and Literature," *Love's Knowledge: Essays on Philosophy and Literature* (New York: Cambridge University Press, 1990), 3–53.

[21] This section is drawn from my article "Principles and Particularity: The Roles of Cases in Bioethics," *Indiana Law Journal* 69 (1994): 983–1014.

[22] T. Quill, "Death and Dignity: A Case of Individualized Decision Making," *New England Journal of Medicine* 324 (1991): 691ff.

profession, a man courageous enough to "take small risks for people he cares about." He explores the roles that the players occupy: a doctor trained to preserve life rather than end it; a patient who is also a wife, mother, and respected friend. He tells us about their prior and ongoing relationship, how he had witnessed and rejoiced over Diane's past triumphs over adversity and anguished with her over the current threat. He describes his own doubts and hopes for Diane's future and the future of their ongoing relationship. He wonders whether prescribing a lethal dose might restore her spirits and give her more emotional comfort in her final struggle. And he alludes to the institutional and social context, albeit in my opinion not sufficiently,[23] with references to the current state of the law.

Although a reconstructed principlist might object at this point that all the above matters can and should be folded into a principlistic analysis as components of "the case," it remains true, I think, that the partisans of moral theory and principlism have not given many of these issues their due. This is especially true of Quill's concern to sketch the moral character of his players, the nature of their past and future relationships, and the fine details of their institutional and social context. As Bernard Williams has argued, most of the received moral theories operate with impoverished or empty conceptions of the individual.[24] In order to bring the moral individual into clearer focus, he claims, we must attend to his or her differential particularity, to the desires, needs, and "ground projects" that coalesce into the character of the person. But if we are concerned with the depiction, understanding, and assessment of character, we can do so only by telling and retelling stories.[25]

It is important to note, however, that a salutary concern for the role of character in ethics need not precipitate a wholesale rejection of principles and theory. Although some commentators have contended that an appropriate concern for character and its narrative environment should lead us to reject principle-based ethics,[26] one could just as well view reflection on character as a necessary supplement or extension of an ethic of principles. So understood, narrative ethics emerges once again as an adjunct to standard, principle-based ways of doing ethics.

[23] Indeed, in my opinion, Quill's major failing is to have inadequately considered the implications of introducing the practice of assisted suicide within the context of a society that fails to provide adequate health care, including pain relief and treatment for depression, to millions of potential candidates.

[24] B. Williams, "Persons, Character, Morality," *Moral Luck* (New York: Cambridge University Press, 1981), 1–19.

[25] For a more fully developed statement of the fit between narrative and the depiction of character, sec T. Siebers, *Morals and Stories* (New York: Columbia University Press, 1992), 15.

[26] Burrell and Hauerwas, "From System to Story."

HISTORICAL NARRATIVE AND ETHICAL JUSTIFICATION

The second major conception of narrative ethics I want to consider is a good deal less accommodating to principle-based ethics and poses a greater challenge to principlism's conceptions of moral justification.[27] This view, perhaps best represented by Alasdair MacIntyre and Stanley Hauerwas, constitutes a frontal assault on the so-called Enlightenment project of establishing a rational basis for ethics beyond the constraints of traditions and culture. According to such critics, reason unmoored to a historical community with its own specific canons of rationality is incapable of providing an adequate basis for morality. Reason and rationality, they claim, are always characteristic of a certain historical tradition, whether it be that of Ancient Greece, medieval Paris, or eighteenth-century Edinburgh. Our capacity to view things as reasonable, valuable, noble, appropriate, interesting, and so on is developed within the context of a certain narrative tradition that subtly shapes all our knowing and valuing. Thus reason and rationality will take on as many forms as there are basic historical traditions; there is no one model of rationality that might be used as a critical vantage point from which to pass judgment on the vast panoply of what Wittgenstein called "forms of life." The Enlightenment project of making ethics "scientific," objective, and rational by stripping it of all subjective elements borne by narrative is, they conclude, a philosophical dead end.

In place of the Enlightenment's deracinated conception of reason, the champions of historical narrative would found ethics on stories and tradition. To be sure, they acknowledge that not just any story will qualify as a ground for our ethical life. Rather, they have in mind what one might call "foundational stories" such as the traditions of Greek or Norse epic poetry, the Bible and traditions of biblical commentary (such as the Talmud and Mishnah), or Confucianism. No matter how much one may strive for a universal and objective picture of things, they claim, at some point one simply has to have faith in a story.[28] The reasoning has to end somewhere, and it ends where it began, with a narrative account of who we are as a people and how we got to be this way. Importantly, even the Enlightenment-inspired projects that attempt to rise above the particularities and vagaries of tradition and culture often betray a nascent awareness of the importance of narrative by portraying themselves as the inheritors of a distinct philosophic tradition—for example, of liberalism, utilitarianism, or social contractarianism.[29]

---

[27] I say "conceptions" here to underscore the fact that principlism embraces both correspondence and coherentist approaches to moral justification.

[28] S. Fleischacker, *The Ethics of Culture* (Ithaca, NY: Cornell University Press, 1994).

[29] See J. Rawls, *Political Liberalism* (New York: Columbia University Press, 1993), xxi–xxix.

On this rival view, ethical justification is a matter of squaring one's actions with a social role (or roles) that is, in turn, justified by a fundamental narrative. Far from being justified before some court of abstract reason, our actions are ultimately sanctioned by appeal to the norms, traditions, and social roles of a particular social group. Obversely, according to MacIntyre and Hauerwas, to lack such a distinctive story is to lack a rationale for one's actions, character, and life.[30] For example, a doctor contemplating Timothy Quill's narrative might well object to the latter's embrace of physician-assisted suicide on the ground that throughout history, beginning with the Hippocratic Oath, physicians have defined themselves exclusively as healers, rather than as healers who might on occasion also kill their patients. When confronted with the proposition that our laws against physician-assisted suicide ought to be changed, such a doctor might well respond not by invoking this or that principle or philosophical theory but, rather, by recalling the physician's role in our society, which is, in turn, explicated and justified by an account of the Hippocratic historical tradition.[31]

This aspect of narrative ethics, understood in this stronger sense, generates an ethic that is highly concrete and effectively action-guiding in a manner unavailable to such standard Enlightenment theories as utilitarianism and Kantianism. Because the latter develop their criteria of right and wrong in a realm beyond the particularities of any specific time and place, they provide significant critical leverage; but they do so at the price of an abstractness and remoteness that often render them incapable of definitively guiding action in specific circumstances. The winds of utilitarianism notoriously blow in all sorts of different directions,[32] often simultaneously justifying contradictory positions on important matters of individual morality and public policy, as does Kant's categorical imperative, which seems to function better (at best) as a necessary condition of morality, telling us what we cannot do, rather than as a sufficient condition, telling us what we must do in specific circumstances. For the partisans of this more robust version of narrative ethics, one's story effectively provides the rationale for one's action. ("We are doctors. We don't kill!" "We help the needy, just as Christ bade us to do in the story of the Good Samaritan.")

---

[30] "[M]an is in his actions and practice, as well as in his fictions, essentially a story-telling animal. . . . I can only answer the question 'What am I to do?' if I can answer the prior question 'Of what story or stories do I find myself a part?" A. MacIntyre, *After Virtue* (Notre Dame, IN: Notre Dame University Press, 1981), 201.

[31] W. Gaylin et al., "Why Doctors Must Not Kill," *Journal of the American Medical Association* 259 (1988): 2139–2140.

[32] G. Sher, "Justifying Reverse Discrimination in Employment," *Philosophy & Public Affairs* 4, no. 2 (1975): 159.

The difficulties inherent in this particular narrativist project are predictable and serious. While the concreteness of the fundamental narrative indisputably paves the way for a truly practical ethic, it also sets the limits for any given story and thereby serves, in spite of itself, as a vehicle of transcendence beyond the merely local to other stories telling of other times, places, and ways of knowing and valuing. In the first place, foundational stories not only tell us who we are, they also tell us who we are not. In telling us the story of "our people" with our own particular exemplars of good and evil, for example, such stories also tell us about other peoples against whom we define ourselves. We usually do not define ourselves *tout court*; rather, we define ourselves against neighboring families, tribes, cities, states, and nations. Thus, the Israelites defined themselves against the gentiles, Protestants against Catholics, Southern whites against African Americans, and in the neighborhood where I grew up, the Irish defined themselves against everyone else. At the heart of our own self-conception, then, lies a conception of the Other.[33]

Now, ordinarily this Other figures in our own self-conception not as a subject with his or her own story to tell but, rather, as an objectified element in our own story. Thus, for contemporary Palestinians, the only relevant story is the history of their oppression at the hands of the Jewish state; conversely, for contemporary Israelis, the relevant foundational story is the history of Palestinian aggression and terrorism. The subjects of these historical narratives are thus locked in a perpetual struggle, not only over land but also over the meaning of their common history. This kind of struggle for narrative supremacy can obviously go on for a long time; sometimes (as in the Balkans) it can last for centuries. Once the realization sinks in, however, that the Other is not about to simply go away, the road to moral and political progress will usually involve an attempt on the part of warring traditions to hear and attempt to understand the story of the other party. But once one actually sits down to listen to the other's story, one opens oneself to the possibilities not simply for acquiring sympathy and tolerance but also for radical self-transformation. It could well turn out, once I have heard your story, that I judge it to be a better story than the one I was taught as a child.

In this way, an awareness of other stories leads to an awareness of the limits of our own. Obviously, we must begin with our own story, which we learn at our parents' knees and which conditions our entire outlook; but contact with the wider world

[33] This dialectical aspect of self-definition has received its most memorable expression in Nietzsche's *On the Genealogy of Morals*, trans. W. Kaufmann (New York: Vintage, 1969). See especially the "First Essay: Good and Evil, Good and Bad," 24–56. See also Hegel's *Phenomenology of Mind*, trans. W. Wallace and A. V. Miller (Oxford: Clarendon Press, 1971).

of other stories usually leads us to question our own story and the various social roles to which it gives rise. Thus, a physician trained in the Hippocratic tradition might be exposed to her patients' stories of suffering, which themselves point to a wider political story of individual freedom struggling to remove the traditional constraints imposed by the heavy hands of religion, custom, and professional codes of ethics. Such a physician might then experience a genuine moral conflict. In addition to her initial repugnance for physician-assisted suicide ("We're doctors. We don't kill.")—a repugnance founded upon her social role dictated by the story of Western medicine—she may now be attracted by other social roles (for example, that of patient advocate) generated by other stories (for example, that of the tradition of political liberalism). This physician then must confront the difficult business of choosing between social roles with their corresponding foundational stories. Whatever she decides, once the complexity of modern societies is acknowledged, a narrative ethic in this stronger sense no longer seems to offer a ready-made action-guiding solution. Just as the moral theorist must attempt to sort out, say, the respective attractions of various competing *prima facie* obligations in a complex situation of moral choice, so the proponent of narrative ethics not only must ask which story should control her actions in a given situation but also must eventually confront the ultimate question of what makes any story morally compelling and worthy of our allegiance. How, in other words, are we to know that the story with which we begin is a "good story" or a better story than the available alternatives?

One way to solve this deep and vexing problem is to set out criteria for the evaluation of stories. Burrell and Hauerwas, for example, contend that "[t]he test of each story is the sort of person it shapes."[34] They elaborate on this answer by positing four additional desiderata that any good story, they assert, will have to display:

1. Power to release us from destructive alternatives;
2. Ways of seeing through current distortions;
3. Room to keep us from having to resort to violence;
4. A sense for the tragic: how meaning transcends power.[35]

While one could quibble with this list of criteria by questioning either the appropriateness of each item or the comprehensiveness of the entire set, the more basic problem for narrative ethics involves the very idea of resorting to a set of abstract criteria for resolving conflicts among plausible stories. For if we are truly able to pick and choose among competing stories by deploying a set of criteria, then

[34] Burrell and Hauerwas, "From System to Story," 136.
[35] Ibid., 137.

it would appear that the criteria themselves, and not the narratives, are fundamental to the critical function of ethics. Although the above list does appear to be rather idiosyncratic, we could easily translate some of its criteria into the traditional language of principles and theory. Thus, criteria (1) and (3) above could be recast into the language of nonmaleficence (that is, do no harm). The second criterion (bearing on release from distortions) could quite plausibly be read as a restatement of Marx's strictures against "false consciousness" a critical position owing more to a theory of social reality and its ideological distortions than to any narrative.[36] By supplementing Burrell and Hauerwas's list with, say, a principle of beneficence, with respect for individuality or autonomy, or perhaps with an ideal of "human flourishing," we could compile a set of criteria that might look something like W. D. Ross's list of *prima facie* duties,[37] which could then be applied to the various fundamental stories competing for our allegiance. Narrative ethics must on this account have recourse to an independent set of abstract criteria bearing either on the rightness of actions or on the kinds of characters that our stories ought to foster. But the problem with this approach is obviously that it forfeits the supremacy of narrative over abstract principle, thereby returning us to the more benign conception of narrative ethics as a supplement to (or dialectically incorporated ingredient of) principles and theory.

Another way of sorting out the rival claims of competing stories, one more consonant with the whole idea of a robust narrative ethics, is to claim that some narratives do a better job of solving the problems that have claimed the attention of other narratives. As developed by Alasdair MacIntyre, this claim boils down to the notion that the only corrective for a bad, inadequate, or incoherent narrative is a better narrative, not some set of abstract principles. MacIntyre develops this suggestion through his conception of "epistemological crises,"[38] in which the members of a narrative tradition come to see that tradition as ultimately unable to resolve its problems or inner tensions. MacIntyre views the fundamental narratives as engaged in a quest to discern "the good life for man." At a certain stage in its development, a narrative tradition may experience an epistemological crisis or breakdown in which its resources no longer prove adequate to the task at hand. At this point, the members of such a tradition might look to other narratives as resources

[36] K. Marx, "Preface to a Critique of Political Economy," in *Karl Marx: Selected Writings*, ed. D. McLellan (Oxford: Oxford University Press, 1977): 388–391.

[37] W. D. Ross, *The Right and the Good* (Oxford: Clarendon Press, 1930). This approach to ethics was a formative influence on Beauchamp and Childress's version of principlism.

[38] A. MacIntyre, *Whose Justice? Which Rationality?* (Notre Dame, IN: University of Notre Dame Press, 1988), 362. MacIntyre also addresses this theme in "The Relationship of Philosophy to Its Past," in *Philosophy in History*, ed. R. Rorty, J. B Schneewind, and Q. Skinner (New York: Cambridge University Press, 1984), 44.

for solving the very problems that had proved so intractable within their inherited story. Adherents of the original narrative may find that the new tradition shows them not only a new story with new social roles to supplant the old ones but also a way out of their former epistemological impasse.

Importantly, MacIntyre contends that when an outside narrative assumes this role, epistemological and moral progress has taken place. We have not merely witnessed the abandonment of one story and accompanying social roles for another story and other roles. If that were all that has happened, then we could speak only of the temporal succession of one story by another, and narrative ethics would have to remain silent on the fundamental question of which story might be better than another, thereby settling for a disquieting relativism. Rather, MacIntyre wants to claim that we have moved from a relatively narrow and (by now) dysfunctional narrative to a more encompassing and more adequate story that effectively solves the problems of the first tradition. When this happens, we have, in effect, moved from the particular to the (more) universal without abandoning our commitment to narrative as the driving force behind ethics. In other words, narrative ethics can remain critical without ultimately abandoning narrative in the fashion of Burrell and Hauerwas.

In order to maintain this position, MacIntyre must insist that the adherents of the faltering story be able to see the succeeding story as holding the key to the resolution of their former problems. They must, moreover, be able to see the new story as constituting an advance over the old story in terms that would be comprehensible to the adherents of the old story.[39] Without this sort of linkage, we would be back to a mere succession of stories instead of the hoped-for moral progress from the particular to the more encompassing view.

While this is not the place for a full-blown critique of MacIntyre's position, it should be noted that his view on narrative and justification is controversial and problematic. In particular, if foundational stories of the meaning of human life are to have the sort of globally pervasive influence that MacIntyre ascribes to them, if they condition our modes of thought, language, sensibility, and frames of reference, then it is hard to understand how the substitution of a new foundational

[39] MacIntyre plays out this theme in the context of the philosophy of science in the following way: "[T]his solution can now be formulated as a criterion by means of which the rational superiority of one large-scale body of theory to another can be judged. One large scale of theory—say, Newtonian mechanics—may be judged decisively superior to another—say, the mechanics of medieval impetus theory, if and only if the former body of theory enables us to give an adequate and by the best standards we have true explanation of why the latter body of theory both enjoyed the successes and victories that it did and suffered the defeats and frustrations that it did, where success and failure, victory and defeat are defined in terms of the standards for success and failure, victory and defeat provided by what I earlier called the internal problematic of the latter body of theory. . . . It is success and failure, progress and sterility in terms both of the problems and the goals that were or could have been identified by the adherents of the rationally inferior theory." MacIntyre, "The Relationship of Philosophy to Its Past," 43.

narrative for a faltering story could leave intact all those old modes of thought and evaluation that are supposed to evaluate the new story in terms of the old.[40]

NARRATIVE AND POSTMODERN ETHICS

So far we have canvassed two distinct approaches to the question of narrative ethics and its relation to ethical justification. The first, articulated by Rita Charon, conceived of narrative ethics as an enriching supplement to the more standard forms of principle-based ethics. On this view, ethical justification resides either in the conformity of our actions to various ethical rules and principles that are themselves justified by some deeper philosophical theory, or in the process of reflective equilibrium. According to the second approach, represented by Hauerwas and MacIntyre, ethical justification must be sought in social roles, which are themselves grounded in foundational historical narratives. I now want to take up a third approach to narrative and ethical justification under the rubric of postmodern ethics. As I shall try to show in this final section, the postmodern storyteller has come to see narrative not as a substrate but, rather, as a substitute for the entire enterprise of moral justification.

What Is a Postmodern Ethic?

As I (dimly) understand it, postmodernism can be understood from one angle as a wholesale retreat not only from traditional theories—such as Marxism, Freudian psychoanalysis, or utilitarianism—but also from attempts at achieving some sort of grand coherence in our epistemological, ethical, and social views. In the place of theory and overarching coherence, the postmodernist asserts the virtues of the *petit récit*, or "little narrative." Instead of probing history, for example, for its "deep structure" or laws of social development, the postmodernist historian dwells on small-scale narratives and anecdote. Thoroughly disabused of grounding or justifying his discourses on such basic and traditional distinctions as between fact and fiction, knowledge and custom, truth and ideology, the postmodernist observer (historian, anthropologist, philosopher, literary scholar, legal theorist, and so on) seeks a kind of legitimation through the telling and retelling of stories.[41]

---

[40] For a fuller development of this criticism, see Furrow, *Against Theory*, 49–59.

[41] Simpson, *The Academic Postmodern*, 62. Lyotard remarks in this connection "narrative knowledge does not give priority to the question of its own legitimation and . . . certifies itself in the pragmatics of its own transmission without having recourse to argumentation and proof." Lyotard, *The Postmodern Tradition a Report on Knowledge*, 27.

Richard Rorty's endorsement of an "ironist culture" provides an illuminating example of this eclipse of explanation and justification by narrative.[42] While Rorty concedes that on the most mundane level, within a particular narrative or historical tradition (for example, the common law), we can still make use of the notion of justification, he argues that at the more global level, where rival narratives, vocabularies, and traditions clash, we cannot speak meaningfully of justifying any one of these rival views by anchoring it in the bedrock of a true theory of history, human nature, or the natural world. When confronted with a sustained narrative that now shows signs of budding incoherence or newly perceived insensitivity to the sufferings of others—for example, a society (such as ours) that has traditionally and systematically degraded women—Rorty's "liberal ironist" must resort not to logical argument but, rather, to a kind of poetic redescription that allows us to see the world in new ways. Instead of presenting one's interlocutor with a logical argument that cannot be denied on pain of self-contradiction, the feminist must work with other like-minded people to forge a new vocabulary, a new set of meanings, and encourage others to begin to describe the world in similar ways.[43] For Rorty, then, the poet, not the traditional philosopher, is the vanguard of the human species.[44]

The ultimate goal of Rorty's culture of liberal ironism is not the replacing of falsity and distortion with truth (about "Man," "human nature," "History," "Reality") but, rather, the mere continuation of the "conversation." Whereas both explanation and justification seek and require closure at some point—always lusting after that "QED"—Rorty's notion of conversation desires only its own continuation in a limitless quest for novelty. It refuses to seek a final resting place in some moral, social, or scientific bedrock that will put an end to disputation and conversation once and for all. One important ethical maxim that Rorty would have us derive from his notion of conversation—a kind of postmodern categorical imperative, if you will—is thus that we should always strive to keep "moral space" open for more dialogue.[45]

Another way to depict the implications of postmodernism for ethics is to describe it as an "ethics of voice."[46] In contrast to the standard brands of Enlightenment ethics that highlight either the content (for example, utilitarianism) or form (for

---

[42] Rorty, *Contingency, Irony, and Solidarity*; see also Rorty, *The Consequences of Pragmatism* (Minneapolis: University of Minnesota Press, 1982). For more on Rorty's views in connection with bioethics, see chapter 5 this volume.

[43] R. Rorty, "Feminism and Pragmatism," in *The Tanner Lectures on Human Values*, vol. 13, ed. G. B Peterson (Salt Lake City: University of Utah Press, 1992), 3–22.

[44] Rorty, *The Consequences of Pragmatism*, 150; Rorty, *Contingency, Irony, and Solidarity*, 20.

[45] For a compelling development of this view as applied to clinical ethics, see M. U. Walker, "Keeping Moral Spaces Open," *Hastings Center Report* 23, no. 2 (March/April 1993): 33–40.

[46] A. Frank, *The Wounded Storyteller* (Chicago: University of Chicago Press, 1995), xiii. Later on, Frank writes, "The idea of telling one's own story as a responsibility to the commonsense world reflects what I understand as the core morality of the postmodern" (17).

example, Kantianism) of what is said, postmodernist ethics seems to be primarily concerned with who gets to tell the story. More specifically, the postmodern categorical imperative seems to come down to an insistence that everyone gets to tell his or her own story. Thus, Arthur Frank, a self-described postmodernist, sets out in his remarkable book, *The Wounded Storyteller*,[47] to rescue the first-person illness narratives of his fellow cancer sufferers from the "colonialism" of modernist (that is, scientific) medicine. According to Frank, those who suffer should be allowed and encouraged to speak for themselves, to find their own voice, rather than submit to the reductionistic and objectifying categories of modern medicine. Instead of the professionals' "case studies," narratives that objectify the experience and sufferings of people grappling with illness, Frank advocates the "case story" in which the "ill are allowed to discover for themselves what it means to be a good person by telling and then reflecting on their own story.[48]

At this point, one might very well be moved to exclaim irreverently, "Nice story, but so what?" What is the connection, in other words, between all this storytelling and what might quaintly be called "the truth" or moral justification? According to Frank, the stories that convey the subjective quest of the ill person "are their own truth," and he confesses to being unsure "what a 'false' personal account would be."[49] While prepared to grant that some personal narratives might be "evasive," Frank considers this evasiveness to be their truth. The more I reconstruct (distort?) the details of my own story, the more I manifest the truth of my desire to have experienced a different narrative course in my life.[50] Against an ethic of principles and rules, Frank claims that narrative ethics offers the ill person the freedom or "permission" to allow his story to lead in different directions in order to facilitate the process of self-discovery through the trial of illness.[51] And lest the reader begin to wonder about the potentially solipsistic consequences of such a view of truth in narrative, Frank concedes in the end that narratives are ultimately based upon an appeal to something more than our desires: "What is testified to remains the really real," he writes, "and in the end what counts are duties towards it."[52] Still, although the act of providing "testimony" forges a connection for Frank to the "really real," this particular kind of postmodern testimony makes no pretense of grasping the whole or presenting a full panorama connecting my testimony to that of others. We are left with the ill person's *petit récit*.

---

[47] Ibid.

[48] Postmodernism is characterized by Simpson as exhibiting a nostalgia for the preprofessional. See Simpson, *The Academic Postmodern*, 47.

[49] Frank, *The Wounded Storyteller*, 22.

[50] Ibid., 22.

[51] Ibid., 160.

[52] Ibid., 138.

As I mentioned at the beginning of this essay, this postmodernist privileging of the "little story" has both an epistemological and an ethical dimension. We ought to favor such narratives, first, because we can't do any better. It is an epistemological error to believe that we can transcend the local, anchoring our science and ethics on the bedrock of the objectively and universally real. But we also have an ethical motivation to prefer the "little story" in the tendency of larger or more "totalizing" narratives, such as Marxism or Frank's portrayal of modern medicine, to silence, coerce, or, at the extreme, physically annihilate those who do not conform to their norms and expectations. As Lyotard mordantly observes, "The nineteenth and twentieth centuries have given us as much terror as we can take. We have paid a high enough price for the nostalgia of the whole and the one."[53]

Some Problems and Reservations

While I do not consider myself sufficiently well versed as yet in the literature of postmodernism to hazard a global assessment of this movement and its implications for ethics, the brief sketch I have presented above should provide us with a rich agenda for further elaboration, reflection, and critique. I will therefore limit myself to the expression of some initial doubts and worries regarding the promise of a postmodern ethic founded on *petits récits*.

The Threat of Subjectivism

As developed by Arthur Frank, postmodern ethics risks sacrificing ethics at the altar of personal self-development. Not entirely satisfied with Rita Charon's portrayal of narrative ethics as a necessary adjunct to an ethic of principles, Frank argues that beyond the delimited sphere of "patienthood," in which the suffering individual is subjected to the norms and projects of health-care providers, narrative ethics achieves autonomy and completeness in its own sphere, which is the sphere of "personal becoming."[54] As noted above, this ethic cannot provide us with guidelines or principles; instead it provides each suffering individual with the moral space and "permission" to develop his or her story in ways that seem appropriate to her or his own life. While Frank says many important and interesting things on this theme, the overall effect of his argument seems to privilege the search for individual coherence

[53] Lyotard, *The Postmodern Condition*, 81. In this connection Simpson notes that even Hegel, the great Satan of postmodernism, saw a need to allocate some role in his totalizing system to the individual, to "the little guy." According to Simpson, the distinctive claim of postmodernism is that "[i]n these times we are all little guys." Simpson, *The Academic Postmodern*, 60.

[54] Frank, *The Wounded Storyteller*, 158.

over one quite central function of ethics, traditionally conceived, which is the passing of judgment on actions, policies, and character traits.

For example, Frank confesses to being unsure what a "false" personal account might be. I must admit to having a lot less trouble on this score. Although every one of us no doubt shades the truth or even intentionally distorts crucial facts in the stories we tell about our own lives, one need think only of the life story or personal testimony of Ronald Reagan to find a staggering example of duplicity and self-deception. As recounted and amply demonstrated in Gary Wills's fine biography,[55] Reagan was chronically and systematically incapable of telling fact from fiction about any of the defining events in his own life. Whether the issue concerned his boyhood days in Illinois, his wartime "service" in Hollywood, his behavior as president of the Screen Actors' Guild during the McCarthy era, or (I might add) during the Iran-Contra affair, Reagan seemed congenitally incapable of telling a story about his own life that was even remotely related to what had actually happened. In each case, the story told had more to do with what Reagan *wished* were true than it did with people and events in what might be referred to as the real world. But this, of course, should come as no great surprise. Although Reagan was perhaps more doggedly systematic in his penchant for self-deception and buffing his personal record than most people, all of us tell stories that deviate in greater or lesser measure from what really happened. Come to think of it, psychiatrists would probably be out of a job if all of us were more truthful, self-aware, and trustworthy in the stories we tell about ourselves.[56] If correspondence to what actually happened—making due allowance, of course, for the necessity and vagaries of interpretation—is an indispensable measure of the verisimilitude of stories, then it would seem that we have no more reason to place unquestioning trust in these "little narratives" than in some of the theorists' metanarratives.[57]

Frank seems willing to concede our penchant for self-deception, but he immediately spots "the truth" involved in distorted narratives—that is, our desire for a reformulated story. While I would agree with Frank that duplicitous or self-deceptive narratives (truly) betray a desire on the storyteller's part to have a

---

[55] G. Wills, *Reagan's America: Innocents at Home* (Garden City, NY: Doubleday, 1987).

[56] For an amusing novelistic portrayal of this fallible human tendency, see I. D. Yalom, *Lying on the Couch* (New York: Basic Books, 1996).

[57] Simpson is particularly discerning on this point: "There is nothing whatever in our participation in little narratives, our own or those of a few natural hearts or professional colleagues or fellow sufferers, that guarantees an avoidance of the blind spots or even of critical errors. Telling one's own story, or the story of one's imagined group or subculture, with an implicit or explicit reliance on the dubious category of 'experience,' has in itself no more or less authority than the grandest of grand narratives." Simpson, *The Academic Postmodern*, 30.

different story from the one he or she has lived out and for which she or he is (in part) responsible, this is certainly not the only or the main thing we mean when we say that a story is "truthful." It appears that Frank is so eager to give suffering individuals sufficient "moral space" and "permission" to develop their own personal stories that he risks undercutting our ability to make moral judgments. It sometimes seems as though he is willing to substitute the "authenticity" of the storyteller for the more traditional concern for ethical justification. So long as the narrator has suffered and claims the mantle of authenticity, that in itself justifies the story told.

We encounter here a broader and more fundamental problem with narrative as a vehicle for ethics. We have already seen, through Rita Charon's work, just how important narrative is to ethics as traditionally conceived. Narrative provides us with a rich tapestry of fact, situation, and character on which our moral judgments operate. Without this rich depiction of people, their situations, their motives, and so on, the moral critic cannot adequately understand the moral issue she confronts, and any moral judgments she brings to bear on a situation will consequently lack credibility. To paraphrase Kant, ethics without narrative is empty. But if all we do is strive to comprehend, if we are exclusively concerned with discerning coherence within a person's narrative, then we have no moral space left over for moral judgment. And this becomes a problem as soon as we realize that some internally coherent stories may yet be morally repugnant and fit objects for moral disapproval. To round out the allusion to Kant, we might say here that ethics without judgment is not ethics. Pace Frank, stories may well have their own (internal) truth, but that is not the only truth with which we must be concerned if we mean also to do ethics. The partisans of narrative ethics must therefore begin to think harder about the implications of "bad coherence" for their enterprise.[58]

Localism and Social Criticism

A related problem for Frank, and more generally for postmodernism, is the temptation to fetishize "little narratives" at the expense of broader social understanding and critique. While there is unquestionably an important place for such narratives,

---

[58] In Frank's defense, one might recall his apparent acknowledgment of a referent for narrative ethics beyond the subjectivity of the individual storyteller: "What is testified to remains the really real, and in the end what counts are duties towards it" (Frank, *The Wounded Storyteller*, 138). The problem with this, however, is that "what is testified to" remains precisely the pain and suffering of the individual storyteller, presumably as interpreted by that storyteller. So what began as a possible link to some tangible external check on the truth of stories ends up being one more manifestation of the subjectivistic nature of Frank's approach.

and while Frank's book makes an eloquent and powerful case for them within the context of an often-stifling modernist medical culture, it is also no doubt true that an overemphasis on the little story can render us purblind to larger social patterns and events that must also be grasped and understood if we are to achieve a fully rounded and adequate picture of our social world. It is an enduring temptation for Frank and the postmodernists, in their single-minded embrace of creativity, empathy, and compassion, uncritically to buy into the essentially romantic myth of the isolated individual or group, and thereby to ignore larger patterns and relationships that a more critical and socially attuned approach might recognize. At the very least, someone like Frank should be concerned not just with individual stories but also with larger sets of relationships or recurring patterns that might cast new light on these stories and suggest common strategies for social improvement.

One might also entertain doubts in this connection about the extent of the postmodern critique of transcending the local. It is certainly true, as Lyotard points out, that a "totalizing" mentality has often led to oppression of dissenting minorities, but it is equally true that the rationalist tendencies of the Enlightenment tradition have also had a profoundly liberatory effect in many instances. Indeed, important movements of liberation from the provinciality of custom and tradition may well find themselves theoretically eviscerated by the postmodernist embrace of the local.

Consider the case of feminism. In contrast to Rorty's assessment,[59] many thoughtful feminists see theirs as an essentially modernist movement opposed to the arbitrary authority of men over women, as an assault on every social norm or institution resting on the ideology of male superiority.[60] Whereas Lyotard views a dogged attachment to the local and the *petit récit* as a liberation from the enslavement of "master narratives," these feminists see the Enlightenment ideals of freedom and equality as liberatory from the enslavement of women manifested in just about every local culture known hitherto. While communitarians like MacIntyre uncritically accept the social roles handed down by tradition and foundational narratives, feminists are bound, in the words of Sabina Lovibond, sooner or later to call the parish boundaries into question.[61] For them, the total reconstruction of society along rational lines—assuming the rationality of gender equality—is not so much a shopworn and discarded Enlightenment ideal as an indispensable blueprint for fundamental and desperately needed social reform. Crucial to this

---

[59] Rorty, "Feminism and Pragmatism."

[60] S. Lovibond, "Feminism and Postmodernism," *New Left Review* 178 (1989): 5–28; S. Benhabib, "Feminism and the Question of Postmodernism," in *Situating the Self: Gender, Community and Postmodernism in Contemporary Ethics* (New York: Routledge, 1992), 203–241.

[61] Lovibond, "Feminism and Postmodernism," 22.

agenda is the critical idea of false consciousness—that is, the ability of dominant social classes to impose their own values and ideals on all other groups so that the latter are often impaired in their ability to discern their own true best interests. For many contemporary feminists, the gradual but systematic transcendence of pervasive local rationales for male domination constitutes the first order of business in social theory. To be sure, these feminists seek out and honor the individual experiences of individual women; that indeed is a large part of what "consciousness raising" is all about. But it is also about linking the common experiences of individual women into a cohesive and global social critique and accompanying program for large-scale social action. For such activists and theorists, the postmodern attachment to the local represents a fundamental threat to feminism as a *critical* theory of society. Defenders of the postmodern outlook in ethics thus need to reflect on the implications of their localism for the prospects of effectively criticizing pervasive, ideologically inspired injustices. And we all need to think much harder about how to acknowledge our individuality and situatedness without abandoning the possibility of social criticism. Instead of just noticing (and even celebrating) our differences, we also need to understand better how our differences are intertwined in a larger social tapestry. In spite of the manifest virtues and attractions of the *petit récit*, there is still room, in other words, for considering the bigger picture.

SUCCESS?

In this chapter I have canvassed three distinct approaches to the relationship of narrative ethics to ethical justification. I have come to the provisional conclusion that the first approach, which conceived of narrative as an essential element in any and all ethical analyses, constitutes a powerful and necessary corrective to the narrowness and abstractness of some widespread versions of principle- and theory-based ethics. The second approach, staked out by Burrell, Hauerwas, and MacIntyre, is initially plausible, but risks either falling back into a more principled version of ethics (see Burrell and Hauerwas's search for abstract criteria) or sinking into a relativistic slough of incommensurable fundamental narratives (MacIntyre). Finally, I have argued that self-consciously postmodern approaches to ethics risk mistaking the authenticity of the narrator for ethical truth and often ignore the larger social picture. While it should be obvious by now that narrative and narrative methods of inquiry are pervasive and indispensable for ethical analysis, it remains less clear whether any of the more fundamental assaults on principle- or theory-based ethics can be successful. Narrative is thus indisputably a crucial element of all ethical analysis, and we would all do better to be more self-conscious about the literary nature of ethical understanding and assessment. It remains to be seen, however, whether narrative will ever be in a position to supplant an ethic also undergirded by principles and theory.

5

Dewey and Rorty's Pragmatism and Bioethics

HOW TO EXPLAIN the recent surge of interest in pragmatism within the field of bioethics? A large part of the answer, I think, has to do with the widespread perception that the heretofore dominant method of bioethics—*viz.*, principlism—has outlived its usefulness and fails adequately to address a cluster of serious problems besetting the field, especially those stemming from cultural diversity. The spectacle of the perennial champ wobbling on the ropes has no doubt encouraged the partisans of pragmatism, along with a host of other methodological malcontents, to enter the ring.[1]

The precise nature and import of claims from the tradition of American pragmatism for the field of bioethics is anything but clear. This is—at least in large part—because different proponents of pragmatism as a model for practical reasoning in bioethics have been influenced by different figures and approaches within the diverse tradition of American pragmatism. Some have been influenced by John Dewey, others by Richard Rorty. And others, whom I'll call "freestanding

[1] The rise of a distinctly pragmatic strain of bioethical thinking promises to add a new dimension to the methodological ferment that has energized this field for some time. The lingua franca and dominant methodological orientation of contemporary bioethics since the late 1970s has been the "principlism" of philosopher Tom Beauchamp and religious ethicist James Childress (T. L. Beauchamp and J. F. Childress, *Principles of Biomedical Ethics*, editions 1–7 [New York: Oxford University Press, 1979, 1983, 1989, 1994, 2001, 2009, 2013]; see chapter 1 this volume). Instead of grounding moral inquiry in either philosophical theory or the particulars of concrete situations, principlism has sought to locate the crux of moral reasoning in the identification, interpretation, and balancing of "mid-level" moral principles, such as those bearing on individual autonomy, beneficence, and justice. So dominant has been principlism's reign within the field of bioethics that commentators routinely refer to Beauchamp and Childress's articulation of these principles as "the Georgetown mantra."

pragmatists" and discuss in detail in the next chapter, do not see their work as rooted in the writings of the classical cannon of American pragmatism. One important objective of my general project on pragmatism and bioethics[2] is to disentangle and identify these various strands of bioethical pragmatism and then to assess their importance for ongoing methodological debates. Accordingly, I will begin with a pragmatism primer to introduce the reader to some central themes of American pragmatism. I will then explore applications and limitations of Dewey's philosophy and Rorty's philosophy. Getting clearer on the insights and limitations of these classical approaches will pave the way for my consideration of "freestanding pragmatists" in chapter 6.

A PRAGMATISM PRIMER

The classical pragmatist outlook is premised on a rejection of the doctrine of metaphysical realism. Pragmatists claim that we cannot intelligibly posit a realm of reality that exists independently of our own language, conceptual schemes, and practical activity. According to traditional philosophical doctrine, the job of human knowers is somehow to produce an adequate picture or representation of reality by means of ideas or perceptions. Our statements or theories about something are "true" whenever they accurately *correspond to* or *mirror* the state of affairs in question. Pragmatists call this the "spectator view" of human knowledge, and perhaps the only thing on which they all agree is that this traditional philosophical approach to reality and knowledge must be resolutely rejected.

In lieu of the spectator view, pragmatists propose a vision of human knowers as active, embodied social agents whose projects and practices give rise to conceptual schemes through which they see and know the world. In place of the disembodied, disengaged, solitary Cartesian subject who seeks a purely objective and dispassionate knowledge of the real, the subjects of pragmatist philosophy are actively engaged in shaping the world that they attempt to know. The knowledge they gain will necessarily be colored by their interests, their projects, and their conceptual schemes. As James put it: "The trail of the human serpent is over everything."[3] "Truth," for pragmatists, thus has a lot more to do with "warranted assertability" and with what the community of inquirers will eventually settle on than it does with correspondence to a reality that supposedly exists apart from our dealings

---

[2] In addition to the present chapter, see J. D. Arras, "Rorty's Pragmatism and Bioethics," *Journal of Medicine and Philosophy* 28 (2003): 597–613; and J. D. Arras, "Freestanding Pragmatism in Law and Bioethics," *Theoretical Medicine and Bioethics* 22, no. 2 (2001): 69–85. See also chapter 6 in this volume.

[3] W. James, "Pragmatism: What Pragmatism Means," in *Pragmatism: A Contemporary Reader*, ed. Russell B. Goodman (New York: Routledge, 1995), 60.

with it. Given our thoroughly *situated* point of view, truth for pragmatists will never be total or absolute. Although our contact with the world and with other people is indisputable for pragmatists, what we know about this world is always fallible, always subject to revision. And while the Cartesian knowing subject attempts to erect a philosophical system on an absolutely secure foundation of indubitable truth, the pragmatist views the corpus of human knowledge more holistically. The plausibility of any new proposition is thus related not to some rock-solid foundation but, rather, to how well it can be integrated into our already existing stock of cognitive commitments.[4]

An important implication of the rejection of the Cartesian spectator view of knowledge is an equally emphatic rejection of many traditional philosophical dualisms. Thus, the dualism of subject and object, so crucial to the Cartesian viewpoint, is swept away in favor of a fully contextualized knowing subject. The dualism of mind and body is replaced by a view of human beings as biological organisms whose thinking is viewed as one means among others of adapting to an environment. Likewise, ethics is taken out of the ethereal realm of the absolute and the *a priori* and is thoroughly naturalized. The study of morality thus ceases to lust after timeless foundational principles in order to ask what actions and forms of social organization will best foster the flourishing of our biological and social natures. An important adjunct to this study is Darwin's theory of natural selection, which helps explain the evolution of ethics itself as an adaptive form of human behavior.

The abandonment of the spectator view and its attendant dualisms has important implications for theorizing in the area of bioethics. One such implication concerns our understanding of the nature of certain pivotal concepts. Take, for example, our concept "death" in the context of our longstanding debate over the respective merits of conceptions of so-called higher versus lower brain death. According to the spectator view, our proper goal in this debate should be to fasten onto the true meaning of death so that we will then be able to determine exactly when it is appropriate to say that a human being has died. In other words, we need to align our concept of death so that it corresponds with the biological or metaphysical reality of death. Fixing on the correct definition of death is thus a

---

[4] Many of these points are nicely summed up by James in "Pragmatism: What Pragmatism Means," 55–56:

> A pragmatist turns his back resolutely and once for all upon a lot of inveterate habits dear to professional philosophers. He turns away from abstraction . . . , from verbal solutions, from bad a priori reasons, from fixed principles, closed systems, and pretended absolutes and origins. He turns towards concreteness and adequacy, towards facts, towards action and towards power. . . . It means the open air and possibilities of nature, as against dogma, artificiality, and the pretence of finality in truth.

matter of *discovering* a truth that is *out there*, regardless of our human projects and practices.

A pragmatic approach to this same problem would begin with the proposition that concepts like "life" and "death" are human constructs that serve certain human purposes. Instead of attempting to discover the meaning of these concepts in some sort of transtemporal and translinguistic realm, the pragmatist will frankly acknowledge that the meaning of the concept "death" is something that we *construct* or *agree upon* in order to advance various purposes, such as facilitating organ transplantation and providing appropriate care to certain categories of patients. The adequacy of any proposed concept of "death" will thus reside not in an imagined correspondence with reality but, rather, in its ability to mesh well with our related intellectual, emotional, and social commitments. For the pragmatist, then, the crucial question has to do with which conception best coheres with the complex web of beliefs, actions, and projects that give shape and meaning to our lives. According to philosopher Martin Benjamin, the answer to this question will depend upon what we feel is most important to the existence of a human being. In other words, do we believe that the ability to spontaneously respire and circulate blood is of primary importance, as the lower-brain conception of death maintains? Or, do we believe that our ability to think, reason, feel, and communicate with others—in short, our "personhood"—is most crucial to our understanding of human life, as the partisans of the higher-brain conception of death maintain?[5] Although Benjamin endorses the personhood approach, his crucial pragmatist point for our methodological debates is that the meaning of problematic concepts like "death" must be determined, not discovered, with a clear view of the human interests involved.

THE PHILOSOPHER'S (AND BIOETHICIST'S) ROLE

The spectator view of knowledge has two implications for the role of philosophers and, by extension, for the role of bioethicists in society. First, the highest form of philosophical activity will be viewed as contemplation. The precise objects of this contemplative attitude will vary from one philosophical school to another. For the ancient Greeks, the proper objects of the philosopher's attention were those "first things"—for example, Platonic Forms—that occupied the highest rungs on the great chain of being, knowledge of which would effectively ground all other

[5] M. Benjamin, "Pragmatism and the Determination of Death," in *Pragmatic Bioethics*, ed. G. McGee (Cambridge, MA: MIT Press, 2003), 191.

knowledge. For Kantians, the objects of philosophical concern are those *a priori* structures of human experience that make knowledge possible. But whatever the objects in question, passive contemplation constitutes the quintessential activity for philosophies built on the basis of a dualism of subject and object.

Second, the spectator view of knowledge implies a very special role for philosophers vis-à-vis other disciplines within the general culture. According to Dewey, a conception of philosophy built on this model will tend to view philosophers as members of a kind of elevated secular priesthood. Armed with the knowledge of "first things," philosophers are uniquely situated, according to this tradition, to expound on what is really real, true, valuable, and beautiful. Armed with a grasp of the *a priori* structures of knowledge, philosophers are uniquely situated to pass judgment on the claims of rival disciplines, such as literature and the social sciences, making sure that they do not transgress the boundaries of their own cognitive limitations.

Rejecting the spectator view of knowledge will thus have interesting and far-reaching implications for pragmatists attempting to "reconstruct" the tasks of philosophy and the role of philosophers. According to Dewey, once we abandon all pretenses of being the discoverers and guardians of "first things," once we begin to envision knowledge as a practical matter involving engaged, embodied, social agents, we will then begin to see that throughout history philosophers have really been preoccupied with important values embodied in existing social institutions and cultures. We will also see that the greatest impetus to philosophy has been not some ineffable confrontation with the "really" real but, rather, historical conflicts between inherited institutions and incompatible ideas borne aloft by new industrial, political, and scientific movements. And once we see this, Dewey concludes, we are then in a position to see that "the task of future philosophy is to clarify men's [and women's] ideas as to the social and moral strifes of their own day . . . and . . . contribut[e] to the aspirations of men [and women] to attain to a more ordered and intelligent happiness."[6]

This pragmatic approach substitutes a much more interdisciplinary and democratic conception of philosophy for the priesthood conception embedded in the spectator view of knowledge. Instead of "discovering" first things and first principles, the philosopher's role is to reflect critically on his or her own culture and on the values embedded therein. Philosophers of a pragmatist bent will analyze and critique human objectives, asking in every case what would likely result for individuals and society from the implementation of those objectives. In addition,

[6] J. Dewey, *Reconstruction in Philosophy, in The Middle Works, 1899–1924*, ed. J. A. Boydston (Carbondale: Southern Illinois University Press, 1982), 12–94.

because emerging technologies tend to outstrip our ability to harness them for genuine human flourishing, philosophers will also have to assume the role of assisting society in the design of humane institutional responses to emerging scientific and technological trends.[7]

Philosophy so understood is a far more interdisciplinary venture than the "logical watchdog" role implied by the spectator view. As we shall see in later sections of this essay, Dewey was particularly keen on forging alliances between philosophy and the social sciences. While philosophers scrutinized the values embedded in various actions, policies, and experiments in living, social scientists would be charged with studying the actual consequences of translating these values into social realities. This knowledge, in turn, could then be used to fine-tune or radically alter our original values and social objectives. In this way, theory and practice—ordinarily conceived as yet another dualism—would be merged, each providing guidance for the other. But in order to make this sort of contribution to intelligent reflection on our public life, philosophers will have to broaden their ambit of learning beyond the usual philosophical canon. In order to work side by side with political scientists, psychologists, sociologists, and economists, they will have to learn a great deal about these fields.

Dewey's conception of philosophy is also profoundly democratic. In stark contrast to Plato's philosopher-king, Dewey's philosopher could perhaps be best described as a broker between the culture at large and the social sciences. In place of such legalistic Kantian locutions as the "tribunal" of reason and the "legitimacy" of knowledge, Dewey prefers metaphors drawn from town meetings and democratic deliberation. Instead of asking about the *a priori* structures of human reason, Dewey asks about what new forms of association we could agree on through the medium of democratic politics.[8]

Having thus briefly sketched a picture of the kind of philosopher Dewey envisages after the fall of the spectator view of knowledge, I must say how striking the resemblance is between this sort of philosopher and the role assumed by bioethicists in the past few decades. Philosophers working in the field of bioethics, and especially those who have had sustained contact with clinical medicine and biomedical research, are in many ways a different breed from their mainstream academic counterparts. They tend to envision their role as one of helping society and the various professions clarify and assess the values embedded in certain social practices. The impetus for much of their thinking is the urgent need to address

---

[7] J. Welchman, *Dewey's Ethical Thought* (Ithaca, NY: Cornell University Press, 1995), 193.

[8] This contrast is nicely drawn in R. Rorty, "Pragmatism and Law," in *The Revival of Pragmatism: New Essays on Social Thought, Law, and Culture*, ed. M. M. Dickstein (Durham, NC: Duke University Press, 1998), 310.

value shifts occasioned by technological change. And they tend to work closely with other professionals, often publishing papers together, which in turn necessitates acquiring knowledge of the vocabularies and methods of other disciplines.

This shift toward a more pragmatic conception of the role of philosophers is most dramatically illustrated in the work of clinical ethicists. As Nancy Dubler, Leonard Marcus, and Jonathan Moreno have observed, philosophers and lawyers working in a clinical context must not only know about theoretical issues embedded in clinical situations but also learn how to work with a wide variety of parties in fashioning mutually agreeable solutions to complex human problems.[9] This, in turn, requires the acquisition of a broad variety of skills ranging from "ethical diagnosis" to dispute mediation. Thus, if bioethicists are seeking a larger philosophical account that will effectively frame and justify their emerging pragmatic and interdisciplinary roles in academia, medical clinics, and policy councils, Dewey's work would be a natural starting point.[10]

DEWEY'S "LOGIC" OF INQUIRY

Anyone in bioethics searching for methodological resources in pragmatism might naturally look to Dewey's theory of experimental inquiry. While his books on ethics and politics discuss the substantive values that should inform our social thought, Dewey's "logical" works sketch a general, all-purpose approach to problem solving that might prove useful to bioethicists seeking to refine their methods.[11] Although most philosophers understand "logic" to be a study of the purely formal relationships between concepts, Dewey conceived of his logic as a general approach for finding fruitful solutions to any kind of scientific or social problem.

Dewey regarded the "scientific method" as a great human achievement that makes it possible for our species to rise above reflex and habit, and to therefore

[9] N. Dubler and L. Marcus, *Mediating Bioethical Disputes* (New York: United Hospital Fund of New York, 1994); J. D. Moreno, *Deciding Together: Bioethics and Moral Consensus* (New York: Oxford University Press, 1995).

[10] This collaborative and democratic model of contemporary bioethical practice contrasts sharply with H. Tristram Engelhardt Jr.'s characterization of bioethicists as illegitimate moral experts and secular priests. See H. T. Engelhardt Jr., "The Ordination of Bioethicists as Secular Moral Experts," *Social Philosophy and Policy* 19 (2002): 59–82. Although Engelhardt tells a plausible story here about the rise of contemporary bioethics to public prominence against the backdrop of our society's loss of faith in technocratic expertise and the public pronouncements of church leaders, his account of the social function of bioethicists is based upon highly selective evidence and bears little resemblance to the everyday practice of most bioethicists.

[11] See G. McGee, "Pragmatic Method and Bioethics," in *Pragmatic Bioethics*, ed. G. McGee (Cambridge, MA: MIT Press, 2003), 19: "John Dewey produced perhaps the clearest account of how pragmatism can revolutionize bioethics in his book about method, *Logic: The Theory of Inquiry*."

control nature and predict the future. Although other pragmatists, such as Peirce, restricted the range of application of this method to the natural sciences, Dewey sought to extend it to moral and social thought as well. Instead of resting the study of morals on mere intuition, Dewey sought to transform it into a field of scientific investigation, a kind of "materials science" of the moral life.[12] Thus, instead of accepting a dichotomy between science and social thought, Dewey proposed that we view natural and social phenomena as two domains approachable through the same intellectual methods. The key similarity uniting the natural and social sciences with moral thought would be a common emphasis on experimentalism.

As Dewey sketched it in his book *How We Think*, this common pragmatic approach to problems involves the following logical steps: "(i) a felt difficulty; (ii) its location and definition; (iii) suggestion of possible solution; (iv) development by reasoning of the bearings of the suggestion; [and] (v) further observation and experiment leading to its acceptance or rejection."[13] I suppose that interesting things might be said about steps (i) through (iv) that would help advance the discussion of methodology in bioethics, but I do not know what they are. The necessity of identifying a serious (i.e., "felt") problem, defining and locating it within a framework encompassing similar problems, rehearsing possible solutions, and trying to figure out in advance the likely implications of each suggested solution seems to me, as it probably did to Dewey, to be nothing more than dressed-up common sense. The fifth step, however, is more promising.

Perhaps the most crucial way in which moral thought needs to become more scientific, according to Dewey, resides in the ongoing experimental testing of its results. It is not enough to have elevated feelings, confident intuitions, well-developed arguments, and even what we today would call reflective equilibrium among our intuitions, principles, and theories. The achievement of the best possible moral results requires, in addition, a continuous process of confirming, discrediting, and refining our hypotheses about what should be done or how society should be organized. Taking great pains to fasten onto a proposed means for solving a problem without bothering to examine how this solution actually works in the real world is, for Dewey, a classic example of unintelligent thought and action. Yet, one could argue that this is often standard operating procedure in bioethics.

Take, for example, the problem of safeguarding the welfare and rights of patients and healthy volunteers enrolled in clinical trials and other varieties of

---

[12] Welchman, *Dewey's Ethical Thought*, 68.

[13] J. Dewey, *How We Think* (Boston: Heath, 1910), 72, quoted in F. Miller, J. Fins, and M. Bacchetta, "Clinical Pragmatism: John Dewey and Clinical Ethics," *Journal of Contemporary Health Law and Policy* 13 (1996): 33.

human experimentation. For decades, bioethicists have been at the forefront of efforts to craft rules and regulations governing the conduct of research on human subjects. Particularly noteworthy are the federal regulations that articulated the relevant ethical principles and rules of conduct and established a vast system of institutional review boards (IRBs) charged with the important task of reviewing the ethical suitability of protocols on the local level. Although this system is currently undergoing increased scrutiny, many years have passed during which it was simply assumed that the system was working as it was designed to do. On the level of local IRBs, committees would dutifully scrutinize the risk/benefit ratios and consent forms of hundreds of protocols each year without ever investigating whether genuine informed consent was actually obtained in the clinic.

Another classic example of this disconnect between theoretical elegance and concrete results is provided by the history of the living will in the United States. A great deal of ink has been spilled by bioethicists on the justifications for using living wills, on their supposed advantages and disadvantages, and on ways to expand their use by means of national and state legislation. But until fairly recently, no one thought it desirable or necessary actually to study the ways in which living wills affected (or, more to the point, failed to affect) clinical practice.[14] As Dewey would have been the first to point out, though, living wills are most likely only one possible way of fostering the effective use of patients' autonomy and helping them to secure a good (or at least decent) death. If studies show that living wills do not really alter physicians' well-worn paths of clinical decision making, then the bioethical community of inquiry needs to rethink its commitment to them. Perhaps some other, more systemic approach—that is, one relying less on the initiative of individual physicians—should be attempted and its comparative efficacy evaluated.

At this point, a resourceful principlist might counter that a concern for the practical consequences of our elegantly articulated and theoretically justified practices could easily be accommodated within the existing methodological paradigm. She might argue, for example, that the principle of beneficence could be used to justify the sort of ongoing experimentalism called for by pragmatically oriented bioethicists. Since that principle encompasses a broad utilitarian concern for securing good consequences, the satisfaction of desires, and human happiness, then surely, it could be argued, it could justify ongoing scrutiny of the IRB system and the role of living wills in the care of actual, terminally ill patients. Indeed, if research

[14] See, e.g., A. F. Connors et al., "A Controlled Trial to Improve Care for Seriously Ill Hospitalized Patients: The Study to Understand Prognoses and Preferences for Outcomes and Risks of Treatments (SUPPORT)," *Journal of the American Medical Association* 274, no. 20 (1995): 1591ff.

subjects and dying patients would be better off in a society that did, in fact, routinely assess and refine its practices in these areas, then the principle of beneficence would *require* this sort of experimentalism—assuming, of course, that the costs of doing so were not excessively high.

In response, contemporary pragmatist bioethicists might contend that although the benefits of periodically assessing and refining our social practices are obvious, principlists have simply been oblivious to them. Principlism can, in principle, accommodate the pragmatists' demand for a more experimental attitude, but this has simply not happened.[15] Why not? My best guess is that principlists have been observing a reasonable but unrealized division of labor. Trained primarily in philosophy, religious studies, medicine, and law, bioethicists have been entirely preoccupied with doing what they do best—namely, engaging in conceptual and normative debates about the best (or least worst) actions and policies to adopt. Although they may have also been vaguely concerned about how their favored policies fared in actual experience, bioethicists have been reluctant to engage in the sort of "outcomes research" for which they are woefully ill-prepared. This kind of research requires the skills of a well-trained social scientist or epidemiologist, not those of the well-trained armchair philosopher. The fault, then, lies not simply with the methodology of principlism but, rather, with the entire field of bioethics, which long ago should have forged productive working relationships with social scientists who could help them, in Dewey's words, to validate their working moral hypotheses regarding the best outcomes.

As Wolf has noted, however, the field of bioethics has recently witnessed the rise of a new and salutary empiricism.[16] Beginning with a few modest clinically based studies of do not resuscitate (DNR) orders in the early 1980s, which later blossomed into some extremely ambitious multi-center studies of informed consent, advance directives, and terminal care in the 1990s, this more empirical branch of bioethics is now supplying the sort of experimentalism demanded by Dewey's method of inquiry.[17] Through such studies, we are now learning about some rather large gaps separating bioethical theory and practice. In moving to fill those gaps with reliable empirical studies, the field of bioethics is beginning to achieve what

[15] An analogous case of principlism failing to exploit its own latent resources has come to light through the feminist critique of bioethics. Although the principle of justice could, in theory, have provided principlists with ample resources with which to reveal and criticize various forms of gender-based inequities in medicine and research, it was not until the advent of the feminist critique that principlists began noticing the existence of a problem.

[16] S. Wolf, "Shifting Paradigms in Bioethics and Health Law: The Rise of a New Pragmatism," *American Journal of Law & Medicine* 20, no. 4 (1994): 403ff.

[17] Typical examples of such empirical studies include the SUPPORT project (see note 14); B. W. Levin et al., "The Treatment of Non-HIV-Related Conditions in Newborns at Risk for HIV: A Survey of Neonatologists," *American Journal of Public Health* 85, no. 11 (1995): 1507–1513; S. E. Kelly et al.,

Dewey envisioned—namely, a marriage between the methods of philosophy and the social sciences.[18]

A PRAGMATIST VIEW OF PRINCIPLES

The aspect of Dewey's moral theory that is perhaps most relevant to contemporary debates about method in practical ethics is his account of rules and principles. In keeping with his rejection of the spectator view of knowledge, Dewey rejects the notion that the objects of moral knowledge are somehow "out there" waiting to be discovered by objective and disinterested moral agents.[19] Indeed, Dewey tends to define his whole approach to morality in opposition to a view of principles as fixed, rigid, and absolute commandments. Such a view, he argues, forgets that principles arose from experience as human constructs; it therefore misconstrues the proper role of principles in our moral experience. Indeed, Dewey regards the most misleading but ubiquitous temptation of moral life to involve the transformation of principles into rules for the easy disposition of hard cases. The Ayala case provides a classic example of this tendency in bioethics. Confronted by a couple who had decided to conceive a child in order to obtain a good match for a bone marrow transplant into their terminally ill daughter, some bioethical pundits immediately declared, prior to any serious investigation of the particulars, that such a scheme would violate Kant's categorical imperative against treating persons as mere means.[20]

Dewey views principles as broad generalizations gleaned from eons of human experience bearing on the sorts of consequences and values that tend to be realized in various situations.[21] In contrast to rules, which he regards as rigid and fixed

"Understanding the Practice of Ethics Consultation: Results of an Ethnographic Multi-Site Study," *Journal of Clinical Ethics* 8, no. 2 (1997): 136–149; and L. J. Blackhall et al., "Ethnicity and Attitudes towards Life Sustaining Technology," *Social Science and Medicine* 48, no. 12 (1999): 1779–1789.

[18] Dewey's emphasis on understanding the social context of moral problems thus meshes nicely with Allen Buchanan's call for the development of a "Social Moral Epistemology." See A. Buchanan, "Social Moral Epistemology," *Social Philosophy & Policy* 19, no. 2 (2002): 126–152.

[19] Dewey's rejection of the kind of objectivity demanded by the spectator view did not lead him to reject any and all conceptions of moral objectivity. Rather, he sought objectivity in our capacity to resolve conflicts and achieve agreement on shared values. Dewey would have thus fully concurred with Hilary Putnam's dictum: "[A]ccess to a common reality does not require access to something preconceptual. It requires, rather, that we be able to form shared concepts." See H. Putnam, *Pragmatism: An Open Question* (Cambridge, MA: Blackwell, 1995), 21. I thank Frances Kamm for requesting clarification of this point.

[20] For more on the Ayala case, see "Two Having a Baby to Save Daughter," *New York Times*, February 17, 1990, 10.

[21] J. Dewey and J. H. Tufts, *Ethics*, rev. ed. (New York: Henry Holt, 1932), 304. See also J. Dewey, "Logical Method and Law," *Cornell Law Quarterly* 10 (1925): 22 ("[G]eneral principles emerge as statements of generic ways in which it has been found helpful to treat concrete cases").

practical directives that tell us what to do, *principles* are viewed as flexible tools for analyzing moral situations. Principles thus provide us with general ideas for organizing our moral experience and making sense of what is at stake in particular situations.[22] Importantly, principles do not dictate right answers; they do not tell us what to do. They do, however, help us think through situations so that we might make responsible decisions. Answers are thus provided not by the principles themselves in isolation from experience but, rather, by the situation in its entirety, including, of course, the weight and bearing of relevant principles.[23] In this sense, principles, for Dewey, are best conceived as being one important ingredient in the mix of raw materials for moral judgment. There is no mechanical substitute for judgment amid a welter of particulars, a fact often brushed aside by our quest for simplicity and certainty.

Whereas the impulse to apply rigid universal formulas with absolute certainty to particular cases appears to stem from a mathematical ideal, Dewey drew his inspiration from the experimental sciences. In a celebrated and often-quoted passage from *Human Nature and Conduct*, Dewey observes that principles are best conceived as *hypotheses* with which to experiment.[24] Viewed as predictions of how things are likely to go if certain values are deployed in particular situations, principles in Dewey's scheme thus require testing and verification through ongoing experience. No final judgment on the appropriateness of invoking any particular principle can be made until we discover its concrete effects on our characters and our communities. Principles are thus useful—but merely presumptive and provisional—guides to conduct.

An important implication of regarding moral principles as tools is that they must be constantly adapted and upgraded to meet the challenges of new experiences. Just as ordinary household tools, such as screwdrivers and socket wrenches, are constantly being modified and improved by their manufacturers, so moral communities must constantly reassess and refine their moral principles in light of their current needs and social conditions.[25] Principles adapted to the resolution

---

[22] Bernard Gert et al. charge that Beauchamp and Childress's principles function as mere "chapter headings"—i.e., as categories of important values to consider as we make moral choices—as opposed to precise, action-guiding rules of conduct. See B. Gert, C. Culver, and K. D. Clouser, *Bioethics: A Return to Fundamentals* (New York: Oxford University Press, 1997). Interestingly, Dewey would side with Beauchamp and Childress in this debate, challenging the belittling qualifier "mere." Thus, even though contemporary pragmatists have opposed much in the method of principlism, the latter's principal exponents agree with Dewey that principles are initially framed at such a level of generality that they cannot be definitively action-guiding in the absence of additional specification, balancing, and good judgment.

[23] Note in this connection Moreno's claim that within a naturalistic or pragmatist approach to ethics, facts tend to overwhelm theory. See J. Moreno, "Bioethics Is a Naturalism," in *Pragmatic Bioethics*, ed. G. McGee (Cambridge, MA: MIT Press, 2003), 13.

[24] J. Dewey, *Human Nature and Conduct* (New York: Modern Library, 1957), 221.

[25] See Dewey and Tufts, *Ethics*, 313; and Dewey, *Human Nature and Conduct*, 221.

of quandaries in one time and place may be completely unhelpful, inappropriate, and counterproductive when applied to novel situations. A good example is the Catholic Church's longstanding moral prohibition of usury. Such a ban made good sense during most of human history, when it functioned as an impediment to the exploitation of vulnerable and needy people. But in the late Middle Ages, the rise of a mercantile economy, based on long-term investments and the assumption of great risks, transformed this restriction into an unjust and otiose obstacle to human flourishing.[26] Thus, the principle concerning exploitation gradually came to be seen as simply no longer applicable to this category of money lending; the scope of the principle had changed.

Miller, Fins, and Bacchetta have seized on Dewey's theory of the nature and function of moral principles in their critique of principlism. Echoing Dewey's denunciations of principles conceived as "absolute" and "fixed" rules of conduct, Miller et al. suggest that bioethicists would do well to begin viewing principles as flexible tools that are constantly being refined until they are capable of giving our experience "the guidance it requires."[27] Although this restatement of Dewey's theory has the ring of plausibility to it, there are two problems confronting this particular pragmatist contribution to the bioethical method wars. First, it is unclear who the enemy is in this picture. While Dewey was engaged with real antagonists, both in philosophy (for example, Kant) and popular culture, who apparently believed that any deviation from fixed and absolute moral principles would result in moral anarchy, Miller et al. are addressing a community of bioethical inquirers that has by and large enthusiastically embraced the plasticity of principles. Admittedly, the early editions of Beauchamp and Childress's *Principles of Biomedical Ethics* unfortunately featured a flow chart moving from moral theory to principles, to rules, and finally to case judgments; such a diagram might have suggested that the origins of moral principles lay in some empyrean realm untouched by time and contingency. However, Beauchamp and Childress have long since explicitly repudiated both that diagram and the account of moral principles implied by it.[28] In response to the assertion of contemporary casuists, such as Jonsen and Toulmin, that principles not only apply to particular judgments but also actually grow out of them, the exponents of principlism have affirmed the dialectical relationship between principles and particular judgments, and have thereby embraced the widely endorsed method of "reflective equilibrium" advanced by philosopher John Rawls and his

---

[26] For an instructive account of this episode in moral history, see Jonsen and Toulmin, *The Abuse of Casuistry* (Berkeley: University of California Press, 1990).

[27] Miller et al., "Clinical Pragmatism," 142.

[28] For an account of this transformation within principlism, see chapter 1 this volume.

followers.[29] Thus, if pragmatists believe that moral principles are both action-guiding and the products of continual refinement in the crucible of concrete cases, then Beauchamp and Childress are pragmatists. For all its verisimilitude, then, the "clinical pragmatist" theory of principles advanced by Miller et al. turns out to be a mere restatement of principlism as presently understood by its chief exponents.[30] It may be the best way to think about principles, but it can hardly be counted as an advance beyond or a contribution to the debate over method in practical ethics.[31]

A second problem with adopting Dewey's theory of principles for bioethical purposes goes to the heart of Dewey's view. Suppose we grant that principles should be conceived as *hypotheses* for further experimentation and verification. The question then arises: How do we know when the deployment of any given principle has been vindicated by experience? Unlike experiments in science, it is unclear what would count as a successful or fruitful result that would validate, post hoc, an ethical experiment. Certainly those of a Kantian persuasion will reject the suggestion that any amount of good consequences accumulated through future experiences can redeem, say, the widespread violation of human rights. Take, for example, the question whether members of religious or ethnic minority groups, such as Christian Scientists or the Hmong, should be allowed to withhold medically necessary treatments from their children. Suppose that a bioethicist proposes that in such cases legal coercion compelling treatment is justified as a last resort. The question then arises: What sort of results would demonstrate that the operative

[29] According to Rawls, principles are developed both to systematize our firmest intuitions about particular propositions and to extend our judgments in less clear cases. Importantly, however, he observes that principles can also be revised or rejected on the basis of particularly firm moral intuitions. The goal of moral reflection, he claims, is to continually adjust our principles, our firmest intuitions, and our background theories of persons and society until they harmonize in "reflective equilibrium." See J. Rawls, *A Theory of Justice* (Cambridge, MA: Harvard University Press, 1971), 20–22. (See also chapter 8 this volume.)

[30] This is not to say that everyone operating within the field of bioethics always employs principles in this flexible way. Secular thinkers of a more traditional bent, such as Leon Kass, or conservative Roman Catholics, Protestants, and Jews are far from embracing pragmatist modes of moral thought. See, e.g., L. Kass, *Toward a More Natural Science* (New York: Free Press, 1985); J. J. O'Connor, "Abortion: Questions and Answers," *Human Life Review* 16, no. 3 (1990): 65–96; P. Ramsey, *Ethics at the Edges of Life* (New Haven, CT: Yale University Press, 1978); and D. Bleich, *Bioethical Dilemmas: A Jewish Perspective* (Hoboken, NJ: Ktav Publishing, 1998).

[31] Indeed, perhaps the most interesting link between pragmatism and a theory of practical reasoning in bioethics is to be found not in the writings of Dewey but, rather, in the "pragmatic" writings of post–World War II Harvard philosophers W. V. O. Quine and J. Rawls. Quine conceived of human knowledge as a "web of belief," while Rawls eschewed foundationalism in moral theory in favor of reflective equilibrium. I thank Christopher Morris for this observation. See W. V. O. Quine and J. S. Ullian, *The Web of Belief*, 2nd ed. (New York: Random House, 1978). I would emphasize, however, that acknowledging such a connection between contemporary versions of pragmatism and current methods of bioethics does not advance the claim under discussion—namely, that we need to develop a pragmatist bioethics in order to improve the way we currently do ethics.

principle here gives our present experience "the guidance it requires"?[32] Certainly, lives will be saved—and that should count for a lot. By the same token, though, a great cost will be imposed on these groups in terms of their religious and psychological integrity. How should a pragmatist sort out these consequences? Clearly, some sort of criterion of "success" would come in handy, especially when the benefits and burdens of different principles would be mediated through competing conceptions of value and the good life.

Miller et al. try to advance this discussion by proposing that consensus be viewed as the overarching goal of clinical-pragmatic deliberations. An obviously false start in this direction would be for clinical pragmatists to maintain that any and every consensus, no matter what its substantive content or its procedural origins, constitutes a morally respectable terminus of ethical deliberation. But this clearly will not do, and Miller et al. realize this. We could, for example, imagine a consensus reached between two or more parties of vastly unequal power, wealth, or information. The weaker party might agree to a manifestly unfair resolution merely because not agreeing might make its situation even worse. In order to avoid such a scenario, the clinical pragmatists insist on certain qualifications. Consensus is still described as the goal of pragmatic deliberation, but only consensus that "can withstand moral scrutiny"[33] or consensus reached through a "thorough process of inquiry, discussion, negotiation, and reflective evaluation."[34] As political theorist Lynn Jansen points out, however, it is unclear whether clinical pragmatism harbors sufficient resources to help us distinguish legitimate from morally suspect instances of consensus. She contends that one way in which more traditional approaches to morality make this distinction is by appealing to fixed moral principles, rules, and maxims.[35] At the very least, the clinical pragmatists owe us an account of what would count as sufficient "moral scrutiny" and what values would animate their "reflective evaluation" of agreements.

The root of the clinical pragmatists' problem here, I think, lies in their conception of moral principles as hypotheses. It is one thing to claim that principles are not fixed, eternal, and absolute, and that they must be adapted and refined by each new generation to meet changing circumstances. It is another thing to claim that principles are essentially *predictions* (if *P*, then *Q*) of what will happen if we uphold certain values. Suppose that a team of social scientists demonstrates that

---

[32] Lynn A. Jansen pursues this line of criticism in her helpful essay, "Assessing Clinical Pragmatism," *Kennedy Institute of Ethics Journal* 8, no. 1 (1998): 23–36.

[33] Miller et al., "Clinical Pragmatism," 130.

[34] J. Fins, M. Bacchetta, and F. Miller, "Clinical Pragmatism: A Model for Problem Solving," in *Pragmatic Bioethics*, ed. G. McGee (Cambridge, MA: MIT Press, 2003), 30.

[35] Jansen, "Assessing Clinical Pragmatism," 27.

Q is what you get when you pursue moral principle *P*; that is, to use Dewey's formula, suppose they have *validated* the original hypothesis that if you act on a certain set of values, you will get a corresponding moral character or social structure. What then? Suppose that there are other, competing visions of what our characters and our society should look like. How are we to choose among them? This, I take it, is the traditional role allotted to moral principles in ethics and the theory of justice. This role is normative, not predictive. While it is true that principles exist in the first place in order to foster human flourishing, their role is to help us choose between various possible future states of affairs, not merely to predict their occurrence. This confusion is the result of Dewey's interesting but misguided attempt to recast ethics as a kind of scientific enterprise with all the trappings and vocabulary of experimental methodology.

In spite of the terminological confusion noted above, Dewey was perfectly aware of the need to evaluate competing actions and policies driven by incompatible values. This, after all, is what ethics is largely about. Indeed, in some important sections of his *Ethics*, a text curiously ignored by all the theorists eager to revive pragmatism within bioethics, Dewey develops a standard against which competing individual and social possibilities should be judged. Importantly, this standard is substantive, not merely procedural; it advances a particular vision of the good based on a distinct conception of human nature and its place in the natural and historical worlds, not just on a vague notion of consensus.[36]

According to Dewey, a moral problem is defined as a challenge to an individual's or group's current habits of action. Such a problem poses the question: What sort of being does the agent wish to become? The fundamental question for Dewey's ethics is thus a matter of character development or self-realization. A good person's character, according to this view, is naturally harmonious, flexible, and stable. In choosing between actions, and the habitual dispositions to which they give rise, Dewey contends that the good person will opt for social or other-regarding dispositions as the only kind that can nurture a character that is harmonious, flexible, and stable.[37] In other words, our happiness and ultimate good are internally linked to the common good. A life based on purely individualistic dispositions of the sort celebrated by libertarian devotees of philosopher Ayn Rand is necessarily "warped," according to this standard.[38]

---

[36] Although Dewey rejected traditional metaphysics, especially its attempt to ground human knowledge and behavior in an absolute, unchanging realm of being, he did develop a rival metaphysics of human nature based instead on our thoroughly contingent biological, social, and historical existence. See Dewey, *Human Nature and Conduct*.

[37] Welchman, *Dewey's Ethical Thought*, 162.

[38] A. Rand, *The Virtue of Selfishness* (New York: New American Library, 1974).

It is well known that the concept of *growth* figures prominently in Dewey's ethics and political philosophy. Contrary to some popular misconceptions of it as an egoistic or narcissistic doctrine, Dewey's conception of growth stressed the importance of self-realization through a common form of life with family, friends, and the larger community. An important objective of moral action, Dewey thinks, ought to be the liberation of individuals for the realization of their capacities as rational, autonomous beings. In contrast to the merely negative image of freedom animating much liberal thought, Dewey's notion of freedom is positive, involving not just protection of others' private space but their capacity for self-realization as well. Importantly, such a positive notion of *effective* freedom would naturally include a concern for the social, economic, and psychological preconditions of everyone's self-realization. A society that maximizes the capacities of individuals to grow in this way is Dewey's notion of the good society, and I take this to be the standard against which he would judge competing actions and social policies. As Dewey himself puts it:

> The moral criterion by which to try social conditions and political measures may be summed up as follows: The test is whether a given custom or law sets free individual capacities in such a way as to make them available for the development of the general happiness or the common good. This formula states the test with the emphasis falling upon the side of the individual. It may be stated from the side of associated life as follows: The test is whether the general, the public organization and order are promoted in such a way as to equalize opportunity for all.[39]

At the foundation of Dewey's ethics, then, lie the metaphysical propositions that humans are naturally social creatures and that the good for individuals is a social good. In contrast to the rather thin procedural notion of consensus posited by Miller et al. as the objective of clinical pragmatic thinking, Dewey elaborates a robust substantive standard that contemporary bioethical pragmatists might consider as a measure of the relative value of various actions, policies, character dispositions, and experiments in living. Such a standard would, I think, yield quite felicitous recommendations in many areas of bioethics, especially those that have been marred by excessive individualism and a lack of concern for our sociality.

On the downside, however, Dewey's ultimate ethical principle—namely, the claim that individual growth (in the deepest sense) can only be achieved in the

[39] J. Dewey, *Ethics* (New York: Columbia University Press, 1908), 431, quoted in M. Festenstein, *Pragmatism and Political Theory: From Dewey to Rorty* (Chicago: University of Chicago Press, 1997), 59.

context of social action—might face stiff opposition in the contemporary philosophical milieu. Resting squarely on a manifestly metaphysical and teleological view of human flourishing, this principle, although not incoherent by any means, would nevertheless be regarded by many as being quaintly out of fashion. Others would note that this moral conception, when pressed into the service of Dewey's political philosophy, would constitute an affront to ethical pluralism. Great artists like Gauguin provide evidence that some idiosyncratic routes to self-realization might not take a wholesomely social direction.[40] And political philosophers like Rawls and his followers would note that Dewey's political thought, grounded as it is in a controversial theory of human nature, expresses a "comprehensive moral view" of the sort that should not be imposed by the state on the free and equal citizens of a liberal polity. Although Dewey sincerely believed that philosophical reflection on human nature and culture would reaffirm his conclusions, many of our philosophical contemporaries find that reflection is more likely to yield differences and discord.

PRAGMATISM, DEMOCRACY, AND PROCESS IN BIOETHICS

Another aspect of Dewey's work that should be freighted with bioethical consequences is his political philosophy—more specifically, his theory of democracy. As Miller et al. point out (see previous section), democracy for Dewey means not simply one formal mechanism of government as opposed to others but, rather, a lofty moral ideal involving mutual participation and cooperation in a common life. Democracy, for Dewey, is thus best conceived as a "way of life" in which citizens deliberate together about common problems and their solutions.

Notwithstanding its initial attractiveness to modern ears and its all-American appeal, Dewey's conception of democracy is by no means obviously right. It has faced stiff competition in the marketplace of ideas, both in Dewey's time and our own. Indeed, comparing and contrasting Dewey's theory of democracy against two alternative political theories will help us sharpen our understanding of its most important features. One longstanding alternative to Deweyan democracy is rule by elites. In this Platonic alternative, the claim is that governing is a tricky business—one requiring great knowledge and skill. Just as we would not leave the training of an expensive racehorse to a rank amateur, so society should not entrust its public governance to those lacking the requisite expertise in the craft

[40] Festenstein's example; see M. Festenstein, *Pragmatism and Political Theory: From Dewey to Rorty* (Chicago: University of Chicago Press, 1997), 61.

of governing.[41] This, it might be argued, is especially true in an age like our own, characterized by rapid technological change in which many public issues, such as global warming and the use of nuclear power, appear to dwarf the comprehension of the average person. If democracy means the rule of the great mass of unskilled citizens, then according to this view it is a defective form of government.

Dewey's response to this Platonic vision of politics is to note that a ruling class of "experts" would soon become isolated from knowledge of the needs that they are supposed to serve. Before long they would begin ruling so as to make the government serve their own interests as a specialized class. He argues that there is a legitimate, even indispensable, role for experts in discovering and disseminating knowledge about the factual bases of social policy, but that the actual making of policy should depend upon people who can judge the relevance of these factual investigations for the overall good of society.[42] Dewey complemented this response to elitism with an argument based upon the value of freedom to individuals. Even if an elite ruling class were to somehow find a way to discern the genuine interests of the great mass of people, such a good "procured from without" would ignore the interest we all have in governing ourselves.[43]

A second competing political theory agrees with Dewey that democracy is the best way to organize society, but this preference is based on democracy's capacity to aggregate the preferences of disparate individuals. Voting, majority rule, and frequent elections ensure that everyone's preferences will be counted and considered in the formulation of public policy. This "atomistic individualistic" conception conceives of the common good as nothing other than the result of aggregating a great host of individual preferences. Public choices are thus made on the basis of the sum total of so many private acts of voting. Since this view does not conceive of the common good as being anything other than the aggregation of private choices, there is no need for communal deliberation about shared societal goals. Indeed, the political process on this view is primarily a domain of self-interested bargaining and deal making by various private interest groups.[44]

For Dewey, by contrast, a democracy is first and foremost a community of people who engage in practical deliberation over the common good. This implies that democracy has an educational function. By participating in public discussion and debate, each of us must learn to cast our own desires and interests in the language of the common good. As we do so, we may discover that what is good for

---

[41] Plato, *The Republic*, 473c–489a.

[42] J. Dewey, *The Public and Its Problems* (Athens, OH: Ohio University Press, 1927), 202–209.

[43] See Festenstein, *Pragmatism and Political Theory*, 81.

[44] Ibid., 8.

us is not necessarily good for our society, and we learn that others have interests that must be recognized as well. As a result, instead of simply registering our own private wants and needs in the shrouded secrecy of the voting booth, the citizens of a Deweyan democracy must use their critical intelligence to forge common solutions—a process that often leads to the transformation of their original interests. Contrary to those who hold that there is no common interest or public good, but only individual wants and needs, Dewey is convinced that there is a common good. He recognizes, however, that the demands of the common good are often obscure. In order to achieve clarity concerning a society's proper goals, Dewey asserts that our highest priority should be to improve the methods and conditions of public debate and discussion. Instead of searching for experts to do this job for us, the citizens of a democracy must sharpen their skills of critical intelligence and persuasion. This, he says, is *the* problem of the public.[45]

Hilary Putnam, a contemporary philosopher who regards Dewey as one of his heroes, extends this line of reasoning into what he calls an "epistemological justification of democracy."[46] In contrast to Dewey, who appears to have grounded his political philosophy in his own naturalistic and teleological conception of the individual, Putnam argues that democracy is a precondition for the exercise of critical intelligence in the service of solving social problems. That is, if we wish to harness our individual resources in a collective effort to solve our problems in the best way possible, we must also wish to do this within the context of a democratic public space. In opposition to political regimes that govern by fiat or appeals to authority, Dewey and Putnam argue that the most effective way actually to solve social problems is by means of intelligent experimentation.

Two things are necessary, though, in order to accomplish this task. First, we must have the freedom to experiment that democracy makes possible; second, we must have an educated public, not one that merely submits to authority. For Putnam (and implicitly for Dewey), all forms of authoritarianism are thus cognitively self-defeating. What we have here, then, is an epistemological (as opposed to a moral) justification of democracy.[47]

What is the relevance of these Deweyan reflections on democracy for our current methodological debates within bioethics? Given Dewey's insistence that democracy is a way of life and not simply a governmental structure, we should expect its

---

[45] Dewey, *The Public and Its Problems*, 208.

[46] H. Putnam, "A Reconsideration of Deweyan Democracy," reprinted in *Pragmatism: A Contemporary Reader*, ed. Russell B. Goodman (New York: Routledge, 1995), 184–204.

[47] To squeeze Putnam into our grid of old versus new pragmatists, it would perhaps be best to label him a "new old pragmatist"—new because he is our contemporary, and old because unlike Rorty he is trying to forge a philosophical argument for the justification of democracy that Dewey himself could have endorsed.

moral ideals to extend well beyond legislative chambers to encompass the making of health policy, the work of hospital ethics committees, and the physician–patient relationship. According to Miller et al., whose work constitutes by far the most sustained and penetrating effort to wring bioethical implications out of Dewey's corpus, the Deweyan account of democracy carries vital lessons for the ethics of the physician–patient relationship. Dewey's embrace of deliberative processes of self-government and his corresponding critique of all forms of authoritarianism could provide additional justification for the doctrine of informed consent understood as a process of shared decision making. Rather than merely imposing "doctors' orders" on patients, physicians must enter into a dialogue with them as full partners in the healing enterprise. Furthermore, although Miller et al. do not call attention to this, one could note that Dewey's theory of the proper role of experts in a democratic society uncannily prefigures the division of labor that is allotted to physicians and patients in the modern legal doctrine of informed consent. Just as it is the Deweyan expert's job to secure the technical facts that will later be subsumed into democratic deliberations about the common good, so the physician's proper role in this legal doctrine is to provide the patient with all the facts he or she needs in order to make a reasonable judgment. Dewey would no doubt also note, however, that experts and citizens, physicians and patients, can educate each other in their respective encounters and thereby soften the rather strict division of labor noted above. Physicians can help patients see that their original preferences might be counterproductive, while patients can help physicians see the larger humanistic dimensions of their calling.

Deweyan democracy has also served as the inspiration for the clinical pragmatists' important "process model" of bioethics. Miller et al. observe that the standard brands of bioethical reasoning—including both principlism and casuistry—converge in what they call a "judgment model." According to this model, the task is simply to find the right answer to any given moral problem. The bioethicist wields various principles or paradigmatic cases in an effort to discern what ought to be done in a particular case. Crucially, note the clinical pragmatists, this is a task that could theoretically be performed by a single individual in the privacy of her study. Although they do not denigrate the need for this sort of critical reflection on principles and cases, the clinical pragmatists wish to stress what might be called the "process dimensions" of most bioethical quandaries. The typical case involves not simply an isolated thinker who comes to a judgment but, rather, a whole panoply of players—including the doctor, the nurse, the patient, the medical team, the patient's family, and in many unfortunate cases, the hospital's administrators and attorneys—who must work together to forge a decision that will ideally be acceptable to everyone. Although they are all working toward a final judgment, these people must first engage in a shared process of discussion, negotiation, compromise, and consensus.[48] They must not only do the "right thing," considered as an intellectual abstraction; they must also see to it that everyone with a legitimate stake in a given case is allowed his or her say, so that when all is said and done, the participants will be able to continue working with each other and respecting each other as moral equals. Sometimes judgments that seem right in the abstract no longer strike us as right all things considered.

Having established that Dewey's pragmatic theory of democracy has implications for various issues in bioethics, we must now ask to what extent this theory makes a valuable contribution to our methodological debates in bioethics. Or as Dewey's pragmatist colleague, William James, would have put it, what is the "cash value" of Dewey's democratic theory for us today? This question needs to be unpacked into two separate issues. First, there is the question of whether Dewey's ideas about democracy are valid, interesting, or attractive in their own right. Second, we need to ask whether these ideas will enrich our ongoing discussions about method.

As for the validity or ongoing appeal of Dewey's theory, I would argue that his view of democracy as a way of life is an extraordinarily powerful idea full of implications for contemporary societies. In its emphasis on democracy as a deliberative community, Dewey's theory bears a striking resemblance to contemporary work under the rubric of deliberative democracy.[49] Both these "old" and "new" perspectives stress the transformative dimensions of deliberative communication, the existence of a common good, and the centrality of deliberation to the legitimacy of political decisions broadly construed. Furthermore, the clinical pragmatists' emphasis on shared decision making and their "process model" strike me as being quite legitimate extrapolations of Dewey's theory and as important foci for contemporary bioethical theory and practice.

Determining the "cash value" of these contributions, however, may lead to a more guarded endorsement. In the first place, although it is true that our contemporary notion of shared decision making is fully consistent with Dewey's democratic theory, it is not at all clear that we need Dewey's theory to vindicate or even clarify our current understandings of informed consent and physician–patient communication. In view of the pivotal and dispositive role of various Kantian and

---

[48] Fins et al., "Clinical Pragmatism," 43.

[49] See J. Bohman and W. Rehg, eds., *Deliberative Democracy* (Cambridge, MA: MIT Press, 1997). It should be noted, however, that much of the current literature concerning the theory of deliberative democracy seems to owe a lot more to the influence of John Rawls's later work than it does to Dewey, whom it rarely mentions. See Rawls, "The Idea of Public Reason Revisited," reprinted in J. Rawls, *The Law of Peoples* (Cambridge, MA: Harvard University Press, 1999), 129–180.

utilitarian theories of autonomy in the ultimate vindication of our moral and legal theories of informed consent, it is hard to imagine why anyone today would need to invoke this aspect of pragmatism. Doing so at the clinical pragmatists' insistence would merely amount to gratuitous theoretical overdetermination.

The same might also be said of the clinical pragmatists' "process model" of bioethical decision making. Again, this emphasis on process, consensus, and compromise involved in reaching responsible clinical decisions can plausibly claim a direct lineage back to Dewey, but the importance of process hardly comes as a revelation to the bioethical community at the turn of the twenty-first century. Numerous important studies have already been devoted to the interpersonal dimensions of bioethical decision making at all levels, from national and state bioethics commissions, to hospital bioethics committees, and finally to clinical ethics consultations at the bedside.[50] It is noteworthy that none of the authors of these studies felt compelled to invoke Dewey's theory of democracy as a way of life in order to justify or buttress his or her own emphasis on process. An alternative explanation for the recent emphasis on process in bioethics might stress the resemblance between clinical bioethics consultation and various forms of hospital-based social work and psychological counseling in which process values tend to predominate.

Thus, although Dewey articulates a powerful vision of democracy with definite implications for the process of doing bioethics, the values embedded in those implications are by no means unique to Dewey's thought. They have, in fact, been available for years under different descriptions, both in our general culture and in our specific bioethical community. The crucial questions, then, are: What is to be gained by attaching the label "pragmatist" to this increasingly widespread emphasis on process? Would we gain any additional clarity or insight by linking our current notions of process to Dewey's account of democracy? At the very least, Miller et al. owe us a more convincing answer to these questions.

My skepticism about the value of invoking Dewey's accounts of moral reasoning and democratic theory for current bioethical inquiry should not be read as a dismissal of his abiding importance and influence as a philosopher and cultural commentator. In a curious way, the fact that we do not need to invoke Dewey today may constitute the best evidence of his pervasive and enduring influence

---

[50] See, e.g., Moreno, *Deciding Together*; S. Wolf, "Ethics Committees and Due Process: Nesting Rights in a Community of Care," *Maryland Law Review* 50 (1991): 798–858; S. Wolf, "Toward a Theory of Process," *Law, Medicine, and Health Care* 20, no. 4 (1992): 278–90; M. Benjamin, *Splitting the Difference: Compromise and Integrity in Ethics and Politics* (Lawrence: University Press of Kansas, 1990); R. E. Bulger et al., eds., *Society's Choices: Social and Ethical Decision Making in Biomedicine* (Washington, DC: National Academy Press, 1995); and Dubler and Marcus, *Mediating Bioethical Disputes*. See also A. Gutmann and D. Thompson, *Democracy and Disagreement* (Cambridge, MA: Harvard University Press, 1998); and Gutmann and Thompson, *The Spirit of Compromise* (Princeton, NJ: Princeton University Press, 2014).

on American political thought. It may well be that we do not need to invoke him precisely because his ideas have already permeated every corner of American life and now strike many of us as just so many commonsensical features of our political landscape.[51] The question remains, however, how dusting off our old copies of Dewey's major works will actually advance our current understandings of moral reasoning, informed consent, or the processes of bioethical decision making. In my view, it will not, but there are still plenty of good reasons for reading and appreciating Dewey's contributions to philosophy and democratic theory.

RICHARD RORTY'S PRAGMATISM

Richard Rorty venerated Dewey. But as I will explain, there are also a number of ways in which he parted company with Dewey on important issues. As a result, his potential contribution to the field of bioethics is different from that of Dewey.

With the publication of *Philosophy and the Mirror of Nature* in 1979, Rorty began an ambitious and spectacularly successful intellectual reclamation project. In Rorty's retelling of recent intellectual history, Dewey emerges alongside Heidegger and Wittgenstein as one of the greatest philosophers of our century. Downplaying Dewey's enthusiasm for scientific method and his metaphysics of experience, while upgrading Dewey's rejection of dualisms and foundations in epistemology, Rorty went on to develop in a series of widely read and highly influential studies[52] a revitalized image of pragmatism at the cutting edge of American intellectual life. Needless to say, Rorty's version of pragmatism was highly idiosyncratic, and some partisans of "old-fashioned" pragmatism have repeatedly accused him of hijacking the name and reputation of pragmatism for the dubious brand of "postmodernism"—a label Rorty has vehemently rebuffed. But whatever the historical merits of Rorty's appropriation of pragmatist authors and themes, it remains true, I think, that the proliferation of contemporary neopragmatisms and the widespread revival of interest in the original American pragmatists have been in large measure Rorty's doing.[53]

---

[51] Evidence for this hypothesis can be found on the back cover of my edition of Dewey's *The Public and Its Problems*, which features a blurb from that hippie bible of the 1960s and '70s, *The Whole Earth Catalogue*: "[I]n this book, the dazzlement [of Dewey's ideas] is fully let loose in a series of far-out proposals for experimenting with altered life styles!" Far out, indeed.

[52] Rorty's many other publications include: *The Consequences of Pragmatism* (Minneapolis: University of Minnesota Press, 1982); *Contingency, Irony, and Solidarity* (Cambridge: Cambridge University Press, 1989); *Objectivity, Relativism, and Truth: Philosophical Papers* (Cambridge: Cambridge University Press, 1991); *Essays on Heidegger and Others: Philosophical Papers*, vol. 2 (Cambridge: Cambridge University Press, 1991); and *Philosophy and Social Hope* (New York: Penguin Books, 1999).

[53] For an alternative view that underscores the continuities between "old" and "new" pragmatisms, see R. Bernstein, "American Pragmatism: The Conflict of Narratives," in *Rorty and Pragmatism: The Philosopher Responds to His Critics*, ed. H. J. Saatkamp (Nashville, TN: Vanderbilt University Press, 1995), 54–67.

Rorty's unrelenting attacks on foundations and the normative status of principles have occasioned vigorous methodological debates and challenged longstanding disciplinary assumptions in such fields as literary studies, sociology, political theory, religious ethics, and law.[54] Is bioethical principlism the next "standard methodology" due for subversive reappraisal? Owing to its resolutely practical nature, its habitat in the medical environment, and its resulting relative isolation from the intellectual fads of American academia, bioethics has only recently begun to assess the relevance of pragmatism to its own methodological debates.

In spite of this routine acknowledgment of Rorty's ubiquitous influence, those who have invoked his name en route to advancing their case for a pragmatist bioethics have not given us a very clear picture of exactly how Rorty's work might actually contribute to methodological discussion in this field. I try to provide such an account here, with the following caveat. Given the impressive depth and scope of Rorty's work, I make no pretense of presenting either a comprehensive or a novel interpretation of his project.[55] My primary aim here is simply to sketch what I take to be the implications of Rorty's neopragmatism for our methodological debates within bioethics.

RORTY'S CRITIQUE OF FOUNDATIONS

As I explained at the start of this essay, the diverse figures in the American pragmatism tradition are united in their rejection of the "spectator theory of knowledge." Rorty takes this critique of objectivist forms of knowledge several steps further in his version of pragmatism. He begins with an attack on the traditional philosophical project of developing a faithful representation of reality upon which various human practices and institutions, such as morality and politics, might be grounded. Stressing the need to adapt Dewey's pragmatism to the environment of a very different postwar philosophical culture, Rorty subjects pragmatism to a thoroughgoing "linguistic turn." According to this view, language and human interpretations color everything that we can know. Rorty uses the powerful metaphor of a mirror of nature in order to encapsulate what he thinks is wrong with the aspirations of the traditional, spectator theory of knowledge: the human mind cannot act as a mirror, faithfully reflecting reality, because it cannot escape from

[54] A notable omission from this list is the field of philosophy, which has by and large simply ignored Rorty's frontal assault on its claims to intellectual respectability (let alone supremacy).

[55] Good, all-purpose secondary sources on Rorty's work include: A. Malachowski, *Richard Rorty* (Princeton, NJ: Princeton University Press, 2002); R. Brandom, ed., *Rorty and His Critics* (New York: Routledge, 2000); and D. L. Hall, *Richard Rorty: Prophet and Poet of the New Pragmatism* (Albany: State University of New York Press, 1994).

its own webs of interpretation. Importantly, language for Rorty does not and cannot function as a medium through which a human mind can make solid contact with the world the way it "really" is apart from our interpretations of it. Instead, he views language and our various conceptual schemes as tools that we use to get a grip on our environments. Some tools, such as Newtonian physics, have proved themselves to be more useful than other tools; but no set of tools can be presumed to afford us some sort of unfiltered access to "the real." Consequently, Rorty holds that there are no entities out there, such as an "order of things" or "the meaning of history," and no entities in here, such as a soul or human nature, that could serve as a source of justification in ethics or politics.

In place of Dewey's metaphysics of "experience," Rorty thus substitutes a thoroughly anti-metaphysical conception of language. Borrowing from Wittgenstein's notions of language games and forms of life, Rorty contends that all meaning and attempts at justification require a certain context in which things can "hang together" and make sense. He calls these linguistic contexts "vocabularies." Examples would include such things as Darwinian biology, Christian fundamentalism, Ptolemaic astronomy, Freudian psychology, Aristotelian physics, and feminism. Now, instead of playing the traditional game of trying to establish which of these vocabularies best connects with or faithfully tracks "reality"—whether this be conceived as the order of nature or women's intrinsic human dignity bequeathed to them by their human nature—Rorty announces that no such argumentative justification of any one of these basic or "final" vocabularies is possible. While things make sense and can be justified within any final vocabulary, just as defendants in our courts of law may be rightly convicted or acquitted according to the canons of ordinary legal interpretation, final vocabularies themselves cannot be justified in this way. In fact, says Rorty, they cannot be justified at all, in the sense of being connected to reality or being derivable from some true universally applicable principle.

This "democratization" of final vocabularies points up another major difference between Dewey's pragmatism and Rorty's. Within the latter's scheme, it would appear that romantic poetry and modern physics are both simply two different vocabularies vying for our attention. In spite of what William Blake or Isaac Newton might have thought, neither of these disciplines or practices can be said to give us privileged access to the realm of the really real. As a result, Rorty refuses to follow Peirce and Dewey in thinking that modern scientific method provides us with the ultimate exemplar of human reason in action. Since he rejects the very notion of a world beyond our language and conceptual schemes that the human mind can discover or represent, Rorty rejects the collateral idea that there must be a true or reliable method to get us there. Hence his call for a "pragmatism without method."[56] Whereas Dewey idealized science and tried to fit ethics out in the finery of experimentalism, Rorty views science as just another contribution to the general cultural mix, and not a terribly interesting one at that. Rorty would no doubt admit that science is helpful in the pursuit of various practical interests, but he resists the temptation to follow Dewey in giving it pride of place within the disciplines of knowledge.[57]

RORTY ON PRINCIPLES AND PRACTICES

The upshot of Rorty's "linguistification" of pragmatism and his attack on the mind as the mirror of nature is a thoroughgoing historicism. There simply are no transhistorical standards of rationality, right and wrong, or the correct way to organize society. Contrary to Dewey's attempt to ground morality and democratic politics in a theory of human nature, and contrary to Hilary Putnam's contemporary attempt to justify democracy as a precondition of reliable knowledge,[58] Rorty contends that our moral and democratic practices cannot be justified by philosophical argument. We cannot, for example, say that slavery, oligarchy, or patriarchy are wrong because they fail to honor the innate "human dignity" of every person, whether he be a slave or she a woman. Or, if we do say such things within the context of our own liberal culture, we cannot appeal to some objective or neutral foundation in an effort to convince people from different cultures who disagree with us.[59]

Principles, both scientific and moral, undergo a corresponding deflation in this historicist tableau. Instead of viewing principles as objective, normative standards against which our disparate practices are to be judged, Rorty sees them as mere post hoc rationalizations of the values and habits already embedded in our existing practices. At most, he contends, principles can serve us as mere "reminders" of a consensus that we have already reached in science, morality, or politics. As such, they lack the sort of normative punch usually claimed for them in moral, political, and bioethical theory.

If we cannot move from one final vocabulary to another—for example, from Aristotelian to Galilean physics or from entrenched medical paternalism to a new bioethics based upon autonomy—by means of principles, good reasons, or reliable methods of inquiry, how do we account for scientific and moral progress? Since

[56] Rorty, *Objectivity, Relativism, and Truth*, 63–77. For Dewey, the very notion of "pragmatism without method" would have been unthinkable.

[57] Rorty, "Science as Solidarity," *Objectivity, Relativism, and Truth*, 35–45.

[58] H. Putnam, "A Reconsideration of Deweyan Democracy," 184–204.

[59] Thanks to Chris Tollefsen for this clarification.

Rorty has already excluded the possibility of explaining change and progress through closer and closer approximations of our physical, moral, or political concepts to "the world" or "human nature," he opts for an explanation in terms of new metaphors or new descriptions of familiar experiences. Change and progress are brought about by people like Freud and Marx, who invent new ways of describing things—ways that elicit new and different emotional responses that, in turn, can motivate others to substitute new practices for the old. Crucially, these new metaphors are simply new vocabularies, new ways of talking, that literally *change the subject* by helping us shed our old repertoire of concepts and emotional responses.

One of Rorty's favorite examples of this phenomenon is provided by contemporary feminism. Instead of saying that old-fashioned patriarchal ways of thinking and talking are flawed because they fail to acknowledge women's true human nature, Rorty lauds theorists such as Catherine MacKinnon who, he says, are trying to create new metaphors and a new group identity for themselves by telling counter-narratives about women's experiences. These new ways of speaking will eventually lead to new practices, like our laws against sexual harassment, that will provide future sources of new standards and criteria for relations between the sexes. As always in Rorty's work, practices ground or justify principles, not the other way around.

One rather disturbing implication of Rorty's account of the transition between ultimate vocabularies is that the criteria for embracing one account over another are primarily aesthetic rather than rational. Since we cannot reason our way from one vocabulary to another by means of logical argument, we must rely on more rhetorical forms of persuasion to make the new vision look good, and the old vision look bad, in the eyes of the relevant public. As Rorty puts it with characteristic frankness, "The method is to redescribe lots and lots of things in new ways, until you have created a pattern of linguistic behavior which will tempt the rising generation to adopt it."[60] Notwithstanding his attacks on scientific and other interpretive methods, then, Rorty does turn out to have a method of sorts; but it is a method that seeks to cause a change of viewpoint in one's interlocutors by nonrational means of persuasion.

THE ROLE OF PRAGMATIST PHILOSOPHY AND PHILOSOPHERS

Just as Dewey's attack on the spectator theory of knowledge had direct implications for the nature of philosophy and the role of philosophers, so Rorty's attack on the metaphor of the mind as a mirror of nature leads him to articulate a new

[60] Rorty, *Contingency, Irony and Solidarity*, 9. One of my colleagues in philosophy at the University of Virginia once remarked to me, in an outburst without the slightest hint of irony, that Rorty, then a colleague of ours at Virginia, was corrupting our youth!

conception of the philosopher's role within contemporary culture. Given Rorty's subversive conception of language, philosophical topics like epistemology, metaphysics, and ethics find themselves divested of their traditional subject matters. Rather than attempting to solve traditional philosophical problems in these areas, Rorty spins historical narratives that attempt to show us why these problems should no longer bother us.[61] The only remaining task for the pragmatist philosopher, then, is to criticize other philosophies that still take "foundations" seriously and thereby impede the creation of new metaphors by new social "prophets" like Freud, Marx, and MacKinnon. The primary role of the pragmatist philosopher, then, is the negative task of clearing the rubbish left by traditional philosophers who continue to insist on discovering the "grounds" of this, the "foundations" of that, or the "conditions of possibility" of everything. In response to those who complain that his brand of philosophical pragmatism lacks "critical bite," Rorty is quick to reply that no philosophy can bite into reality. Thus, the only kind of bite his philosophy can manage is into other (foundationalist) philosophies. And in response to Cornel West's call for a "prophetic pragmatism," a call echoed by bioethicist Susan Wolf,[62] Rorty tartly observes that if pragmatism is taken in what he calls the "professorial sense"—i.e., as a technical device for criticizing the overinflated claims of traditional philosophy—then the term "prophetic pragmatism" will sound as odd as "charismatic trash disposal."[63]

PRAGMATISM AND PROPHECY: RORTY'S CONSTRUCTIVE PROGRAM

Rorty thus agrees with Dewey that philosophers need to be knocked off their priestly pedestals; but whereas Dewey envisioned a quite significant public role for philosophers in conjunction with social scientists, Rorty conceives of philosophers as mere underlaborers of the social prophets, poets, and other creators of new visions. But at this point, a serious question arises concerning which prophets are worthy of being followed. Into whose service should the contemporary philosopher cast his or her lot? This is an important question since, strictly speaking, Rorty's "professorial pragmatism" is limited to foundationalist "trash removal"

[61] Were one tempted to boil Rorty's approach down to a slogan, it might read, "Philosophy—Get Over It!"
[62] Wolf, "Shifting Paradigms," 395–415.
[63] R. Rorty, "The Professor and the Prophet," *Transition: An International Review* 52 (1991): 75. Rorty elaborates on this metaphor elsewhere: "The 'new' pragmatism should, I think, be viewed merely as an effort to clear away some alder and sumac, which sprang up during a thirty-year spell of wet philosophical weather—the period that we now look back on as 'positivistic analytic philosophy.'" See R. Rorty, "The Banality of Pragmatism and the Poetics of Justice," *Southern California Law Review* 63, no. 6 (September 1990): 1815.

and, as such, it is theoretically neutral between the respective prophecies of democrats and fascists, of Franklin D. Roosevelt and Mussolini.[64]

Rorty contends that the only kind of "justification" a political standpoint can have is the frankly "ethnocentric" fact that it meshes well with the beliefs, intuitions, and values of those who espouse it. The kind of liberal democracy now institutionalized in Western Europe and North America is the end product of many historical contingencies that could well have worked themselves out in very different political directions. Had our history been significantly different, we would all have very different beliefs and intuitions about the value of individual freedom. But as good liberals, we are committed to beliefs in individuality and freedom in spite of the fact that these cannot be given a rational or transhistorical justification.

Borrowing a line from political philosopher Judith Sklar, Rorty contends that the basic stance that defines liberals is their opposition to cruelty and humiliation.[65] These, he says, are the worst things that humans can do to each other, and liberalism as a political program seeks to build a society as free as possible from their baleful presence. Another way to put this, underscoring Rorty's emphasis on language and vocabularies, is that a liberal society will oppose all forced "redescriptions" or coercively imposed stereotypes of other persons, such as the widespread images imposed upon African Americans for so long in our society as lazy, shiftless, primitive, promiscuous, and childlike.[66] In a liberal society, everyone is permitted to pursue his or her own path to self-realization just so long as the individual's chosen means do not interfere with the freedom and self-development of others. Apart from this important constraint elaborated long ago in Mill's *On Liberty*, Rorty believes that liberalism should be single-mindedly devoted to the protection of individual rights and to the self-realization of individuals.[67] Thus, although he cannot provide a philosophical argument in favor of this kind of society, Rorty believes that the planting and nurturing of this kind of garden is eminently worthy of the pragmatist philosopher's humble ground-clearing efforts. As he sometimes puts it, pragmatist philosophy's goal is to clear away other philosophical distractions so that people can get on with the important tasks of ending cruelty and humiliation, and in "getting what they need."

---

64 Ibid.

65 Rorty, *Contingency, Irony, and Solidarity*, xv.

66 This theme meshes nicely with Arthur Frank's postmodernist spin on the ethical importance of telling one's own story. See A. Frank, *The Wounded Storyteller* (Chicago: University of Chicago Press, 1995), and chapter 4 this volume.

67 R. Rorty, "Pragmatism as Romantic Polytheism," in *The Revival of Pragmatism: New Essays on Social Thought, Law, and Culture*, ed. M. M. Dickstein (Durham, NC: Duke University Press, 1998), 33.

Rorty thus has a positive program—a "prophetic pragmatism," if you will—but there are two important caveats. First, Rorty's prophetic vision of democracy is, as we have seen, a completely ungrounded leap in the dark. There are, in other words, no philosophical reasons to prefer Thomas Jefferson's Declaration of Independence to Mao's *Little Red Book*. His visions and those of other likeminded liberals thus represent a kind of groundless "social hope" for a better future. This program, then, amounts to a difficult—some would say impossible—balancing act. On the one hand, Rorty is a good liberal committed to the standard litany of liberal values, including toleration, individual freedom, and social solidarity in the face of human finitude and death. But, on the other hand, Rorty is an "ironist," a philosophical character beset by unremitting skepticism regarding the ultimate justification of his or her own final vocabulary and most deeply held values.[68] Whether Rorty is capable of actually sustaining this dual commitment to liberal values and to skepticism regarding the grounds of those same values is, not to put too fine a point on it, a matter of continuing conjecture and disputation. Whereas Rorty holds that the outlook espoused by liberal ironism places us in a "meta-stable" situation, wherein it is hard to take ourselves and our values seriously owing to their ultimate contingency,[69] others might describe such a stance as an invitation to intellectual schizophrenia.[70]

Second, Rorty concedes that there is nothing distinctly pragmatic about his own or anyone else's social visions. When confronted with the plethora of Deweyan texts that attempt to do much more than clear metaphysical junk from the roadway of democracy, Rorty splits his favorite philosopher into two distinct personages. On the one hand, there is Dewey the pragmatist philosopher, making the world safe from the spectator theory of knowledge and foundationalism; on the other hand, there is Dewey the social visionary, prophet, and poet of left-wing democracy.[71] The latter Dewey, Rorty insists, is not derived from and does not need the former.[72]

---

68 Rorty defines an "ironist" as someone who meets three conditions: (1) due to her acquaintance with the ways of people from other times and places, she has continuing doubts about her own final vocabulary; (2) she realizes that these doubts cannot be dissolved by any argument emanating from her own final vocabulary; and (3) she has given up on the notion that her own final vocabulary is in any way "closer to reality" than others, that it is in touch with a power not herself. See Rorty, *Contingency, Irony, and Solidarity*, 73.

69 Ibid., 73–74.

70 I owe this formulation of the problem to Jeffrey Blustein (personal communication).

71 Rorty, "The Banality of Pragmatism and the Poetics of Justice," 1816.

72 Frank Miller observes that, as Dewey saw things, the experimentalism of science provided the bridge between these two different aspects of his work (personal correspondence).

BIOETHICAL IMPLICATIONS OF RORTY'S PRAGMATISM

One aspect of Rorty's prophetic program has clearly defined and, on the whole, quite salutary implications for medicine and bioethics. Recall that, for Rorty, liberalism stands for liberty and individual self-expression, while opposing coercion, cruelty, humiliation, and forced redescription. One rather straightforward medical application of this view would be the proposition that health-care professionals should not forcibly redescribe the identities of their patients. This proscription would obviously encompass the practice within Soviet psychiatry of labeling many political dissidents as being mentally ill, but it would also include more ordinary assaults on the identities of patients in the everyday practice of medicine. Rorty's proscription of forcible redescription has been eloquently and comprehensively articulated for the world of medicine by sociologist Arthur Frank. In his admirable book *The Wounded Storyteller* (1995), Frank attempts to articulate an avowedly postmodern "ethic of voice," according to which everyone should be allowed to "tell their own story."[73] Patients facing chronic illnesses (such as cancer, AIDS, heart disease, etc.) should be assisted in reclaiming and asserting their own voice and personal experiences with illness in the face of medicine's depersonalizing language and categories.[74]

Given the general anti-foundationalist, anti-epistemological, and anti-metaphysical views sketched above, it should come as no surprise that most other implications of Rorty's views for bioethics are largely negative or critical. In the first place, his version of philosophical neopragmatism would target any vestiges of foundationalism and naturalism remaining within the field of bioethics. Views based upon conceptions of natural law, natural rights, the "inherent dignity of persons," or foundationalist moral/political theory of any kind would have to go. This blanket rejection would also include moral theories and principles based upon a metaphysical conception of the self as an identifiable and stable entity that endures through time. Thus, any bioethical principle based upon a Kantian notion of the self that gives near absolute priority to autonomy over other considerations would also fall within the sweep of this critique. Examples of bioethical work that Rorty's views would discredit include Leon Kass's naturalistic ruminations on the nature of health, the moral status of embryos, and on the family in its relation to society; H. Tristram Engelhardt's early work insofar as it was inspired by Robert Nozick's theory of nearly absolute "side constraints" on public action; and any and all religious views that claim a transcendent source and guarantor of

[73] Frank, *The Wounded Storyteller*. See also chapter 4 this volume.

[74] Frank's self-described "postmodern" ethic is not without problems of its own; see chapter 4 this volume.

their bioethical conclusions.[75] Importantly, this list should also include the early editions of Beauchamp and Childress's *Principles of Biomedical Ethics*, which Rorty would claim are tainted by nostalgia for philosophical foundations.

Rorty would also no doubt take a dim view of efforts by philosophically inclined bioethicists to engage in "conceptual analysis." Such bioethicists typically explain their work as consisting in both conceptual analysis of notions like "autonomy," "coercion," "person," and "suicide," and in normative examination of substantive moral questions, such as "Is abortion wrong?"[76] Rorty would say, with regard to the former effort, that philosophical bioethicists really do not have much to offer practicing physicians, except perhaps the possibility of suggesting to them new vocabularies and the prospect of some new alternatives. Toward this end, they can tell the perplexed doctor about what some illustrious philosophers, such as Plato, Kant, Mill, and Rawls, might have said about "freedom" or "truthfulness." But this will not, Rorty suggests, tell the doctor what she "really meant," or what presuppositions she must be relying on, or what was "really" in question in any given case. Rorty rejects the notion, often voiced by bioethicists, that physicians may use a concept like "paternalism" or "autonomy" in some sort of confused way, but that it falls to the philosophically trained bioethicist to really analyze and clarify the concept in question. The most they can do, he claims, is to help enlarge the troubled doctor's linguistic and imaginative possibilities, just as any other humanistically trained literary or historical scholar would do. Beyond this rather modest task, Rorty sees no special contribution of philosophers to the moral problems confronted by ordinary working-stiff physicians, just as he sees no use of philosophers of law for ordinary working-stiff judges. No special contribution, that is, beyond the typical lawyerly and sophistic task of "provid[ing] an argument for whatever our client has decided to do, mak[ing] the chosen cause appear the better."[77]

One important remaining question here is whether and to what extent Rorty's pragmatism poses a threat to Beauchamp and Childress's still-dominant principlist approach to bioethical method. As noted above, the early editions of *Principles of Biomedical Ethics* (*PBE*) would certainly have fallen under Rorty's generalized attack on foundationalism, but what about their later editions that attempt to

---

[75] See, e.g., Kass, *Toward a More Natural Science*; H. T. Engelhardt Jr., *The Foundations of Bioethics*, 2nd ed. (New York: Oxford University Press, 1996); P. Ramsey, *The Patient as Person* (New Haven, CT: Yale University Press, 1970).

[76] See J. D. Arras, "The Owl and the Caduceus: Does Bioethics Need Philosophy?," in *Biomedical Ethics Reviews*, ed. F. G. Miller, J. C. Fletcher, and J. M. Humber (Totowa, NJ: Humana Press, 2003), 1–42.

[77] R. Rorty, "Philosophy in America Today," *Consequences of Pragmatism*, 222–223. It's hard to imagine bioethicists rushing to embrace this conclusion.

develop a nonfoundationalist but still principle-based bioethics? We need to recall here that beginning with their fourth edition, Beauchamp and Childress abandoned any pretense of grounding their principles in some sort of philosophical or theoretical foundation. Instead, they now claim that the principles they discuss have their origins in an historically rooted "common morality," a bow toward historicity and contingency that Rorty might welcome.[78] In addition, the later editions of *PBE* explicitly embrace Rawlsian reflective equilibrium, a method that attempts to weave our intuitions, principles, and theories into a coherent fabric while denying foundational or privileged status to any one of these ethical raw materials.[79] Since Rorty enthusiastically supported Rawls's apparent admission that ethics and political theory are really about the coherent ordering of our time-bound intuitions through reflective equilibrium, he would likewise welcome this development in *PBE*.[80]

The remaining sticking point seems to be Beauchamp and Childress's abiding commitment to the normative status of ethical and political principles. In spite of their admission that principles are ultimately rooted in the history of our communal life and their endorsement of nonfoundationalist reflective equilibrium, Beauchamp and Childress still cling to the notion that principles can guide action, that they are not "mere (post hoc) reminders" of consensus that we have already reached. The difference between Rorty and Beauchamp and Childress appears to be that the former does not believe that moral, political, or scientific principles do any actual work, whereas the latter believe that they do. For Rorty, principles merely tell us what we already know; they serve only to highlight the values that cement our allegiance to our ongoing social practices and institutions. For Beauchamp and Childress, principles can help shape, criticize, reform, or revolutionize ongoing practices.

It is worth noting here that Rorty's rejection of the normativity of principles is more nominalist than it is pragmatist, at least if we understand pragmatism as Dewey did. Recall that in spite of his emphasis on the temporality and flexibility of moral principles, Dewey viewed principles as abbreviated statements of those actions or policies that have been found to work in the past. Although he had no use for a mechanistic view of principles as algorithms, rigid rules, or substitutes for good judgment, Dewey did consider principles to be action-guiding in the sense that they could help inform intelligent choice. This difference between Rorty

[78] Although it is doubtful that Rorty would approve of Beauchamp and Childress's lingering insistence that the dictates of this common morality are in some sense universal.

[79] See chapter 8 this volume.

[80] For Rorty's expropriation of Rawls's method of reflective equilibrium, see, e.g., "The Priority of Democracy to Philosophy," *Objectivity, Relativism, and Truth*, 175–196.

and Dewey can be brought into sharper focus by recalling Dewey's description of principles as tools for analyzing a special situation.[81] According to this account, principles function ideally as a kind of ethical flashlight, helping us illuminate the morally relevant aspects of our situation and to think through that situation in an intelligent and effective way.

Dewey's view of principles thus appears to have a lot more in common with the more mature work of Beauchamp and Childress than it does with Rorty's "mere reminder" view. In later editions of *PBE*, principles function very much like Dewey's tools, helping us sort out what to attend to in a morally freighted situation. Beyond this highlighting function, however, principles also resemble tools here in the sense that they are deployed along with other tools. Just as one needs to coordinate the use of a hammer, eye hooks, tape measure, wire, and a level in hanging a framed picture, so in complex moral situations one must invoke several moral principles or maxims, specifying as far as possible the concrete meaning of each one, and then carefully weighing their respective claims in the context of a rich factual narrative. For Dewey and Beauchamp and Childress, then, one must do things with principles, which are like tools scattered around one's living room. For Rorty, by contrast, principles appear to bear more resemblance to the framed facsimile of the Bill of Rights on the wall. It reminds us of something we agree on, but it pretty much just hangs there.

Rorty's "reminder view" of principles will also prove less than entirely helpful in the usual context of difficult choices for individuals and societies. If the only function of moral and political principles is to remind us of a consensus that we have already forged, they cannot be expected to be very helpful when we are faced with morally problematic situations involving serious conflicts among values and principles. Rorty says remarkably little about this ubiquitous feature of our moral and social lives, contenting himself with the observation that such "intra-societal tensions" are usually satisfactorily resolved not by means of general principles but, rather, by convention and anecdote.[82]

The positive flip side of Rorty's critical pragmatism is his claim that once we clear away the detritus of foundationalism we will then be free to create

---

[81] Dewey and Tufts, *Ethics*, 309.

[82] R. Rorty, "Postmodernist Bourgeois Liberalism," *Objectivity, Relativism, and Truth*, 201. Rorty's discussion of principles in this text actually approaches the view I have attributed to Dewey and Beauchamp/Childress: "The political discourse of democracies, at its best, is the exchange of what Wittgenstein called 'reminders for a particular purpose'—anecdotes about the past effects of various practices and predictions of what will happen if, or unless, some of these are altered." What is the difference between this formulation and Dewey's notion of principles as the pooling and crystallizing in general ideas of the experience of the entire human race? (See Dewey and Tufts, *Ethics*, 304). One difference might be that Dewey still regards principles as "the final methods used in judging suggested courses of action" (309).

new vocabularies, new possibilities, and new practices that will, as he puts it, "work better," "satisfy our needs," or deliver "what we want." Although I would certainly agree with Rorty that many traditional appeals to "objective truth" and "ethical first principles" have had the untoward effect of stunting human flourishing and denying human needs, it is unclear just how helpful Rorty's pragmatism will be to us in its post-trash-disposal phase. In the first place, a mere appeal to "what works" will obviously require supplementation by some vision of the good in order to provide an answer to what we ought to do in any given situation. The question of whether any particular constellation of results can be deemed sufficiently "fruitful" presupposes some sort of value framework that Rorty's pragmatism seems unable and unwilling to provide. Take, for example, the vexing problem of choosing a societal response to the emergence of many new reproductive technologies. According to one side of this debate, we can best "get what we want" by giving individuals the widest possible latitude to join with others—such as doctors, surrogates, baby brokers, and so on—in so-called collaborative reproductive efforts. According to this libertarian outlook, so long as no particular, identifiable individuals are harmed, prospective parents should have near total freedom and discretion in their use of the new technologies.[83] But according to another side of the debate, allowing people this sort of freedom will have subtle but real adverse consequences for individual children, women, and society at large. Viewed from this angle, the new technologies threaten to create a brave but decidedly unpleasant new world in which baby making is transformed into a commercialized and alienating industrial process.[84]

Importantly, it is not at all clear whether either of these competing visions of emerging reproductive technologies is inherently more "pragmatic" than the other. If one is primarily concerned with helping infertile individuals and couples become parents, subject only to the constraint that no identifiable individuals are harmed, then clearly the first perspective is the more pragmatic. But if one is primarily concerned to avoid the commercialization, objectification, and debasement of baby making, then the second perspective will be judged the more pragmatic.[85] Thus, even when Rorty begins to contemplate the positive space opened up by

[83] The *locus classicus* of this reproductive libertarian position remains John Robertson's *Children of Choice: Freedom and the New Reproductive Technologies* (Princeton, NJ: Princeton University Press, 1994).

[84] See J. D. Arras, "Reproductive Technology," in *A Companion to Bioethics*, ed. R. G. Frey and C. H. Wellman (Oxford: Blackwell Publishing, 2003), 342–355.

[85] For a similar assessment of Rorty's pragmatism with regard to the problem of legally regulating hate speech, see M. Rosenfeld, "Pragmatism, Pluralism, and Legal Interpretation," in *The Revival of Pragmatism: New Essays on Social Thought, Law, and Culture*, ed. M. M. Dickstein (Durham, NC: Duke University Press, 1998), 336–337.

the destruction of philosophical foundationalism, the prophetic side of his pragmatism turns out to be singularly uninformative about how we should proceed to grapple with such difficult problems of social policymaking. In the end, it will come down to a poetic contest of vocabularies, with each side trying to attract the attention and approval of the rising generation while also trying to make the opposition look bad.

Beyond the fact that Rorty's pragmatism offers scant positive guidance for individuals and policymakers, there may also be a contradiction between two aspects of his more positive philosophical program. On the one hand, as a good bourgeois, North Atlantic liberal (his description), Rorty is on record opposing revolutionary social change and coercion in the name of social progress. Conversation, persuasion, and unforced redescriptions are the preferred routes to social change. On the other hand, Rorty's liberalism also leads him to oppose cruelty, sadism, and humiliation practiced against the poor and vulnerable. An important question arises when we realize that putting an end to humiliating social conditions, such as lack of access to health care,[86] might well require coercion in the form of forced redescriptions and reallocations of wealth. What does Rorty say to the devotee of Ayn Rand or to H. Tristram Engelhardt Jr., who prizes individual autonomy and self-creation above all else, and who resists the imposition of a societal consensus in favor of alleviating cruel and humiliating social circumstances? Solidarity is clearly a pivotal theme in Rorty's work, but it's unclear that he is capable of mustering the resources to justify, in the face of inevitable libertarian protests, the social coercion required to fund many public expressions of solidarity.

In sum, then, the yield of Richard Rorty's pragmatism for current methodological debates in bioethics is primarily negative, knocking the props out from under any pretensions to foundations and universal principles of right and wrong. His "professorial pragmatism" and philosophical trash-disposal efforts would clearly sweep away some approaches based upon appeals to nature or universal human dignity, and his deflationary nominalist view of principles would threaten the foundations of some influential principlist approaches to bioethics. Apart from these negative contributions, Rorty is characteristically modest about the contributions of pragmatism to the ongoing moral struggles of professionals and ordinary working people. Indeed, if we are seeking new and, it is hoped, more fruitful

[86] I refer the reader here to Michael Walzer's astute observation that, in our society, lack of access to health care is not only dangerous but degrading as well. See M. Walzer, *Spheres of Justice* (New York: Free Press, 1983), 89.

approaches to our moral problems, Rorty seems to think that we will probably do better to look to novelists and poets rather than philosophically oriented practical ethicists. We can always wax prophetic, attempting to create a better society through redescribing lots and lots of things, but these efforts won't have much, if anything, to do with philosophical pragmatism or with bioethics.

6

Freestanding Pragmatism in Bioethics and Law

A NUMBER OF well-established figures in the field of bioethics have recently begun advocating the merits of pragmatism as a method of practical reasoning. Some of these bioethicists have proposed a return to the methodological orientation originally proposed by John Dewey, whose work I discussed in detail in chapter 5.[1] Others have advocated a "pragmatist" approach to bioethics without bothering much to tether their specific conception of pragmatism to the classical canon of Peirce, James, and Dewey.

In one of the first studies to embrace an explicitly pragmatic approach to bioethics, law professor Susan Wolf discerns a pronounced shift in both bioethics and health law away from the abstractions of analytical philosophy and toward a more clinically oriented and empirical mode of analysis.[2] In place of theoretically elegant academic treatises on such topics as advance directives, Wolf endorses empirical research projects that might tell us how advance directives actually work in the real world. In addition to this shift from armchair theorizing to the practical world of the clinic, Wolf also discerns a widespread effort within the field to focus more explicitly than before on feminist issues of power and voice. Feminist critics of the "Georgetown mantra" have examined the power relations between (male) physicians and (female) nurses and patients, explaining how

---

[1] G. McGee, *The Perfect Baby: A Pragmatic Approach to Genetics* (New York: Rowman and Littlefield, 1997); G. McGee, ed., *Pragmatic Bioethics* (Nashville: Vanderbilt University Press, 1999); F. Miller, J. Fins, and M. Bacchetta, "Clinical Pragmatism: John Dewey and Clinical Ethics," *Journal of Contemporary Health Law and Policy* 13 (1996): 27–51. (See also chapter 5 this volume.)

[2] S. Wolf, "Shifting Paradigms in Bioethics and Health Law: The Rise of a New Pragmatism," *American Journal of Law and Medicine* 20, no. 4 (1994): 395–415.

power imbalances contribute to the exploitation of women and the marginalization of their legitimate concerns. Theoreticians representing minority groups, who have charged bioethics with privileging the concerns of white, male patients, have lodged criticisms similar to those raised by feminists of the dominant mode of bioethical discourse. While conceding that skepticism about elegant abstractions, a focus on empiricism and practical results, and a concern for the poor and disenfranchised can all be usefully described in a variety of ways, Wolf argues that *pragmatism* constitutes a particularly satisfying rubric for these disparate phenomena. In order to stress the extent to which this new pragmatism differs from a merely vulgar pragmatic concern for means and "results," Wolf argues that the engine of pragmatic moral analysis should be animated by a vision of social justice and the empowerment of women, racial minorities, and other marginalized groups. Borrowing the self-description of the celebrated African-American neopragmatist Cornel West, Wolf closes her discussion with a call for a "prophetic pragmatism."

Although members of this latter group, of which Wolf is an important figure, might occasionally invoke the name of this or that great pragmatist thinker for rhetorical effect, their views on bioethical method do not appear to require a return to the textual wellsprings of classical American pragmatism. For them, a pragmatic bioethics would emphasize paying heed to the richness of factual detail in which moral problems are embedded, achieving the "best results" in concrete circumstances, an eclecticism with regard to competing philosophical "grand theories," flexibility with regard to the use of moral principles, the denial of foundationalism, and in some instances a stance of solidarity with the marginalized and oppressed sectors of our society.[3] I shall call the former group "canon-dependent" pragmatists, and the latter group "freestanding pragmatists." Admittedly, these groupings are somewhat rough and porous. Sometimes canon-dependent pragmatists sound as though their pragmatism amounted to little more than paying attention to factual details,[4] while some freestanding pragmatists invoke the great tradition of American pragmatism (but without attempting to base their arguments on explicitly Deweyian, Jamesian, or Peircean premises).

[3] M. Benjamin, *Philosophy and This Actual World* (New York: Rowman and Littlefield, 2002; Wolf, "Shifting Paradigms in Bioethics and Health Law," 395–415.

[4] Thus, McGee writes, "Figuring out the solution to a complex social problem through pragmatic philosophy will turn out to be more a matter of immersing oneself in the details of the particular problem than studying Dewey's position on that problem. Therefore, pragmatist scholarship about particular social problems is seldom credited as such." McGee, *Pragmatic Bioethics*, xiv.

One advantage of the relative isolation of bioethics from the fads and foibles of the academic mainstream is that, coming to some of these methodological debates years after they have played out elsewhere, bioethicists are in a good position to learn from the prior impact of pragmatism on other fields. Although the revival of pragmatism hasn't made much of a dent in psychology, the social sciences, or even in contemporary philosophy departments,[5] it has had a significant impact in the area of legal studies. In scores of law review articles and academic symposia, legal scholars have exhaustively debated the relevance and merits of pragmatism's revival for jurisprudence and the work of lawyers and judges.[6] This recent encounter between law and pragmatism may be especially felicitous for our methodological ruminations within bioethics because, unlike literary applications of neopragmatism, both law and bioethics are fundamentally *practical* enterprises in which decisions affecting real people must be made.

One theoretical outgrowth of this encounter of pragmatism and the law, dubbed "freestanding legal pragmatism" by its proponents, may have particular relevance for methodological debates within bioethics. According to this jurisprudential view, most clearly and forcefully articulated by theorists Thomas Grey[7] and Judge Richard Posner,[8] a pragmatic approach to legal reasoning and practice can be defended quite independently of any appeals to distinctly philosophical versions of pragmatism, whether old (e.g., Dewey) or new (e.g., Rorty). I believe that much of the pragmatist work in bioethics today that I have labeled "freestanding" bears a remarkable resemblance to this freestanding pragmatism in legal studies. An elaboration of freestanding legal pragmatism might thus provide us with a fruitful working model of its bioethical analogue. I shall argue in this chapter that when bioethical pragmatism is understood as being "freestanding" in this way, there is a sense in which we are all (or at least most of us are) pragmatists now. And if this is so, then it is unclear how much of a distinctive contribution pragmatism can make to contemporary methodological discussions within bioethics.[9]

---

[5] It is ironic that psychology, the field that Dewey viewed as philosophical pragmatism's chief partner, has apparently had little, if any, use for either the old or the new varieties of pragmatism.

[6] T. Grey, "Holmes and Legal Pragmatism," *Stanford Law Review* 41 (1989): 787–870; M. Dickstein, ed., *The Revival of Pragmatism: New Essays on Social Thought, Law, and Culture* (Durham, NC: Duke University Press, 1998); M. Dickstein, "Symposium on the Renaissance of Pragmatism in American Legal Thought," *Southern California Law Review* 63 (1990): 1569–1928.

[7] T. Grey, "Freestanding Legal Pragmatism," in *The Revival of Pragmatism: New Essays on Social Thought, Law, and Culture*, ed. M. Dickstein (Durham, NC: Duke University Press, 1998), 254–274.

[8] R. Posner, "Pragmatic Adjudication," in *The Revival of Pragmatism: New Essays on Social Thought, Law, and Culture*, ed. M. Dickstein (Durham, NC: Duke University Press, 1998), 235–253.

[9] I argue in chapter 5 of this volume that even the main contentions of canon-dependent pragmatism can be articulated and defended without reliance upon the actual texts of Peirce, James, and Dewey.

COMMON FEATURES

A composite account of freestanding legal pragmatism (henceforth, FLP), drawn primarily from the writings of Grey and Posner, would stress four important features: *viz.*, contextualism, instrumentalism, eclecticism, and theory independence. As good contextualists, pragmatist judges work within the constraints of established practices bearing on judicial interpretation and the administration of justice. They will thus be mindful of past cases as they prepare to render decisions in present cases. This is so for two reasons. First, as Posner points out, cases can and should be viewed as repositories of social values and important judicial insights. Even if judges were not legally bound by the rule of precedent (*stare decisis*), they would be foolish to ignore the fruits of past efforts to deal with analogous problems. Second, consistency is itself an important value. Were judges to veer too far from conformity with past decisions in search of pragmatic solutions, they would undermine the stability of law and thereby preclude legal actors from basing their conduct on a set of reasonably firm expectations. This aspect of FLP obviously bears a striking resemblance to the method of casuistry within bioethics. To some extent, both approaches are concerned with history, with institutional roles and constraints, and above all with rendering present decisions coherent with a body of preexisting case law or case studies.

Notwithstanding its acknowledgment of the importance of historicity, context, and consistency, freestanding legal pragmatism denies that contemporary judicial decision makers are bound by any strict duty of precedence. In contrast to coherentist legal theorists such as Ronald Dworkin,[10] who claim that judges are duty bound to decide present cases according to the principles animating past cases, partisans of FLP are primarily concerned with achieving the best outcomes. Hence, the second crucial feature of FLP is its instrumentalism. Contrary to both "formalist" legal theorists, who would bind judges strictly to the principles embodied in precedent, and those bioethical casuists who would rely exclusively on past analogies to drive present decisions, freestanding legal pragmatists advocate a more empirically informed and forward-looking perspective. For them, the crucial objective of adjudication isn't the most consistent decision but, rather, the best decision—i.e., the one that generates the *best* outcomes for all concerned. The achievement of this overriding objective requires the judge to make good use of "extralegal" sources of information and insight, such as the views of experts in medicine, economics, psychology, and other social sciences. Judge Posner

[10] R. Dworkin, *Law's Empire* (Cambridge, MA: Harvard University Press, 1988).

provides a good example of this commitment to instrumentalism in his assessment of the New Jersey Supreme Court's performance in the famous surrogate parenting case involving Baby M. Contrary to that court's opinion, which relied heavily on the analogy of baby selling (a legally proscribed practice), Posner would have had the judges seek answers to two empirical questions: (1) Do women serving as surrogate mothers tend to experience extreme regret when called upon to give their newborn children up to the contracting couple? And (2) Does poverty drive women into coercive and exploitative surrogacy contracts? According to Posner, surrogate parenting arrangements offer so many manifest benefits to so many parties that both questions would have to be answered in the affirmative to prompt the pragmatist judge to nullify such contracts as contrary to public policy. Thus, the crucial issue for Posner is the overall effect of the practice of surrogate parenthood on all involved parties, not the resemblance of this practice to previously proscribed activities, such as baby selling.[11]

The empiricism of Posner's freestanding legal pragmatism is mirrored in Susan Wolf's recent account of an emerging "pragmatist paradigm" within bioethics. According to Wolf, various empirical studies are beginning to show the inadequacies of the dominant "principles approach," both as an accurate account of how people actually make decisions and as a guide to good social policy. She notes, for example, that the standard approach to surrogate decision making—an approach that calls upon surrogates to decide as the presently incompetent patient would have decided—has been rendered problematic by empirical studies showing that surrogate deciders often fail to connect with patients' own values and choices.[12] The standard autonomy-based model of surrogate decision making has also been threatened by recent studies showing that patients from different cultural backgrounds reject the current bioethical orthodoxy on patient autonomy and truth-telling in favor of a more oblique and family-centered approach to communication.[13] Viewing this shift toward a more empirically based bioethics as a salutary trend, Wolf would thus echo Posner's insistence that mere theoretical elegance and coherence are not enough. We must, rather, measure the adequacy of our theoretical musings against actual attitudes and practices in the world.

The third crucial element of freestanding legal pragmatism is its eclecticism. In contrast to the partisans of "grand theory" in jurisprudence, legal pragmatists eschew total explanations in favor of a more inclusive and democratic attitude

[11] Posner, "Pragmatic Adjudication," 235–253.

[12] Wolf, "Shifting Paradigms in Bioethics and Health Law," 404.

[13] L. Blackhall et al., "Ethnicity and Attitudes Towards Life Sustaining Technology," *Social Science and Medicine* 48 (1999): 1779–1789.

with regard to the multitude of contending theoretical perspectives. According to Grey, FLP occupies a middle ground between warring jurisprudential factions, such as the law and economics movement and the least common denominator of merely "thinking like a lawyer."[14] In contrast to the advocates of grand, holistic theories, the partisans of FLP agree that no one theory has cornered the market on truth; but in contrast to those who would reject the claims of theory entirely, they contend that each of the grand theories nevertheless sheds partial light on legal phenomena. FLP thus makes room for those who see law primarily as policy (e.g., Posner) and those who view it as primarily a body of coherent principles (e.g., Dworkin). Although they are practical, always seeking the best results, they manage to make room for universal human rights and prohibitions against slavery and torture.

This relaxed, inclusionary attitude toward the mutually exclusive claims of rival theories finds a bioethical counterpart in the *locus classicus* of the regnant bioethical paradigm—i.e., Beauchamp and Childress's *Principles of Biomedical Ethics*. From the start, this book has exhibited a remarkable insouciance regarding the claims of ultimate or foundational philosophical theory. In the early editions of the book, the authors contented themselves with noting that their favored middle-level principles could be derived either from Beauchamp's commitment to utilitarianism or from Childress's embrace of a religiously oriented deontology. Later versions of this text, however, have included lengthy expositions and friendly critiques of all the current "grand theories" as applied to bioethics, including utilitarianism, Kantianism, character ethics, communitarianism, casuistry, and feminism. With regard to each of these contenders for methodological supremacy within bioethics, the response of Beauchamp and Childress has been the same: *viz*., to reject their one-sidedness and theoretical excesses while embracing those insights that make sense and contribute to a richer understanding of the whole. Just as the Borg, in *Star Trek: The Next Generation*, relentlessly assimilated vanquished civilizations into their ever-expanding neural network, so Beauchamp and Childress have become the "Borg of Bioethics" by subsuming the partial truths of rival theories into their ever-expanding synthesis.[15]

The fourth element of freestanding legal pragmatism is its alleged independence from any and all distinctly philosophical underpinnings; obviously, it is this feature that makes this version of legal pragmatism *freestanding*. According to Grey and Posner, a legal theorist can embrace all the central tenets of FLP without committing herself in any way with regard to philosophical pragmatism, old

[14] Grey, "Freestanding Legal Pragmatism," 257–258.

[15] See chapter 1 this volume.

(e.g., Dewey, James) or new (e.g., Rorty, Putnam). Conversely, one can embrace the original pragmatist and neopragmatist assaults on epistemological and metaphysical foundationalism without necessarily being led to FLP. Posner notes in this connection that a true philosophical pragmatist, always seeking the best results, might actually prefer that judges pursue a decidedly nonpragmatist decision procedure.[16] It may turn out, for example, that strict adherence to legal rules and precedent will lead to better results in most cases than the untrammeled and ad hoc pursuit of "what works" in every case. Although Grey acknowledges that grappling with concrete legal problems, such as hate speech and the insanity defense, can sometimes generate philosophical puzzlement, he claims that when this happens discussion "hives off" from concrete legal reasoning and joins the enterprise of speculative philosophy.[17] Thus FLP proclaims itself to be an essentially *practical* discipline that remains unaffected by the battles between pragmatist and nonpragmatist philosophers over the nature of truth, objectivity, and the foundations (if any) of morals. That is, one can embrace a limited commitment to contextualism, instrumentalism, and eclecticism with regard to legal theory without having to take one's cue from any version of pragmatist philosophy. As Giovanni Papini once shrewdly observed, pragmatism is a philosophy for getting along without philosophy.[18]

This detachment of pragmatist judging from pragmatist philosophy is mirrored in the detachment of most work in bioethics today from any overarching grand theory. True, there are some exceptions. The bioethical contributions of such authors as Leon Kass,[19] H. Tristram Engelhardt Jr.,[20] and Peter Singer[21] bear the unmistakable marks of their authors' theoretical commitments to, respectively, Aristotelian teleology, Nozickian libertarianism, and utilitarianism. But most work in the field today seems profoundly suspicious of attempts to "apply" the dictates of any grand ethical or philosophical theory straightaway to practical problems in the bioethical trenches. Indeed, Richard Posner has gone so far as to claim that the "best bioethics is the least philosophical." In response to those who criticize Beauchamp and Childress's nonfoundationalist principlism as being insufficiently theoretical, Posner contends that this detachment from moral theory actually constitutes the singular strength of contemporary mainstream bioethics.[22]

---

[16] Posner, "Pragmatic Adjudication," 236–237.
[17] Grey, "Freestanding Legal Pragmatism," 265.
[18] Dickstein. *The Revival of Pragmatism*, 15.
[19] L. Kass, *Towards a More Natural Science* (New York: Free Press, 1985).
[20] H. T. Engelhardt Jr., *The Foundations of Bioethics*, 2nd ed. (New York: Oxford University, 1996).
[21] P. Singer, *Rethinking Life and Death* (New York: St. Martin's, 1994).
[22] R. Posner, "Reply to Critics," *Harvard Law Review* 111 (1998): 1796–1823.

This detachment from theory is also characteristic of much self-consciously pragmatist work in contemporary bioethics. Echoing the commitment of freestanding legal pragmatism to contextualism and instrumentalism, Glenn McGee writes that addressing complex social problems through "pragmatic philosophy" will usually be achieved not by reading and applying lots of Dewey and James but, rather, by immersing oneself in the factual details of the problem at hand.[23]

Our emerging picture of what might be called "freestanding bioethical pragmatism" is nearly complete. In order to round it out, we should mention here two other salient features in addition to its contextualism, instrumentalism, eclecticism, and theory independence. The first involves the abandonment of philosophical foundations for ethics in favor of the method of reflective equilibrium. Thus, rather than seeking justification for moral judgments in some sort of ultimate ethical bedrock—such as God's will, natural law, utilitarian theory, or moral intuition—the partisans of freestanding bioethical pragmatism embrace a method in which justification is sought in the overall coherence of our intuitions, mid-level principles, moral theories, and non-moral philosophical "background" theories (e.g., of personhood).[24] Noting that Dewey was a staunch opponent of philosophical foundationalism in all its forms, Martin Benjamin calls our attention to the pragmatic dimensions of the method of reflective equilibrium.[25] Rather than seeking moral truth in some objective realm detached from human purposes, the pragmatist seeks it within the web of human constructs. Apart from the exceptions noted above, much if not most work in bioethics today either explicitly or implicitly embraces this method.[26] Although some self-described pragmatist insurgents have been highly critical of Beauchamp and Childress's method of principlism, it is interesting to observe that if Benjamin is correct in his assertion that reflective equilibrium constitutes a distinctly pragmatist approach to ethics, then Beauchamp and Childress are pragmatists, as are most casuists and narrativists.

A second (and final) feature of freestanding bioethical pragmatism, also highlighted by Benjamin,[27] is attention to the need for compromise and consensus in

[23] McGee, ed., *Pragmatic Bioethics*, xiv. McGee's own work is surprisingly light on references to Dewey's substantive moral or philosophical doctrines. His "pragmatism" thus seems to be mostly restricted to enthusiasm for Dewey's "logic of inquiry" that emphasized the perpetual testing of the results of moral inquiry against experience (18–29). McGee's explicitly named pragmatist chapter in his book *The Perfect Baby* contains only a few references to Dewey, and the insights he attributes to Dewey there do not appear to be doing most of the heavy lifting in support of McGee's main conclusions. McGee, *The Perfect Baby*, 67–78.

[24] N. Daniels. *Justice and Justification: Reflective Equilibrium in Theory and Practice* (New York: Cambridge University Press, 1996). (See chapter 8 this volume.)

[25] Benjamin, *Philosophy and This Actual World*.

[26] M. Kuczewski, "Bioethics' Consensus on Method: Who Could Ask for Anything More?," in *Stories and Their Limits*, ed. H. L. Nelson (New York: Routledge, 1997).

[27] Benjamin, *Philosophy and This Actual World*.

a world divided by pervasive and deep moral disagreement. As an ever-expanding chorus of moral philosophers and bioethicists might put it, once we give up on the quest for foundational moral principles and acknowledge the ineradicable plurality of values, the search for common ground through deliberative democratic processes replaces the search for universal solutions applicable to all. Instead of being "found," solutions to moral problems must now be negotiated. In place of Kantian metaphors featuring practical reason as a lofty tribunal, reflection on the significance of moral pluralism suggests the town hall meeting, a crucible of consensus and compromise, as the most appropriate metaphor for our common political life.[28]

ASSESSING FREESTANDING PRAGMATISM

The freestanding pragmatist of either a legal or a bioethical orientation is thus committed to contextualism, instrumentalism, eclecticism and value pluralism, and theory independence; while the bioethical freestanding pragmatist also explicitly embraces reflective equilibrium in lieu of foundations. Four questions immediately come to mind: (1) To what extent is there anything *distinctly pragmatist* about this methodological approach? (2) To what extent is there anything novel about it? (3) To what extent can it deliver *normative standards* for thought and action? (4) To what extent is this kind of pragmatism truly *freestanding*?

(1) In contrast to those who would marshal the resources of the great American pragmatist tradition in the service of jurisprudence[29] or bioethics,[30] freestanding pragmatists wish to bracket the import of philosophical theory while remaining somehow decidedly pragmatist. Thus, this will not be an approach that requires us to dust off our volumes of Peirce, James, and Dewey in order to reinvigorate our methodological reflections in practical ethics. In what sense, then, is this a *pragmatist* approach to practical ethics?

The answer to this question isn't at all obvious, especially when we begin to reflect on the range of alternative sources of support for the various elements of freestanding pragmatism.[31] The *contextualism* of both law and bioethics derives from the fact that both disciplines strive for consistency and coherence in their

[28] R. Rorty, "Pragmatism and Law: A Response to David Luban," in *The Revival of Pragmatism: New Essays on Social Thought, Law, and Culture*, ed. M. Dickstein (Durham, NC: Duke University Press, 1998), 304–311.
[29] "Symposium on the Renaissance of Pragmatism in American Legal Thought," 1569–1928.
[30] Miller et al., "Clinical Pragmatism," 27–51.
[31] D. Luban, "What's Pragmatic about Legal Pragmatism?," in *The Revival of Pragmatism: New Essays on Social Thought, Law, and Culture*, ed. M. Dickstein (Durham, NC: Duke University Press, 1998), 275–303.

judgments. Far from being a distinctly pragmatist requirement, this appears to run against the instrumentalist grain of traditional pragmatism; it can, moreover, be based upon a wide variety of moral theories or commonsensical constraints on policymaking. The *instrumentalism* of freestanding pragmatism could, obviously, be based upon the traditional pragmatist canon, but it can also find support in utilitarianism or in the mid-level principle of beneficence. Likewise, the *eclecticism* of freestanding pragmatism can be based upon an appropriately humble recognition that human beings strive for a diversity of moral and non-moral goods that cannot be shoehorned without remainder into some preordained monistic theoretical grid. One need not be a pragmatist to recognize how theories dominated by a single value—such as the efficiency prized by economic analysts of law or H. T. Engelhardt's obsession with unbridled liberty[32]—tend to yield analyses that strain our credulity to the breaking point.

Similar questions can be raised about Martin Benjamin's claims on behalf of reflective equilibrium and value pluralism. According to Benjamin, reflective equilibrium provides the method for a pragmatic approach to ethics, while recognition of value pluralism supplies the key premise for a pragmatist political philosophy. Although Benjamin is no doubt correct that these notions are consistent with the pragmatic spirit, we certainly don't need to read Dewey to understand reflective equilibrium as a method of ethical justification. Indeed, there is quite a robust literature on this theme in practical ethics, most of which could be described as decidedly neo-Kantian rather than pragmatist. As for value pluralism and the virtues of seeking mutual accommodation and consensus, it's also true that this theme can be found in Dewey, but its elaboration in contemporary political philosophy owes more to Isaiah Berlin, Charles Taylor, and the advocates of the "deliberative democracy" movement.[33]

In sum, then, it would appear that what currently passes for a freestanding pragmatic approach to legal and bioethical problems owes its distinctly pragmatist credentials neither to ties to the classical pragmatist canon (remember, it's freestanding) nor to any distinctly pragmatist doctrine or methodological approach. Indeed, if this is what pragmatism amount to—*viz.*, an embrace of contextualism, instrumentalism, eclecticism, and so on—then in a very real sense (nearly) all of us are pragmatists now. In a world in which the later incarnations of Beauchamp and Childress would count as pragmatists, the question immediately

---

[32] Engelhardt, *The Foundations of Bioethics*.

[33] A. Gutmann and D. Thompson, *Democracy and Disagreement* (Cambridge, MA: Harvard University Press, 1996); N. Daniels and J. Sabin, "Last Chance Therapies and Managed Care: Pluralism, Fair Procedures, and Legitimacy," *Philosophy & Public Affairs* 26 (1997): 303–350.

arises: Pragmatist—as opposed to what? I suspect that recognition of the ubiquity of this kind of pragmatism led Richard Rorty to conclude that legal pragmatism, as opposed to his own version of anti-foundationalist *philosophical* pragmatism, was at this point in American history fundamentally *banal*.[34]

(2) To what extent, then, is freestanding pragmatism a novel move—one that can inject fresh, new perspectives into our ongoing methodological debates? Although there is obviously much to be said in favor of the various elements of freestanding pragmatism, it should be clear by now that they do not add up to genuine news. Although Monsieur Jourdain, Molière's bourgeois gentleman, could manage to be genuinely astonished at the news that he'd been speaking prose all his life, it may be somewhat less of a revelation for legal and bioethical advocates of contextualism, instrumentalism, eclecticism, reflective equilibrium, and value pluralism to learn that they've actually been pragmatists all along.

The only apparent exception to this conclusion is the claim of freestanding pragmatism to be freestanding—i.e., independent of any comprehensive moral vision inspired by American pragmatism or any other philosophical theory. From one angle this does represent a somewhat novel development in recent moral and political philosophy. John Rawls appears to have staked out this position in developing his final conception of "justice as fairness," as resting on an overlapping consensus among disparate views of the good rather than on any "comprehensive moral view."[35] Abandoning his earlier attempt in *A Theory of Justice* to ground "justice as fairness" in a neo-Kantian vision of the good life based upon individual autonomy, Rawls now claims that the adherents of differing (reasonable) conceptions of the good can all endorse his two famous principles of justice within the context of a wider democratic and pluralist society. Within the realm of political philosophy, this move to make the principles of justice freestanding in this sense does indeed constitute a novel and quite controversial departure.[36]

But from another angle, that of contemporary bioethics, the "freestandingness" of key moral principles from any one comprehensive vision has been a familiar feature of the "principles approach" for roughly a quarter-century. Indeed, a central tenet of this dominant methodological approach asserts that people wedded to diametrically opposed moral philosophies, such as religious deontology (Childress) and utilitarianism (Beauchamp), can nevertheless reach convergence

[34] R. Rorty, "The Banality of Pragmatism and the Poetry of Justice," *Southern California Law Journal* 63 (1990): 1811–1820.

[35] J. Rawls, *Political Liberalism* (New York: Columbia University Press, 1993).

[36] For an opposing view, see J. Hampton, "Should Political Philosophy Be Done without Metaphysics?" *Ethics* 99, no. 4 (July 1989): 791–814.

on the four "mid-level" principles of bioethics.[37] So again, if a freestanding pragmatism is supposed to represent a new methodological departure or improvement on the principlist status quo, then at least with regard to bioethics (if not law, as well) it's unclear what that new direction might be.

Of course, the key question for any methodological approach to either law or bioethics is (3)—whether it can provide adequate normative guidance for our moral deliberations. With regard to legal pragmatism, Judge Posner cheerfully leaves open the question bearing on the criteria for judging the "best results" within the context of pragmatic adjudication. In stark contrast to John Dewey, for whom the somewhat amorphous notion of "growth"[38] provided the ultimate touchstone for moral and social progress, and even in contrast to his own previous singular allegiance to the economic value of efficiency, Posner now rather astonishingly prescinds from recommending any substantive norms that would guide the deliberations of pragmatist judges. He simply assumes that on most questions there will be a fair degree of consensus among judges about what will constitute the "best results," and that this consensus will relieve them of the burden of relying on philosophically charged conceptions of the good.[39]

Posner's stance here is questionable on a number of grounds. First, it's fairly obvious that consensus does not exist among judges or anyone else on many of the most urgent questions confronting society today. With regard, for example, to Posner's own example of surrogate parenthood, many judges believe that such contracts should be banned as a matter of public policy, while others, including Posner himself, believe that surrogacy contracts should be regulated but not banned. Given this manifest lack of consensus, what is the pragmatist judge to do? More fundamentally, in the absence of a discrete set of norms to guide pragmatist deliberations, Judge Posner's reassuring advocacy for the "best results" in any given case proves itself to be completely vacuous. Again, commercial surrogacy contracts helpfully illustrate the poverty of Posner's freestanding pragmatism. This policy debate presents us with two quite distinct and mutually incompatible estimates of

[37] Alex John London has argued, albeit on different grounds, that a conception of practical ethics as a freestanding enterprise can even be found in classical works such as Aristotle's *Rhetoric*. A. J. London, "The Independence of Practical Ethics," *Theoretical Medicine and Bioethics* 22 (2001): 87–105.

[38] Dewey and Tufts write: "The moral criterion by which to try social conditions and political measures may be summed up as follows: The test is whether a given custom or law sets free individual capacities in such a way as to make them available for the development of the general happiness or the common good. This formula states the test with the emphasis falling upon the side of the individual. It may be stated from the side of associated life as follows: The test is whether the general, the public organization and order are promoted in such a way as to equalize opportunity for all." J. Dewey and J. H. Tufts, *Ethics* (New York: Holt, 1908), 431.

[39] R. Posner, "Pragmatic Adjudication," 247–248.

what will yield the "best results." Proponents argue that such contracts will clearly accomplish the best results. They advance the interests of the contracting couple, the surrogate mother, and, counting existence as a benefit, the child born as a result of such a contract. But opponents argue that surrogacy contracts violate the interests of surrogate mothers and threaten to wreak psychological damage on the resulting children. They also claim that such contracts amount to "baby selling," and thus threaten to commercialize and commodify children, thereby degrading their status as full persons over the long term.[40] It is important to note in this connection that this disagreement hinges not simply on conflicting empirical predictions about what bad effects will happen but also on conflicting conceptions of liberty and human flourishing. In the absence of some normative conception of what constitutes good results, Posner's freestanding legal pragmatism will be completely useless in the adjudication of such disputes.

Thomas Grey's conception of freestanding legal pragmatism is somewhat more modest, and thus more plausible than Judge Posner's. According to Grey, the freestanding pragmatist is not an anti-theorist committed to the view that the various live options in moral and political philosophy are all bankrupt; rather, he or she accepts each of the current major theories as occupying a legitimate (albeit partial) place in our deliberations. Thus, instead of conceiving each of the major theories as mutually exclusive comprehensive accounts, the freestanding pragmatist finds merit in all of them insofar as they succeed in capturing incomplete but complementary truths about our moral and political life. Although Grey, like Posner, does not endorse any particular set of values as uniquely characteristic of freestanding legal pragmatism, his account at least has the merit of implying that glib appeals to consensus will not necessarily see us through, and that the pragmatist judge will have to wrestle with a variety of conflicting norms that lie ready to hand, drawn from various conflicting theories.

The closest bioethical analogues to this way of thinking are the casuistry of Jonsen and Toulmin[41] and the principlism of Beauchamp and Childress.[42] Following a decade of intense mutual criticism and the resulting retrenchment of their more exaggerated claims either for or against the role of theory and principles in bioethics, both of these rival camps now appear to agree that a complex assortment of intuitions, maxims, principles, and moral theories play an important normative role in our interpretation of concrete cases. In contrast to Judge Posner's denial

---

[40] M. J. Radin, *Contested Commodities* (Cambridge, MA: Harvard University Press, 1996).

[41] A. Jonsen and S. Toulmin, *The Abuse of Casuistry* (Berkeley: University of California Press, 1988).

[42] T. Beauchamp and J. Childress, *Principles of Biomedical Ethics*, 4th ed. (New York: Oxford University Press, 1994).

that legal pragmatism itself can offer us normative guidance, Thomas Grey and his bioethical counterparts hope to provide such guidance through the skillful mixing and matching of the various principles and theoretical perspectives readily available in our common moral environment. Although there may be much to recommend this "theory modest" approach to legal and moral interpretation, it is important to note here that there is nothing either especially new or "pragmatist" about it. Indeed, Beauchamp and Childress have devoted seven editions over (roughly) a thirty-five-year period to the elaboration and refinement of their methodological approach without once bothering to mention that it even had pragmatist overtones.

Finally (4), there is the question whether this sort of legal and bioethical pragmatism is genuinely "freestanding." It is important to specify here precisely *from what* this pragmatism is supposed to stand free. Posner and Grey make a convincing case that their respective versions of legal pragmatism need not rely on any *philosophical* conception of pragmatism, whether old or new. Since the central features of their legal pragmatisms—*viz.*, their contextualism, instrumentalism, and eclecticism—are so minimalist and uncontroversial, they clearly need not appeal either to Dewey's or Rorty's "professorial" philosophical refutations of foundationalism or realism in epistemology to proceed with the very practical business at hand of judging particular cases according to the usual canons of evidence and argument. The same conclusion evidently holds true for bioethical pragmatism, even when we add Martin Benjamin's short list of additional core features of pragmatist ethics—*viz.*, reflective equilibrium and value pluralism. As we have seen, a variety of methodological schools within bioethics have embraced all the key features of freestanding pragmatism recommended by Posner, Grey, and Benjamin without even mentioning, let alone depending on, pragmatism as a philosophical critique of foundations.

Whether legal or bioethical pragmatism can stand free of any and all philosophical reflection is, of course, another matter entirely. Judge Posner has flatly declared that philosophical ethics as currently practiced in Anglo-American universities is both useless and downright dangerous.[43] Thomas Grey contends that the outcome of concrete legal disputes should not depend upon the judge's acceptance or rejection of arcane philosophical doctrines in metaphysics, the philosophy of mind, or ethics. He admits that law often gives rise to philosophical puzzles worth considering in their own right—for example, the compatibility of environmental determinants of action with free will and, hence, the possibility of just punishment—but

[43] R. Posner, *The Problematics of Moral and Legal Theory* (Cambridge, MA: Harvard University Press, 1999).

he insists that the ensuing discussions leave the practical domain of law behind and enter the murkier realm of speculative philosophy.[44] Whatever the truth of these claims, I would argue that it's hard to imagine what bioethics would be like without reference to a wide variety of philosophical debates bearing on such disparate issues as the moral status of embryos, the personhood of brain-dead patients, the moral relevance of the distinction between killing and allowing to die, the ultimate rationale of informed consent, the "nonidentity" problem as applied to the question of whether impaired children can be harmed by being born, or indeed the proper method(s) of doing bioethics. Although bioethics might well stand free of pragmatic anti-realism, and may well also follow Rawls by standing free of any overarching "comprehensive" vision of the good, it cannot avoid philosophical entanglement on a host of questions at the very core of the field.

CONCLUSION

In contrast to current attempts to apply the lessons of either classical or contemporary philosophical pragmatism to methodological debates within law and bioethics, the advocates of freestanding pragmatism have attempted to develop an approach that holds overarching philosophical theories (including pragmatism itself) at arm's length without settling for "merely thinking like a lawyer" or its bioethical equivalent. The main problem in assessing freestanding pragmatism as a method of legal and bioethical thought has been to determine in what sense, if any, it constitutes a truly distinctive contribution to our "method wars." Freestanding pragmatism seems most successful in distinguishing itself from those approaches that still cling to a single overarching comprehensive philosophical theory such as utilitarianism, Kantian deontology, libertarianism, Marxism, or Aristotelian teleology. This doesn't get us very far, however, because (especially with regard to bioethics) defenders of these methodological approaches are now increasingly hard to find. Once we bracket such theories, the potentially distinctive contributions of freestanding pragmatism become difficult to discern. As we have seen, the various elements usually associated with this sort of pragmatism are by now pretty much standard methodological fare within the field of bioethics. If even Jim Childress, the avatar of embattled principlism, could recently affirm that in a sense, "We're all pragmatists now,"[45] then this sort of pragmatism increasingly begins to resemble the proverbial night in which all cows are black.

[44] Grey, "Freestanding Legal Pragmatism," 265.

[45] Personal communication.

These deflationary reflections prompt us to ask in what sense freestanding pragmatism can properly be called a method of moral inquiry. With regard to other widely recognized methodological approaches to practical ethics such as cost-effectiveness analysis, principlism, casuistry, or feminism, one has every reason to expect that the application of a given method will have some sort of predictable bearing on the outcome or procedures of the inquiry. If one deploys a cost-effectiveness analysis in a debate over health-care priorities, for example, we can be quite certain that the end result will reflect an attempt to maximize utility or quality-adjusted life years. Likewise, were someone to engage in a principlist, casuist, or feminist analysis of assisted reproductive technologies, we can bet that such analyses will yield, respectively, an interpretation and balancing of rival ethical principles, an analogical argument based upon prior paradigm cases, or a critique of existing gender-based patterns of domination and oppression. But if someone were to announce that he was going to apply freestanding pragmatism to a legal case or bioethical problem, I would be hard pressed to anticipate what such an analysis would attempt to do or say beyond simply eschewing appeals to some grand theory. Thus, while some contend that cost-effectiveness analysis should be rejected because its moral vision is excessively constricted, one might well conclude that freestanding pragmatism is too amorphous and ill-defined to offer any meaningful constraints on ethical analysis.

At most, the freestanding pragmatist might be able plausibly to claim that her analysis will exhibit two distinctly pragmatist motifs. First, the analysis will manifest a concern for the consequences of theory upon our lives. As Susan Wolf reminds us, we must always pause to ask whether our current theoretical approach to a problem is actually making life better for people. If our theories of informed consent and surrogate decision making currently distort the lived moral experience of various groups in our society or fail to notice what is most important to them, then we should shelve those theories and try to develop better ones. Crucial to any such effort will be the deployment of ethically informed social scientific research on the impacts of current theories as they are embedded in actual policies and protocols.

Second, a freestanding pragmatist approach to moral problems will insist upon the flexibility of moral principles as applied to concrete and often tragic circumstances. As Jane Radin points out, the direct application of ideal moral norms to nonideal moral realities can often mire the theorist in a perplexing double bind.[46] In assessing the phenomenon of contract pregnancy, for example, Radin

[46] Radin, *Contested Commodities*, 123–130.

concludes that standard surrogacy contracts threaten to commodify childbearing and degrade our culture with a manifestly inadequate conception of human flourishing. In a perfect world, we would, she concludes, simply banish such contracts. But we do not live in a perfect world; rather, we live in a world in which access to the role of surrogate parent might constitute one of the few ways by which women of limited means might be able to escape from their precarious economic plight. Thus, both a policy intolerant toward commercial surrogacy grounded in ideal norms of human flourishing and a permissive policy based upon a concern to redress current economic inequalities equally risk subordinating people who are trying to make progress. A pragmatist approach to the double bind will not be inflexibly governed by any preestablished and lexically prior moral norm. Rather, the pragmatist will approach such situations with an acute awareness of the potential for error and subordination in either direction, and will try to forge a practical solution on the basis of each proposal's potential for human betterment at a given time and place.

7

A Method in Search of a Purpose

THE INTERNAL MORALITY OF MEDICINE

SOME RESPECTED COMMENTATORS on medicine and morality claim that a sufficiently robust medical ethic can be derived entirely from the contemplation of medicine's proper nature, goals, and practice.[1] For them, physicians have no need of moral values, principles, or theories stemming either from common morality or, worse yet, from the fevered brains of philosophers or theologians; instead, according to this view, physicians may obtain all the moral guidance they need from a morality internal to medicine. But other, equally respectable commentators contend that there is no such thing as an internal morality of medicine.[2] They contend that all judgments in bioethics must be guided and ultimately justified by ethical norms external to the practice of medicine. This is indeed a curious state of affairs. How is it that equally perceptive observers of the medical scene could have come to such diametrically opposed conclusions about the most fundamental methodological question in medical ethics?

Something else is quite curious. Among the more moderate partisans of an internal morality of medicine are theorists who claim that this morality exists in a state of perpetual historical dynamism "in conversation" with external moral

---

[1] L. R. Kass, "Regarding the End of Medicine and the Pursuit of Health," *The Public Interest* 40 (1975): 11–42; L. R. Kass, "Thinking About the Body," *Hastings Center Report* 15 (1985): 20–30; and E. D. Pellegrino and D. C. Thomasma, *For the Patient's Good: The Restoration of Beneficence in Health Care* (New York: Oxford University Press, 1988).

[2] R. M. Veatch, "The Impossibility of a Morality Internal to Medicine," *Journal of Medicine and Philosophy* 26 (2001): 621–642.

norms derived from a wide variety of sources.[3] These moderate internalists contend, moreover, that the successful resolution of contemporary moral problems in medicine will depend upon a judicious balancing of both internal and external moral norms. They thus deny that internalism in medical ethics can function as a comprehensive, stand-alone methodological approach. This crucial concession in effect appears to reconcile internalism with the views of one of its sharpest externalist critics.[4] How is it that this other set of equally observant proponents of rival methodological approaches could end up saying the same thing?

In this commentary I shall explore how the various participants in this debate over method can have reasonably arrived at their respective positions. I shall agree with internalists that there may well be a core of good sense in the idea of an internal morality of medicine, but I shall agree with the externalists that the successful resolution of any and all contemporary problems in bioethics will require resort to a host of moral norms external to medicine. This undertaking will require a much closer look at the typology of internalism—i.e., the various kinds of internalism that, I shall argue, have only been partially mapped by the participants in this debate. More importantly, however, it will also require a much more explicit and thorough inquiry into the various possible functions that an internal morality of medicine might serve. Against the backdrop of these analytical inquiries, I shall conclude that one likely explanation for the possible misunderstanding between the various partisans in this debate is that they have been insufficiently attentive to *the point* of an internal morality.

DEEPER INTO THE TYPOLOGY OF INTERNALISM

A review of the literature on this subject yields the following different varieties of moral "internalism" in medicine:

- "Essentialism," according to which a morality for medicine is derived from reflection on its "proper" nature, goals, or ends.[5]
- "The practical precondition account," according to which certain moral precepts are derived as preconditions of the practice of medicine.

[3] F. G. Miller and B. H. Brody, "Professional Integrity and Physician-Assisted Death," *Hastings Center Report* 25 (1995): 8–17.

[4] T. L. Beauchamp, "Internal and External Moralities for Medicine," *Journal of Medicine and Philosophy* 26 (2001): 601–619.

[5] Pellegrino and Thomasma, *For the Patient's Good.*

- "Historical professionalism," according to which the norms governing medicine are decided upon solely by the practitioners of medicine—an ethic about physicians, by physicians, and for physicians.
- And, finally, an "evolutionary perspective," according to which professional norms in medicine evolve over time in creative tension with external standards of morality.[6]

Essentialist Accounts

Let us take a closer look at these types of moral internalism, beginning with the essentialist perspective. This is by far the most robust, but also the most controversial, of the internalist approaches. Essentialism claims, in brief, that careful reflection on the very nature of medicine as a practice, including reflection on its ends or goals, can yield a serviceable medical ethic. For example, such reflection might highlight the nature of medicine as a *healing* profession whose members *proclaim their commitment* to caring for the sick. From these basic premises, one might then move to a consideration of various practical problems in medicine, such as determining the morality of physician-assisted suicide (PAS), performing cosmetic surgery or abortion, or physicians' obligations to dangerous or contagious patients. Some plausible applications of essentialism to such problems might, then, yield the following practical conclusions:

- Physicians have a moral duty to treat HIV-infected patients. This follows from the proposition that physicians are healers; they care for the sick and vulnerable among us. Those unwilling to shoulder such burdens does not know what it *means* to be a physician; or, if they do know what it means to be a physician and are yet unwilling to shoulder such a burden, then they have chosen the wrong profession for themselves.
- Physicians should not cooperate with HMO-inspired mandates to ration health care at the bedside. The physician's job is to minister to the needs of individual patients, not to solve social problems at her patients' expense.
- Physicians should not participate in PAS. The end of medicine is to heal, cure, or alleviate suffering by licit means. Killing patients contradicts the true end of medicine.

---

[6] F. G. Miller and H. Brody, "The Internal Morality of Medicine: An Evolutionary Perspective," *Journal of Medicine and Philosophy* 26 (2001): 581–599.

- Physicians should not perform abortions, cosmetic surgery, or cognitive (or other bodily) enhancements. Such actions do not advance the above goals of medicine, so they fall outside the bounds of the proper procedures physicians should perform.

This kind of internalist medical ethic derives additional specificity and strength from the very notion of a *profession* and the ethical duties attendant upon being a *professional*. In contrast to those engaged in ordinary trades, such as selling stamps or repairing auto mufflers, a professional is bound by more stringent duties than those governing contractual relations within a market economy. Because the relationship between professionals and those they serve is asymmetrical with regard to knowledge, power, and vulnerability, lawyers, physicians, and nurses have a duty *as professionals* to subordinate their own self-interests to the welfare of their clients or patients. Combined with the traditional medical obligation to "do no harm," this professional duty creates a very strong sense of fidelity or loyalty to the best interests of one's patients.[7]

The Practical Precondition Account

This approach simply amounts to asking what the essential *preconditions* are for the practice of medicine. It asks, in other words, what the virtues and norms are without which the practice of medicine would cease to be a going concern. This approach to the development of an internal morality seems to have been somewhat neglected in the bioethics literature.[8]

A classic example of this method at work would be the acknowledgment of a duty of confidentiality in medicine. Whether or not violating patient confidences also violates the nature of "healing" or of some other essential goal of medicine, it certainly makes it *practically impossible* for physicians to maintain a relationship based upon trust with their patients; and in the absence of trust, patients either will not disclose information vital to the healing enterprise or will simply refuse to seek the services of a given physician. Note that this approach does not appear to commit us to speculative and controversial claims concerning the essential nature of medicine and its goals; all we need to assume is a very thin account of the goals of medicine (for example, one that accepts the desirability of

---

[7] C. Fried, *Medical Experimentation: Personal Integrity and Social Policy* (New York: American Elsevier, 1974).

[8] Robert M. Veatch and Franklin Miller, eds., Special issue, "The Internal Morality of Medicine: Comment," *Journal of Medicine and Philosophy* 26, no. 6 (2001): 555–662, where this chapter originally appeared as a commentary on the other articles in the symposium.

an ongoing patient–physician relationship). It simply asserts that, whatever we think about medicine's "true" purposes, the enterprise of medicine as a practical activity won't be able to get off the ground without scrupulous adherence to the duty of confidentiality.

There is an interesting and instructive analogy to this approach in the legal theorist Lon Fuller's celebrated "internal morality of law."[9] In contrast to those who would ground the moral force of law on some speculative scaffolding—such as might be available, for example, in Thomistic natural law theory or Rawls's Kantian theory of justice—Fuller sought the moral bedrock of law in an account of "the morality that makes law possible." So, instead of grounding law in a theory of rationality or natural human tendencies fraught with implications for the resolution of substantive problems in constitutional or criminal law, Fuller attempted to articulate a theory of the practical preconditions of successful lawmaking. Unlike Aquinas and Martin Luther King Jr., who attacked wicked and unjust laws on the ground that they contradicted a "higher law," Fuller elaborated a set of eight preconditions without which law could not be successfully made in the first place. His list included the following:

- There must be rules.
- The rules must be promulgated.
- Except when necessary to remedy a past injustice, laws should not be retrospective or ex post facto.
- Laws should be clearly and coherently articulated.
- There should not be contradictions in the laws.
- Laws should not require the impossible.
- Laws should be maintained constant through time.
- And, finally, there should be congruence between official action and declared rule.[10]

Instead of viewing law through a Hobbesian-Austinian positivist lens—that is, as an exercise of sheer power of the stronger party over the weaker—Fuller insisted on viewing law as a purposive social practice wherein citizens are given norms to shape their future conduct. Insofar as evil rulers, such as the Nazis, failed to abide by the above norms of successful lawmaking, they didn't simply make bad laws that need not have been obeyed; rather, Fuller asserts, they actually failed to make law in the first place. It is noteworthy that this morality has to do exclusively

[9] L. L. Fuller, *The Morality of Law* (New Haven, CT: Yale University Press, 1969).
[10] Ibid., 46–81.

with the *making of* law *tout court*, and it is thus noncommittal with regard to any and all more specific controversies bearing on the morality or justice of particular laws. In other words, the internal morality of law is fully in place well before we have even begun to debate the vagaries of capital punishment, affirmative action, and the economic analysis of law. Anyone who wants to make law, whether he be Taliban, Marxist, or Christian Democrat, must first attend to the craft of lawmaking, which is strictly speaking *neutral* between these different ideological engines for the direction of law. The disturbing consequence of this is that a given regime might succeed in formulating genuine laws according to all eight of Fuller's criteria while the content of those laws remained manifestly unfair and perhaps even wicked. (South Africa's apartheid regime comes to mind.)

Historical Professionalism

This method of deriving an internal morality looks to the medical profession's efforts over the course of history to define its own specific virtues, vices, and codes of conduct. In contrast to externalism's mode of deriving duties, this approach embraces a historically evolving core of norms determined exclusively by physicians to constitute a professional morality. And in contrast to essentialism's mode of deriving duties from atemporal essences and unchanging goals, the primary source of historical professionalism's internal morality resides not in claims bearing on the essential nature and goals of medicine but, rather, in a temporally conditioned *agreement* among physicians on what they consider to be right and virtuous conduct. Thus, in opposing PAS, for example, this approach would stress the medical profession's nearly universal and historically continuous opposition to this practice stretching back to the Hippocratic Oath.

An Evolutionary Perspective

Miller and Brody deploy what is, to my mind at least, the most plausible and attractive model of medical internalism advanced so far.[11] Eschewing both the Platonic essentialism of Pellegrino's account and the historicism of a purely social constructionist view of professional morality, Miller and Brody propose a theory of professional medical goals and duties conditioned by the evolving demands of history and (external) social cultural influences. They thus argue that there is indeed a core ethic developed on the basis of reflection on medicine's specific goals and

[11] Miller and Brody, "The Internal Morality of Medicine: An Evolutionary Perspective."

duties, but that this core ethic develops historically as a result of a dialectic or conversation between the medical profession and the larger society.

One interesting feature of this evolutionary internalism is its openness to historical change and development in the received core values, goals, and duties of medicine. There is no reason whatever to believe that medicine exhibits some eternal essence, unmodified by time, place, and culture. Miller and Brody are thus open to the acknowledgment of new goals and duties—for example, the prudent shepherding of society's medical resources under conditions of fiscal scarcity—and to the reinterpretation of the relative strength or importance of existing elements of the internal morality. An example of the latter phenomenon, the authors assert, is their own embrace of PAS based upon a reinterpretation of the relative weights of the traditional admonitions not to kill, on the one hand, and to relieve pain and suffering, on the other.

Another noteworthy feature of this approach is its frank acknowledgment of the interaction between medical values and (external) social norms and influences. The very idea of an unchanging essence of medical practice unaffected by the vagaries of history and culture as it meanders through the ages is, to modern sensibilities at least, rather implausible on its face. Miller and Brody's evolutionary account embraces the idea that the morality of medicine is always forged in a dialectical relationship with the surrounding (external) worlds of common morality, law, commerce, technology, politics, and so on. This concession to the claims of externalist morality permits a much more satisfying explanation of the gradual development of various medical norms, such as the duty to treat dangerous or contagious patients. Whereas the essentialist account would have us believe, implausibly, that a timeless "duty to treat" derives entirely from reflection on the goals of medicine, this evolutionary approach would be much more sensitive both to historical accounts of physicians' behavior in time of plague and to the changing social expectations of physicians. It would note, for example, that in many previous historical epochs, physicians basically served rich patrons. Should the plague strike a city, physicians (like Sydenham) would traditionally decamp to the countryside with their patrons, leaving their ordinary patients behind. Sometimes citizens would be highly critical of physicians who abandoned their posts, but there was by no means a single, unitary norm governing the behavior of physicians through the ages.[12]

---

[12] J. D. Arras, "The Fragile Web of Responsibility: AIDS and the Duty to Treat," *Hastings Center Report* 18, no. 2 (Supplement; 1988): 10–20. Given the often extremely harsh and ineffective treatments meted out to patients during former times of plague, patients whose physicians fled the scene were in many ways the lucky ones.

Such an account would also note how the duty to treat was forged in part as a response of the medical profession to the expectations of society. In an era when only the rich could expect help from physicians, or when medicine as we know it existed side by side with a plethora of alternative approaches to health and disease, we should not expect physicians to conceive of a rigorous duty to treat all in need. But this is just what we would expect, for example, in the contemporary era when health care is nearly universally regarded as a *social need* akin to fire and police protection, and when various licensing provisions have given physicians a *de jure* monopoly on treating the sick. Indeed, the dialectical interplay between the duty to treat and licensure is quite striking in the modern era. In exchange for the exclusive and legally enforced privilege to practice medicine, physicians have (largely voluntarily) assumed the responsibility to treat all in need, including patients with contagious diseases. Thus, the duty to treat is best viewed as neither a pure internal duty nor a purely externally imposed norm; rather, it is the concrete, historically determined outcome of a dialectic between medicine's internal morality and a host of social expectations.

PUTATIVE FUNCTIONS OF AN INTERNAL MORALITY OF MEDICINE

Having briefly surveyed the various candidates for an internal morality of medicine, we come now to the question of what might be reasonably asked of any such approach. What, in other words, is an internal morality of medicine *for*? One salient answer, which seems to constitute an implicit premise of much of the literature, is that medical internalism should provide us with the tools we need to resolve important issues in bioethics, such as abortion, PAS, confidentiality of genetic records, the duty to treat AIDS patients, and so on. I shall argue, on the contrary, that medical internalism either cannot satisfactorily perform this function or, if it can, it must give up its claim to be a species of internalism. I shall also argue that there nevertheless remains another function of medical internalism—a product of professionalism in general and the practical precondition account—that is both legitimate and important. In brief, I shall side with Robert Veatch[13] and Tom Beauchamp[14] on the question whether an internal morality of medicine is useful for contemporary bioethics (No, it's not), but I shall also side with Ed Pellegrino,[15]

[13] Veatch, "The Impossibility of a Morality Internal to Medicine."

[14] Beauchamp, "Internal and External Moralities for Medicine."

[15] E. D. Pellegrino, "The Internal Morality of Clinical Medicine: A Paradigm for the Ethics of the Helping and Healing Professions," *Journal of Medicine and Philosophy* 26 (2001): 559–579.

Frank Miller, and Howard Brody[16] on the question whether such a morality exists and can perform a valuable service for physicians.

Problem Solving with an Internal Morality of Medicine

I begin with my negative thesis—*viz.*, that none of the versions of internal morality thus far surveyed will prove useful in the resolution of contemporary bioethical problems or, if one or another does prove useful, it thereby ceases to be a bona fide version of internalism. Let us begin with Pellegrino's essentialism.

Essentialism

As a number of commentators have pointed out, among them Miller and Brody, essentialist internalism is a nonstarter, for several reasons. First, in spite of its advocates' best efforts, certain indispensable elements of contemporary medical morality, such as a duty to obtain the informed consent of patients, simply cannot be derived from an analysis of the concept or primary goals of medicine.[17] As legions of physicians correctly but futilely complained during the protracted legal battle over informed consent in the early 1970s, the doctrine of informed consent did not grow organically out of the very practice of medicine but, rather, was imported from the external camps of law and liberal political philosophy.[18]

Second, this kind of essentialist internal morality lacks the resources to determine the limits of (or resolve conflicts among) norms that might, for the sake of argument, be postulated as belonging to this internal morality. Three likely candidates for this status are the duty of confidentiality, the proscription of active killing, and the duty to alleviate suffering. As for confidentiality, even if it can be shown that such a duty belongs to this internal morality (more on this later), that morality by itself is incapable of determining the strength and limits of this duty as it collides with other, clearly external obligations to other parties. If we agree that psychiatrists have a "duty to warn" third parties of their patients' credible threats of violence, our agreement is premised on considerations having nothing to do with the nature and goals of medicine, but everything to do with the protection of vulnerable others. Here the prerogatives of equal citizenship and common decency show the way, not deeper reflection into the heart of medicine.

With regard to the proscription of killing and the duty to alleviate suffering, defenders of essentialist internalism must come to terms with the possibility of

[16] Miller and Brody, "The Internal Morality of Medicine: An Evolutionary Perspective."
[17] Pellegrino and Thomasma, *For the Patient's Good*, 214.
[18] J. Katz, *The Silent World of Doctor and Patient* (New York: Free Press, 1984).

head-on conflict among internally generated norms. We have already seen how the condemnation of PAS and euthanasia can be derived from the physician's profession as a healer ("We're doctors, we heal; we don't kill"), but we must now contemplate the possibility that a positive duty to aid patients in their own suicides may with equal plausibility be derived from physicians' obligation to alleviate pain and suffering. Just as physicians have a moral duty to prescribe effective painkillers for patients following surgery, so they may in certain extreme situations, when all other alternatives have failed, have a duty to help patients overcome their intractable suffering by means of a mercifully delivered prescription of lethal dose. If Miller and Brody are correct, either reading of the internal morality of medicine is plausible, but they cannot both be true at the same time and place. In order to adjudicate the conflict between these internal norms, we will have to appeal to values, principles, and norms outside the medical sphere (for example, the principle of self-determination). There is no clearly articulated hierarchical principle within medical morality, so defined, that could settle this debate on purely internalist terms.

Internal Morality as Practical Precondition

As we saw in our account of the legal analogue of this kind of internal morality, *viz.*, Fuller's "morality that makes law possible," an internal morality of law is really more akin to a theory of legal craftsmanship than to a critical *moral* theory. It tells us what judges must do in order to successfully make law, whether the laws we wish to make pertain to the mandatory destruction of graven religious images, the restoration of property to the proletariat, or entitlements under the welfare state. Fuller's internal morality of law is not only fully in place before we get to the question of law's substantive morality, it is also of little, if any, use in the resolution of that question in the context of debates over problematic laws and governmental policies. Presumably, in order to make progress in our familiar debates about affirmative action, the death penalty, and so on, we will have to invoke one or another explicitly external morality of law, whether it be the common law, Thomistic natural law theory, legal realism, a Rawlsian theory of fairness, Marxism, the Koran, the wisdom of Dr. Phil, or some other approach. Thus, Fuller's theory of an internal morality of law can only help us determine how to actually create law as a responsive social interaction between those who make law and those governed by it. The actual content or direction of law can only be settled by appeal to various moral sources external to law.

The practical precondition approach to internal medical morality differs somewhat from Fuller's legal analogue because some of the things that "make practicing medicine possible"—for example, the duty of maintaining patients' confidentiality—are also elements of substantive morality that figure in contemporary bioethical debates. Whereas Fuller's internal morality of law cannot help us decide among rival but indisputably lawlike solutions to problems in the various branches of law, medical internalism harbors norms, such as "do no harm" and "keep confidences," that are at least relevant to many practical problems. This advantage over Fuller's version of internalism ultimately proves insufficient, however, for two reasons.

First, the indisputably action-guiding norms inherent in this version of internalism, such as confidentiality, may be valued by patients and society at large for other reasons than those given by internalism, and this may have implications for the resolution of problems at both the bedside and policy levels. As we have seen, this version of internalism values the duty of confidentiality in purely instrumental terms—*viz.*, as a norm that makes the practice of medicine possible. Although this is certainly a crucially important consideration, it completely ignores other explanations for the importance of confidentiality based upon *patient-centered* values, such as self-determination and privacy. Thus, internalism may enjoin physicians to do the right thing for the wrong reason—or at least for an incomplete set of reasons—or, on some occasions, the medial practice-centered account of confidentiality may yield conclusions different from a more patient-centered or philosophical account. An example of the latter type of problem would be the challenge to confidentiality posed by the sexually active yet irresponsible HIV-infected patient. Whereas a medical practice-centered approach would most likely enjoin physicians to maintain strict confidentiality in such cases, on the grounds that violations of confidentiality will disrupt the physician–patient relationship, other approaches might contend that patients who demand confidentiality while recklessly exposing others to a lethal disease thereby contradict themselves—that is, autonomy is good for them, but not for others—and thus prove themselves undeserving of the full protection of medical confidentiality.[19]

Another, even more serious problem threatens to undermine this practical preconditions approach. A set of norms must not only be relevant to the resolution of practical problems; it must, in addition, harbor the requisite resources to provide for the specification and balancing of competing values. Although the value of confidentiality is certainly highly relevant to many bioethical disputes today, in order to *solve* those problems internalism would have to take into account a plethora of external considerations, including externally articulated moral and

[19] G. Gillett, "Aids and Confidentiality," *Journal of Applied Philosophy* 4 (1989): 15–20.

political norms bearing on the protection of third parties and the public's health. Since it cannot do this and remain an internal morality, the practical precondition account of internalism cannot function as a useful guide to contemporary bioethical problems.

Historical Professionalism

If internalist essentialism founders because it attempts, somewhat preposterously, to plane above the contingencies of history and culture, then historical professionalism fails because it never rises above the level of the guild toward a genuine ethics. Founded upon historically contingent understandings of the nature of medicine and its goals, this kind of moral internalism is notorious for giving medicine a bad name.

Note first that historical professionalism is an internal morality in a sociological sense. A particular group of people—physicians—define an ethic to govern their own conduct in splendid isolation from the norms governing the rest of society. As we shall see momentarily, this disjunction between the medical and all other sources of morality (e.g., religious, legal, customary, etc.) creates enormous problems for historical professionalism, but I want first to stress the point that this kind of isolationism also has a tendency to give rise to a kind of guild mentality that mistakes economic self-interest for morality. A classic case in point is the American Medical Association's (AMA's) longstanding, but now legally defunct, opposition to advertising. Prior to 1981, the AMA condemned any and all varieties of advertising on the part of physicians as grave violations of the most sacred tenets of medical morality. Although there was no doubt something to be said for this stance as a bulwark against the encroachments of a kind of sleazy self-promoting commercialism ("Come on down! We've got your colon covered!"), the law and ordinary patients have tended to view it as a classic case of restraint of trade, motivated at least in large part by concern for physicians' incomes.[20]

The salad days of historical professionalism are obviously those epochs in which there is fundamental harmony between the internally derived medical ethic and external social values. (Is Doctor Welby in the house?) Severe problems arise, however, whenever individuals and groups in the larger society call into question medicine's understanding of its own proper nature, goals, and means. When these outsiders begin asking "Why?," the professionally derived internal morality of

---

[20] American Medical Association, *Petitioner, v. Federal Trade Commission*, Respondent; *Connecticut State Medical Society and New Haven County Medical Association, Inc., Petitioners, v. Federal Trade Commission*, Respondent. Nos. 995, 1050, Dockets 79–4214, 79–4226; US Court of Appeals, Second Circuit. 638 F.2d 443; 1980 US App. Lexis 13300; 1980–2 Trade Cas. (CCH) P63, 569.

medicine begins to appear reactionary at worst, or at best, merely quaint. When the partisans of this internalism fail to acknowledge the widening gap between their own deeply held norms and those of the rest of society, their thunderous pronouncements, although taken seriously at the time, usually end up years later sounding preposterous or even comical. Here are three representative cases in point; scores of other examples could easily be provided.

- En route to coercing Dax Cowart to accept surgery, one of his physicians, Dr. Duane Larson, declared that he has "the knowledge and the means of caring for this patient so that he does survive, and you're asking me not to do this. Why am I in medicine?"[21] Now, nearly forty-five years later, this physician is universally portrayed in introductory bioethics courses as Exhibit A of an overweening and unethical paternalism.
- At the dawn of the women's liberation movement, breast cancer surgeons routinely imposed the radical and disfiguring Halstead mastectomy on their patients, refusing even to discuss less aggressive measures. Dr. Jerome Urban of the Memorial-Sloan Kettering Memorial Hospital in New York imperiously declared that "Lesser surgery is done by lesser surgeons."[22] Defenders of the status quo in medical ethics mocked those surgeons who would disclose their uncertainties to patients and give them a share in decision making.[23] Again, thirty years later, physicians are legally obliged to obtain the consent of such patients following a frank and comprehensive discussion of the various alternative procedures and their respective risks and benefits. True/false examinations for board certification in surgery today would count those aggressive surgeons of the *ancien régime* as having given the *wrong* answer.
- During the comparative clinical trials of the clot-busting drugs Streptokinase and tPA, a physician declared that his duty as a physician is to give his patients the best proven drug, irrespective of cost—even if tPA proved to be only a fraction of a percentage point more effective in preventing repeat heart attacks at a cost of roughly $2,000 more per patient.[24] Now, roughly twenty years later, this kind of insouciance with

[21] D. Andersen, R. Cavalier, and P. Covey, *A Right to Die?: Teachers Guide* (Oxford: Routledge, 1997).

[22] B. Lerner, *The Breast Cancer Wars: Hope, Fear and the Pursuit of a Cure in Twentieth-Century America* (New York: Oxford University Press, 2001), 78.

[23] For a good example of this kind of haughty but currently laughable criticism, see E. G. Laforet, "The Fiction of Informed Consent," *Journal of the American Medical Association* 235 (1976): 1579–1585.

[24] B. Brody, *Ethical Issues in Drug Testing, Approval, and Pricing: The Clot-Dissolving Drugs* (New York: Oxford University Press, 1995).

> regard to the financial consequences of medical choices is widely regarded as a case study in irresponsibility and injustice to the other citizens of the medical commons.

The root problem here for this species of internalism is its obliviousness to values that have come to occupy center stage in the wider society. In these cases, those key values are self-determination and equity in the distribution of health-care resources. One important consequence of this detachment of internalism from the wider world of values and norms is that it puts physicians in the position of unilaterally making health-care decisions that, from the perspective of this wider world, they have no right to make. Although Dax Cowart's physicians saw themselves as answering to the highest standards of medical morality, Dax and the rest of us object that their unilateral imposition of unwanted treatment on him constituted a violation of his ethical and common law rights of autonomy and bodily integrity. And although an HMO physician might proudly proclaim her allegiance to an "ethic of loyalty" to patients by ordering a hugely expensive drug with only a scintilla of additional benefit over the cheaper standard of care, her superiors are now likely to remind her that she does not own the resources that she dispenses so freely, and that she therefore has no right to make unilateral decisions that adversely affect the medical commons.[25]

Finally, the historical professionalism approach to internalism faces an insuperable problem of moral justification. As we have seen, the duties acknowledged within this kind of medical morality are grounded in an agreement among physicians about the proper goals of medicine; and we have seen that, in contrast to essentialism, the contents of this agreement are subject to historical change. Now, although it might make a great deal of sense for a profession or any voluntary organization to have its own code of behavior to govern the behavior of its members, as soon as the behavior of such a group becomes, to use Mill's phrase, "other regarding" in the sense that it impinges on the interests and lives of those outside the group, a major problem arises. For those outside the group—in this case, the world of patients and those who pay for health care through insurance premiums or taxes—the mere fact that physicians have agreed on a set of duties does not suffice to justify physicians' behavior based upon those duties. Indeed, for every instance of professional agreement one can raise the question, "Yes, that's what physicians have agreed on, but is it right?" Another way to state this problem is to claim that medical internalism so defined commits the so-called naturalistic

[25] H. Morreim, *Balancing Act: The New Medical Ethics of Medicine's New Economics* (Washington, DC: Georgetown University Press, 1995).

fallacy of attempting to derive an "ought" from an "is." The bottom line here is that codes of professional conduct are not self-justifying. They must be subjected ultimately to moral and political standards of justice, however those might be defined. Many elements of professional codes will no doubt prove consistent with such standards. Even those elements that might initially seem to contradict standards of impartiality and universality, such as physicians' traditional ethic of loyalty to their patients, might ultimately be justified by the fair apportionment of different roles to different social institutions. But other norms of professional behavior—such as physicians' longstanding reluctance to inform patients of their diagnosis, prognosis, and alternatives, or their longstanding and destructive opposition to group practice (a.k.a. "socialism")—will be found wanting by external norms of justice. Historical professionalism, then, proves utterly insufficient as a source of solutions to practical problems in bioethics and health policy.

The Evolutionary Account

We have seen how the evolutionary approach of Miller and Brody represents a distinct advance over Pellegrino's essentialist version of internalism. Whereas the latter's theory yields a set of medical duties *sub specie aeternitatis*, this updated version of internalism embraces history and the gradual evolution of an internal ethic based upon medical goals and duties. Significantly, Miller and Brody also embrace the need to complement internalism with values and norms derived from external sources. They argue, in effect, that the ethic we actually bring to the resolution of practical problems should represent a fusion of internal and external elements. This move will enable their more expansive and eclectic theory to successfully resolve most of the problems that embarrassed all the other versions of medical internalism. Thus, in contrast to both the practical precondition and historical-professional accounts, the evolutionary model opens medical ethics up to the full range of external values and norms and, in so doing, it transcends internalism's chronic failures with regard to both justification and the specification of duties.

Unlike all other variants of internalism, the evolutionary model cannot be criticized for ignoring crucial external values, such as self-determination, or for attempting to base medical ethics on the mere fact of physicians' agreement on a set of duties. The evolutionary account also provides internalism with the requisite resources to effectively delimit the scope and boundaries of various internally developed duties. Here again, the duty to treat provides an apt case in point. Assuming it's true that reflection on the nature and goals of medicine could somehow deliver the conclusion that physicians have a duty to treat contagious patients, neither the essentialist nor the practical precondition accounts could advise physicians on the limits of this duty. Must physicians expose themselves to any and all risks encountered in the course of their practice? Are some risks too great, or is the likelihood of their occurring too certain, to charge physicians with a duty to expose themselves to them? If physicians have a duty to be moderately courageous, do they also have a duty to become martyrs for medicine? Do they have a strict duty to treat SARS and Ebola patients at the start of these epidemics and in the absence of reliable modalities of self-protection? Answers to such important questions will not be found through abstract inquiries into the nature of medicine and its proper ends. Instead, we will have to look to history and culture to determine the levels of risk that have been expected of various professional groups, such as police officers, firefighters, and physicians, at various times and places. Because it is prepared to acknowledge the role of such social expectations bearing on the medical profession, the evolutionary account of internal morality can succeed where the other internalist accounts failed.

Evolutionary internalism's success in overcoming these persistent problems has been purchased, however, at a very high price. I now want to argue that this theory has been able to avoid the traditional pitfalls of internalism by abandoning internalism itself. In other words, its victories on the fronts of specification and justification have been entirely Pyrrhic. This is so for two reasons: (1) evolutionary internalism has given up any claim to being a comprehensive method of bioethical problem solving, and (2) the substantive content of internalism proper has become virtually impossible to identify.

In contrast to all other species of internalism, Miller and Brody's evolutionary account no longer pretends to offer a fully comprehensive morality for physicians and policymakers. Thus, anyone wishing to come to terms with a specific bioethical problem—e.g., PAS—must bring two distinct sets of tools to the task. First, she must deploy an account of the proper goals and duties of medicine and physicians, and then she must supplement this account with values and norms drawn from such external sources as common morality and the common law. From the former she will perhaps derive the notion that physicians have a duty to relieve pain and suffering (although she may also find there is a centuries-old prohibition of killing), while from the latter she may deploy the duty to honor patients' self-determination. Now, although this eclecticism obviously doesn't disqualify Miller and Brody's theory as a serious and potentially helpful moral methodology—any more than the putative incompleteness of virtue ethics or casuistry disqualifies these methods as important guides to the moral life—it does largely signify that these authors are throwing in the towel on a key issue that has divided internalists and externalists: *viz.*, whether an internal morality is sufficient to guide the moral lives of physicians.

Supposing, then, that evolutionary internalism proposes a fusion of internal and external sources of morality en route to a fully rounded and comprehensive method for bioethics. The question, however, remains: What is the distinct contribution of the internalist element to this larger, more holistic method? In what sense, exactly, does their approach remain internalist? If Miller and Brody still wish to insist that internalism can help resolve practical moral problems, we first need to know what exactly constitutes the internalist phase of the method. Their answer to this question seems to be just this: The internal element of any moral analysis is that part concerned with the proper goals and duties involved in the practice of medicine. So, to use the authors' most explicit example, an analysis of PAS can be factored into an internal and external component—the former having to do with relief of intractable pain and suffering, and the latter with citizens' moral rights to self-determination and legal rights to "privacy." But now a problem arises: If Miller and Brody do not view their internalism as a comprehensive method of moral analysis, if they in fact view their ultimate moral norms as the offspring of a fusion of internal and external elements that have slowly evolved and intertwined over time, then the precise determination of what's internal and what's not in any moral analysis will be extremely problematical. This is because what at any given time physicians consider to be the proper goals and duties of medical practice will itself *already* be the product of a dialectical interaction of internal and external social forces. Recall in this connection how the exact contours of the duty to treat have been shaped by social expectations and licensure statutes, and how physicians' notion of the proper scope of confidentiality has been informed by legal expectations and philosophical applications of the harm principle. So what emerges from Miller and Brody's account is a rather formal conception of an internal morality as that aspect of morality having to do with medical goals and duties, a conception whose *actual content* will always be a product of a complex and historically evolving interplay between "internal" and "external." If this suspicion turns out to be correct, then it will be extremely difficult, if not impossible, to assign a reliable content to what's internal about any particular morality. And if this turns out to be the case, then it becomes fairly vacuous to speak of the contributions of an internal morality to the resolution of practical problems in bioethics.

Perhaps the most interesting test case for this interpretation of Miller and Brody's internalism is their handling of PAS.[26] Although they concede that both internal and external sources of moral analysis are available on this question, they

[26] Miller and Brody, "Professional Integrity and Physician-Assisted Death," 8–17.

suggest that an internalist approach can make a valuable and independent contribution to its proper resolution. If they are right about this, then we may have more reason to hope than I've admitted that an internal morality can be a useful tool in resolving bioethical problems. Their story goes like this: Although for centuries the Hippocratic admonition against killing has dominated the discussion of euthanasia, we are now in a position to see that other medical values, such as the duty to ease the suffering of patients in intractable pain and suffering, might finally tip the scales of moral judgment in the other direction. Viewed from this angle, writing a prescription for a lethal dose (or administering it oneself) can be interpreted as an act falling at the far end of a continuum of actions taken to ease the sufferings of humanity. Thus, the case for PAS can be made to rest exclusively on a basis of (internal) medical values and norms. Miller and Brody then proceed to contrast this internalist account of PAS with the typically externalist accounts of liberal political philosophy and the legal right to privacy.[27] Whereas these latter approaches stress the notion of a right to PAS, their internalist account forswears any and all appeals to rights in favor of a purely internalist interpretation of PAS as a last-ditch attempt to relieve patients of interminable and intractable suffering. This, then, is an ideal test case for their theory because they see it as vindicating the notion of a content-full internal morality.

Although I am impressed, as usual, with the erudition and moral perspicacity of Miller and Brody's treatment of this issue, I am not yet persuaded. My skeptical instincts lead me to ask, "Why now? Why, after all these centuries of loyal and heartfelt obedience to the Hippocratic proscription of killing, should physicians suddenly come to see that a permissive case for PAS can actually be constructed out of elements heretofore marginalized within physicians' own internal morality?" My tentative answer to this question is that entirely external challenges to physicians' traditional ethic have altered the usual balance between the perceived value of not killing and the value of alleviating suffering. Importantly, I think that it is not plausible to attribute these challenges and shifting priorities to physicians' sudden realization that the alleviation of suffering can be more important on occasion than worries about killing patients. Rather, I suggest, they are the result of social phenomena, such as the recent decline in the authority of medicine and religion, the rise of consumerism and patients' rights movements, and an increasingly robust conception of patient self-determination. In other words, my hunch is that Miller and Brody's current sense that a proper appreciation of

[27] R. Dworkin, *Life's Dominion: An Argument about Abortion, Euthanasia, and Individual Freedom* (New York: Alfred A. Knopf, 1993). *Vacco, Attorney General of New York v. Quill et al.*, 1997, 117 S. Ct. 2293 (US 1997 *Washington et al. v. Glucksberg et al.*, 1997, 117 S. Ct. 2258 (US 1997).

medical values now permits PAS in rare instances is largely, if not entirely, the product of external societal forces impinging on traditional medical values—forces that motivate physicians (finally) to assign greater weight on occasion to alleviating suffering and less to avoiding killing. And if this hunch is correct, then even Miller and Brody's best case for the practical usefulness of a purely internal morality of medicine turns out to be largely a product of externalist influences. And if this is so, then there isn't much left to the notion of an internal morality of medicine that can help us solve current bioethical problems.

AN ALTERNATIVE FUNCTION FOR AN INTERNAL MORALITY

Instead of viewing internalist medical morality as a guide to the resolution of substantive moral problems, I propose that we attempt to vindicate internalism by assigning it a more modest function. But given my skepticism about whether the Miller and Brody account is really an internalism in any robust sense, a word might be in order about how I construe the internal morality of medicine. Although I do not have a well-worked-out theory on this subject, I do have some very rough ideas about what elements might go into such an ethic:

- Borrowing a page from Fuller's practical precondition approach, we can say that the internal morality of medicine will emphasize those duties (like confidentiality) that help to make the practice of medicine possible.
- This ethic will also incorporate traditional maxims that might not take us very far as guides to solving moral problems, but are nevertheless useful as general rules of thumb—for example, "Do no harm." One corollary of this maxim is that physicians are not supposed to sacrifice the interests of their patients to those of society at large.
- Finally, this ethic will adopt a set of fiduciary responsibilities derived from the role of *professional*. Given the significant disparities of knowledge and power between physicians and their patients, and given patients' resulting vulnerabilities, physicians assume a strict duty to place the welfare of patients ahead of their own financial (or other) interests.

This is just a start, and I'm sure that others could flesh out this list better than I can. Still, it sets us on the right path toward a much more modest account of the internal morality of medicine. The proper function of this morality is not to solve problems but, rather, to give physicians an identity as professionals, rather than as self-interested tradespeople, and a basic education in some key medical virtues (e.g., courage, compassion, truthfulness, etc.) As Pellegrino and Thomasma suggest, this foundation for medical morality is "necessarily antecedent" to whatever position may be taken in specific moral dilemmas.[28] The take-home lesson of this investigation into moral internalism is that it's possible to have an internal morality of a professional practice that is at once meaningful (as a set of preconditions for the practice itself) and yet also completely inadequate (as a guide to the resolution of current practical problems).

Thus, contrary to Robert Veatch's conclusion that an internal morality of medicine is "impossible"—typical Veatchian hyperbole!—we can now see how such a morality is indeed possible (as a general orientation toward the virtues necessary to practice medicine) without being of much, if any, assistance in helping us resolve knotty moral problems in medicine. The key, as with so much else in this life, is to lower one's expectations.[29]

[28] Pellegrino and Thomasma, *For the Patient's Good*, 219.

[29] I would like to thank Robert A. Crouch for his help with the argument and with this chapter

8

One Method to Rule Them All?

REFLECTIVE EQUILIBRIUM IN BIOETHICS

IN THE WORLD of bioethics, the air is abuzz with reflective equilibrium. Reflective equilibrium (henceforth, RE) is a method of doing moral and political philosophy originally developed by the great political philosopher John Rawls.[1] According to Rawls, the project of justifying ethical beliefs ideally involves the attempt to bring our most confident ethical judgments, our ethical principles, and our background social, psychological, and philosophical theories into a state of harmony or equilibrium. Our most confident moral judgments or intuitions (e.g., "Slavery is wrong") provide a touchstone for the adequacy of our principles; any moral principle that justified slavery would be either reformulated or rejected. Meanwhile, principles invested with a great deal of confidence could be used to reject some conflicting intuitions while extending our ability to judge confidently in less familiar moral settings. We thus zip back and forth, nipping an intuitive judgment here, tucking a principle there, building up or reformulating a theory in the background, until all the disparate elements of our moral assessments are brought into a more or less steady state of harmonious equilibrium. According to this view, moral justification must be sought not in secure, incorrigible foundations outside of our processes of moral reflection but, rather, in the coherence of all the flotsam and jetsam of our moral life.

[1] J. Rawls, *A Theory of Justice* (Cambridge, MA: Harvard University Press, 1971/1999).

Although Rawls limited the deployment of RE to the theoretical construction of his social contract theory—i.e., to the design of his "original position" within which to choose principles of justice governing the basic structure (or constitutional essentials) of a liberal state—applied ethicists in many fields have more recently taken up this method as a vehicle for solving practical moral problems in their respective disciplines.[2] Although this more practical deployment of RE might raise eyebrows among those philosophers who view ethical theory and practical ethics as existing on two entirely different planes, it has made perfect sense for the growing number of practical ethicists who regard their work as existing on a continuum with that of theorists in normative ethics. It has, in fact, become something of a commonplace for philosophers straddling the theoretical and practical domains to remark that their modes of thinking and justification are pretty much identical in both areas, even if the role of abstraction is obviously greater in the domain of theory construction.[3] Although there is no doubt much to be said on behalf of this claimed continuity between practical and theoretical ethics, it remains to be seen whether RE, at least in its most expansive contemporary manifestations, can serve the theorist and practical ethicist equally well. As I explain below, I have some doubts on this score.

One of the many attractions of RE as a method in practical ethics has been its ability to appeal to just about every faction in the method wars. It is agreeably flexible, nondogmatic, and nonfoundationalist in claiming that there are no incorrigible elements of morality on which everything else must be grounded and from which all justification flows. It enforces an appealing egalitarianism with regard to all the various elements of our belief systems, including our beliefs about particular cases, moral principles, and background theories. Within the method of RE, there are no privileged beliefs. Every belief is fair game for pruning or grafting in the service of more confidently held beliefs of the same or other kinds. Thus, casuists are happy to hear that intuitive case judgments are crucially important in moral justification; principlists are pleased with the robust role of moral principles; and high-flying philosophers and social theorists are relieved to hear that

---

[2] See, e.g., M. Benjamin, *Philosophy and This Actual World: An Introduction to Practical Philosophical Inquiry* (Totowa, NJ: Rowman & Littlefield, 2002); M. Nussbaum, "Perceptive Equilibrium: Literary Theory and Ethical Theory," *Love's Knowledge: Essays in Philosophy and Literature* (New York: Oxford University Press, 1992); N. Daniels, *Justice and Justification: Reflective Equilibrium in Theory and Practice* (Cambridge: Cambridge University Press, 1996); W. Van der Burg and T. Van Willigenburg, eds., *Reflective Equilibrium: Essays in Honour of Robert Heeger* (Dordrecht: Kluwer Academic Publishers, 1998).

[3] T. Beauchamp, "On Eliminating the Distinction Between Applied Ethics and Ethical Theory," *The Monist* 67 (1984): 514–531; D. Brock, "Public Moral Discourse," in *Society's Choices: Social and Ethical Decision Making in Biomedicine*, ed. R. E. Bulger et al. (Washington, DC: National Academy Press, 1995), 215–240.

there's even a place for background theorizing about the nature of persons and society.

It thus came as no great surprise, then, when Beauchamp and Childress, confronting that unruly mob of rival methodologists gesticulating from the other side of the moat, hoisted the unifying flag of RE, declaring it to be henceforth *the* method of principlism in bioethics.[4] All our methodological differences would henceforth merely be matters of emphasis. We would all just be fellow bozos on Neurath's boat—out at sea, unable to reach dry dock where foundational work could be done, we patch, mend, and stitch our moral bark with the disparate materials at hand.[5] As Mark Kuczewski observed at the time, "Who could ask for anything more?"[6]

Indeed, who could ask for more than this? As a philosopher, however, my job is to make life more difficult for people, so I will proceed to ask some hard questions about the method of RE in practical ethics. I do this not simply to make trouble but, rather, because this method raises some very difficult and complex questions I shall explore here. I do so with some trepidation and even regret, however, because I have previously recommended a modest version of this very method,[7] and I am very hard pressed to identify a better way of justifying our judgments of right and wrong in practical ethics.

I begin, then, with some preliminary remarks about the general features and basic varieties of RE in moral reflection. I shall then consider a couple of preliminary doubts about this method. One claims that the most plausible interpretation of RE is so comprehensive that it risks paralyzing our thinking, while the other claims that this same version of RE is insufficiently determinate in practical contexts and will thus fail to be sufficiently action-guiding. I then proceed to explicate the sense in which RE qualifies as a coherence theory of justification, and I consider several objections to RE that flow from its reliance on the putative connection between coherence and moral justification. I conclude that in its more ambitious formulation, RE amounts at best to a noble but unattainable

[4] T. Beauchamp and J. Childress, *Principles of Biomedical Ethics*, 4th ed. (New York: Oxford University Press, 1994).

[5] "We are like sailors who on the open sea must reconstruct their ship but are never able to start afresh from the bottom. Where a beam is taken away a new one must at once be put there, and for this the rest of the ship is used as support. In this way, by using the old beams and driftwood the ship can be shaped entirely anew, but only by gradual reconstruction." O. Neurath, "Protocol Sentences," in *Logical Positivism*, ed. A. J. Ayer, trans. G. Schick (Chicago: Free Press, 1959), 201.

[6] M. Kuczewski, "Bioethics' Consensus on Method: Who Could Ask for Anything More?," in *Stories and Their Limits: Narrative Approaches to Bioethics*, ed. H. Nelson (New York: Routledge, 1997).

[7] J. D. Arras, "The Owl and the Caduceus: Does Bioethics Need Philosophy?," in *The Nature and Prospect of Bioethics*, ed. F. G. Miller et al. (New York: Humana Press, 2003), 1–42.

regulative ideal, and at worst to a hopelessly cumbersome, interminable, and indeterminate decision procedure. In between these extremes, a pared-down version of RE may offer us a method well designed for slogging our way through the thickets of practical ethics, but without any assurances of ultimate agreement or ethical justification. As we shall see, we may not be able to do any better, but this method offers no grounds for methodological triumphalism.

STANDARD FEATURES OF REFLECTIVE EQUILIBRIUM

Considered Judgments and Principles in RE

In his first paper devoted to a "decision procedure" in ethics, Rawls elaborated an interesting picture of the relationship between moral principles and the intuitive or "considered" judgments out of which they develop.[8] We begin, says Rawls, with a notion of "competent moral judges"—i.e., people who are intelligent, impartial, reasonable, well informed, imaginative, empathetic, and so on. Now, let us assume, first, that these judges are capable of filtering out their less plausible moral judgments. They are on guard against operating under conditions that usually yield bad or untrustworthy decisions—i.e., they are not judging in haste, under a cloud of intense emotions, driven by their own self-interest, and so on. Let us then suppose that these competent judges confront a wide spectrum of moral situations or cases and deliver judgments based not upon some sort of sophisticated theory or set of principles but, rather, assuming there to be such, simply upon their direct, unmediated intuitions of right and wrong. Later on in *A Theory of Justice*, Rawls calls these responses "considered moral judgments"—i.e., those moral judgments in which we have the most confidence.[9] Although Rawls, as always, is loath to cite concrete examples here, the paradigm cases might be examples of free speech, religious liberty, and racial equality. Putting it mildly, a competent moral judge would look unfavorably upon both the goals and the methods of the Spanish Inquisition. Coercing everyone to abandon his or her own vision of the good and the nature of the universe at the altar of Catholic orthodoxy—and to do so by threatening the rack, thumbscrew, or burning pyre—would definitely strike our competent moral judges as being morally out of bounds. So the initial "data" of moral reflection are these intuitive judgments of competent judges directed at various cases. A good

---

[8] J. Rawls, "Outline of a Decision Procedure for Ethics," in *John Rawls: Collected Papers*, ed. S. Freeman (Cambridge, MA: Harvard University Press, 1999), 1–19.

[9] Rawls, *A Theory of Justice*, (1971) 47.

bioethical example of this would be our intuitive negative responses to the infamous Tuskegee syphilis study.[10]

The next step in the method is to develop moral principles that "match," "explicate," "accord with," "fit," or "account for" the body of intuitions amassed by competent moral judges. Thus, a principle of religious freedom might explicate the fact that various competent moral judges would intuitively condemn the torture and burning of heretics and similar behaviors. Rawls likens this process to the inductive scientific method, whereby inquirers assemble a set of observation statements or data points, and then attempt to formulate a principle or mathematical function that best makes sense of them. According to this interpretation of RE, moral principles are descriptive hypotheses advanced to make sense of the set of considered moral judgments of competent judges. Principles "explain" moral judgments if we could deduce exactly the same judgments just from the principles and relevant facts alone, without the benefit of any moral intuitions or sentiments. In short, moral principles are supposed to yield conclusions in particular cases that would match our considered judgments. If our suggested principles mesh perfectly with our considered judgments, then we are in equilibrium; if they don't fit, then we have to amend either our particular moral judgments or our principles, depending upon which element of our moral system merits the most confidence.

In addition to their explanatory function sketched above, moral principles have normative functions within the framework of RE. First, principles that have been forged over time in the crucible of RE can help us recognize and reject mistaken moral judgments; second, Rawls asserts that principles should help us resolve moral perplexities posed by conflicting intuitions in difficult cases. Deploying a set of firmly held principles can assist us in extending the reach of our convictions, even in those situations where we initially lack confidence in our judgments.

A number of questions arise with regard to this initial Rawlsian sketch of RE. First, it is reasonable to ask whether our considered judgments about cases really present themselves in isolation from more "theoretical" considerations in the way that Rawls initially suggested that they might.[11] I suspect, with Brian Barry, that most such intuitive judgments about cases already harbor the germ of some sort of larger, quasi-theoretical or at least principled reflection. For example, our

---

[10] Although utilitarians are fond of pointing out the fallibility of such considered judgments throughout history, their own favored starting points for moral theorizing have been neither especially helpful nor convincing. It's important to note, moreover, that Rawls never said that such judgments were an incorrigible bedrock; to the contrary, he treats such judgments, rightly in my view, as the most plausible (but always ultimately revisable) *starting points* for ethical and political theory. See T. M. Scanlon, "The Aims and Authority of Moral Theory," *Oxford Journal of Legal Studies* 12 (1992): 14.

[11] Rawls, "Outline of a Decision Procedure for Ethics," 1–19.

repulsion at the burning of heretics or at the withholding of proven treatment from syphilitic black sharecroppers is not some sort of brute "datum," but is rather most likely a reaction already suffused with the "quasi-theoretical" judgment that the Inquisition and Tuskegee violated, *inter alia*, important moral norms mandating equality among human beings.[12] Conversely, it is equally problematic to assert that moral principles can be relied upon to yield, exclusively on the basis of the relevant facts, the very same conclusions yielded by confidently uttered case judgments. Just as case judgments are infused with quasi-theoretical elements, so principles, in order to actually reach practical conclusions in concrete circumstances, must be supplemented with all sorts of judgments, intuitions, and comparisons with other morally similar cases. Although we might be able to "derive" or "deduce" correct practical conclusions from principles in clear-cut cases of moral evil like the Tuskegee experiment, we cannot do so in hard cases involving conflicting principles or difficult problems of interpretation—that is, in precisely those cases that provide the grist for most bioethical reasoning.

A second problem with Rawls's initial formulation of RE is his claim that moral principles should be understood as hypotheses developed to explain or match whatever deeply felt intuitions we happen to have.[13] At the least, proponents of RE need to explain how moral intuitions can play the same justificatory role as observation statements in the physical sciences, each one providing its own particular kind of basic "datum" for further theorizing. (I shall say more about this issue later on.) Even some of the most zealous defenders of RE have abandoned this suggested analogy between observation statements in science and considered moral judgments.[14] More plausible recent expositions of RE simply acknowledge the existence of most of our commonsensical moral principles—e.g., keep promises, respect autonomous choices—and then attempt to show what is valuable and important about the norms they articulate and to state the best reasons why it is wrong to violate them.[15] In other words, instead of deploying RE to discover new principles, these theorists harness RE for the more modest but still crucially important task of becoming more reflective about the meaning, functions, and justifications of whatever moral principles we happen to endorse. Sometimes the process of RE will reveal that we have misunderstood the values protected by a principle, and this will have implications for what the principle is now taken

---

[12] B. Barry, *Theories of Justice* (Berkeley: University of California Press, 1989); Arras, "Getting Down to Cases: The Revival of Casuistry in Bioethics," 29–51. (See also chapter 3 this volume.)

[13] Barry, *Theories of Justice*, 263.

[14] N. Daniels, "Wide Reflective Equilibrium and Theory Acceptance in Ethics," *Journal of Philosophy* 76 (1979): 256–282.

[15] Scanlon, "The Aims and Authority of Moral Theory," 1–23.

to sanction. More rarely, this process may reveal that we have simply given up entirely on the reasons behind a principle ("Shield your patients from troubling diagnoses"), and at that point we jettison the principle.

Finally, and most importantly, it is unclear how RE, as explicated so far, has any serious normative bite. At best, such a bouncing back-and-forth between considered judgments and derivative principles will yield a fully rounded inventory of our collected moral intuitions, but the justification for those very intuitions remains unsettled. It is a commonplace that people often feel supremely confident in their most basic moral judgments; but it is unsettling, to say the least, to acknowledge that some of those very judgments have in the past affirmed the naturalness of slavery, the utter necessity of burning heretics at the stake (for their own good!), and the unsuitability of atheists and women for public office. Construed narrowly to encompass only particular judgments and the principles that explain them, RE offers an easy target to critics, who claim that it is hopelessly parochial and conservative.[16] This suspicion of moral intuitions is nicely captured by James Griffin, who observes that "[i]t is especially in ethics that intuitions have risen so far above their epistemological station."[17] In order to meet this challenge, the partisans of RE reach for a distinction between "narrow" and "wide" versions of the method.

Narrow vs. Wide RE

The version of RE that we have considered so far is called "narrow reflective equilibrium" (henceforth, NRE); it can help us identify our most confidently held moral judgments and the principles that best explain them, but it apparently lacks the resources to actually *justify* those intuitions and matching principles. To do that, RE must expand its inventory of moral considerations and widen its scope. Toward this end, Rawls and Norman Daniels have developed an alternative account of RE that they call "wide reflective equilibrium" (henceforth, WRE).[18] In addition to considered judgments and principles, then, WRE encompasses a wide variety of theoretical considerations, including (1) alternative "moral conceptions" (e.g., utilitarianism, perfectionism, Kantian ethics, etc.) and their respective philosophical warrants; (2) theories of moral personhood; (3) theories of procedural justice; (4) theories of moral development; and (5) empirical theories bearing on

[16] R. M. Hare, "Rawls' Theory of Justice," in *Reading Rawls*, ed. N. Daniels (New York: Basic Books, 1975), 82–107; P. Singer, "Sidgwick and Reflective Equilibrium," *Monist* 58 (1974): 490–517; S. Kagan, *Normative Ethics* (Boulder, CO: Westview Press, 1998), 11–16.

[17] J. Griffin, *Value Judgement: Improving our Ethical Beliefs* (Oxford: Clarendon Press, 1996), 5.

[18] J. Rawls, "The Independence of Moral Theory," in *John Rawls: Collected Papers*, ed. S. Freeman (Cambridge, MA: Harvard University Press, 1999), 286–302.

the nature of society and social relations. In spite of the evident shortcomings of our considered moral judgments with regard to the problem of justification, the partisans of WRE contend that we have no other choice but to embrace them. Crucially, however, they contend that these judgments are only "provisional fixed points" that must be critically scrutinized from every possible angle. So the above theoretical considerations are imported into RE in order to provide just that kind of critical scrutiny. Importantly, Daniels insists that these background theories are not dependent upon our moral intuitions in the same way that our principles are, so they can, he argues, be counted on to provide independent justification for the deliverances of RE.[19]

WRE thus provides us with a highly complex and multilayered approach to moral justification. Considered judgments, principles, and background theoretical considerations incorporate as many moral and empirical beliefs as possible, and allow us to test each of these elements or strata against all the others. Crucially, as mentioned before, no single element or stratum of this dynamic mix of beliefs is considered to be foundational or immune to criticism. We shuttle back and forth from judgments, to principles, to theories, and back again—always adjusting, pruning, and seeking coherence among the widest possible set of relevant beliefs. WRE is thus both a coherentist and a nonfoundationalist approach to moral justification.

WRE and Methods of Bioethics

It's time to pause in our exposition and draw out some important initial implications of WRE for our methodological debates in bioethics. Remember, Beauchamp and Childress have explicitly embraced WRE as the official methodology of principlism.[20] They write, "[W]e have agreed with Rawls that justification is 'a matter of the mutual support of many considerations, of everything fitting together into one coherent whole.'"[21] One important question is whether this move is consistent with their longstanding advocacy of principlism as a distinct methodology. As I understand it, principlism has traditionally emphasized the centrality of moral principles in bioethical reflection. As the very title of their often-revised book implies, for Beauchamp and Childress bioethical reasoning is ultimately about the identification, justification, specification, weighing, and balancing of moral

[19] Daniels, "Wide Reflective Equilibrium and Theory Acceptance in Ethics," 256–282; Daniels, *Justice and Justification*.

[20] See chapter 1 this volume.

[21] Beauchamp and Childress, *Principles of Biomedical Ethics*, 4th ed. (1994), 23.

principles against one another in the context of specific cases. As Beauchamp once remarked to me, principles provide the "spine of ethical analysis."[22]

Now, it may well have been a commendable move for these distinguished partisans of principlism to endorse WRE and thereby usher in the peaceable methodological kingdom, but it is difficult to comprehend how they could do so while still giving pride of place to principles in moral analysis. We must recall in this connection that WRE doesn't play favorites with regard to the various *kinds* of beliefs, whether they are about cases, principles, or background theories. No single stratum or cluster of moral considerations is privileged. What matters, as we go about our business of adjusting, pruning, and rendering our beliefs (at all levels) coherent, is our confidence in them and our degree of commitment to them, rather than the objects of belief or the level of their concreteness.[23] Thus, our beliefs about principles are always subject to revision at the bidding of more confidently held beliefs about particular case judgments or background theories of the person, due process, or society. If this is the case, then principlism seems to have effectively placated and silenced its critics at the cost of its own methodological distinctiveness. Were brevity and aesthetics not factors to consider, the title of their next edition should more properly read: *Considered Case Judgments, Principles, and Background Theories in Bioethics: How They Can All Be Brought into Coherence within the Ambit of Wide Reflective Equilibrium.* Principles no longer deserve top, let alone exclusive, billing.

What's true for principlism is also true for each of the other rival methodologies in bioethics. Just to take one additional example, casuistry can also be taken up into the larger synthesis of WRE, but only at the cost of sacrificing its distinctiveness. According to Albert Jonsen and Stephen Toulmin, the prime movers of casuistry as a rival method to principlism, the primary locus of moral justification and certitude is the paradigm case.[24] Modeling their vision of ethics on the common law, these authors assert that moral knowledge results from the slow accretion of cases and our efforts to distill principles out of them. According to Toulmin, moral principles are just so many afterthoughts trailing behind our intuitive responses to paradigm cases. If we are looking for normativity, we will find it, asserts Toulmin, in the paradigm case—not in principles distilled post doc, and certainly not in abstract ethical theories.[25] Thus, just as principlism gave pride of

[22] Personal communication.

[23] Scanlon, "The Aims and Authority of Moral Theory," 14; M. De Paul, *Balance and Refinement: Beyond Coherence Methods of Moral Inquiry* (London: Routledge, 1993), 157.

[24] A. R. Jonsen and S. Toulmin, *The Abuse of Casuistry: A History of Moral Reasoning* (Berkeley: University of California Press, 1988). (See chapter 3 this volume.)

[25] S. Toulmin, "The Tyranny of Principles," *Hastings Center Report* 11 (1981): 31–39.

place to moral principles (the "spine" of ethical inquiry), casuistry locates the 'real action' in ethical reflection at the level of the paradigm case. Insofar as both of these rival methodologies favor one level of moral belief over others, they both must be disabused of such favoritism before being allowed to play their respective roles in our search for wide reflective equilibrium.

The take-home message here is that if WRE is taken to be the preferred method in moral philosophy and bioethics, then both principlism and casuistry as traditionally understood must be rejected as partial and incomplete moments in a grander, all-encompassing methodological synthesis. As Hegel would put it, both methods are *aufgehoben*—that is, they are shorn of whatever is partial, fragmentary or one-sided about them, while their remaining valuable features are preserved and elevated within a more comprehensive synthesis.

Again, who could ask for anything more? The beauty of WRE is that it makes room for *all* beliefs that might potentially contribute to a richer synthesis. As Michael De Paul notes, WRE is the only fully *rational* method of moral inquiry.[26] Whatever its faults or limitations might be, WRE is uniquely capable of leading the moral inquirer to accept a rational system of beliefs through a set of rational steps. Alternatives to WRE cannot make this claim. This judgment is endorsed by T. M. Scanlon, who contends, not to put too fine a point on it, that "[RE] is the only defensible method: apparent alternatives to it are illusory."[27]

One example of an illusory method might be R. M. Hare's project of grounding ethics on a foundation of meta-ethical propositions bearing on the meaning of moral terms like "good" and "right."[28] According to Hare and other utilitarians, moral intuitions and considered moral judgments are far too untrustworthy to help guide moral reflection in a process like RE. ("Garbage in, garbage out.") He therefore urges us to submit all our moral beliefs, including those suspect intuitions about cases, before the tribunal of epistemic principles and background theories. De Paul asserts that Hare's proposed method is irrational insofar as it would require us to subordinate or jettison our strongly held moral beliefs even if we think, on due reflection, that they are more likely to be true than any theory of moral language that Hare or others might concoct. This, De Paul concludes, cannot be a rational move.[29] (If, on the other hand, the inquirer really does believe that epistemological background theories are more credible than considered moral judgments, then this is simply an example of WRE, not an alternative to

[26] De Paul, *Balance and Refinement*, 107 ff.

[27] T. Scanlon, "Rawls on Justification," in *The Cambridge Companion to Rawls*, ed. S. Freeman (Cambridge: Cambridge University Press, 2003), 149.

[28] R. M. Hare, *Freedom and Reason* (Oxford: Oxford University Press, 1963).

[29] De Paul, *Balance and Refinement*, 124.

it.) The same thing could be said about a method like casuistry that submits background theories and moral principles to the tribunal of paradigm cases. Even if someone were suddenly to come to believe that a moral or political theory (e.g., Marxism) were more likely to be true than any other item in their inventory of beliefs, the casuist might require her to give up her theory if it conflicted with her original moral intuitions about paradigm cases, *even if the born-again Marxist now views those intuitions* (e.g., relating to private property) *to be the products of false consciousness.*

The intuitive attractiveness of WRE, then, rests upon its inclusiveness. If you don't like the way the process of RE is going, if you think that it's leaving out some crucial pieces of the moral picture—such as a different moral outlook or a background theory of social stability—then WRE simply asks you to toss it into the mix alongside all our other beliefs. In this sense, RE has definite colonizing tendencies, but who could ask for a more accommodating method of moral reflection?

PRELIMINARY DOUBTS ABOUT WIDE REFLECTIVE EQUILIBRIUM

Notwithstanding the inclusiveness and intuitive attractiveness of WRE, there are difficulties and objections that must be squarely confronted. Although the most philosophically interesting and important challenges to WRE may relate to its embrace of coherence as the engine of moral justification, I shall begin with worries focused on the scope and action-guiding potential of this method.

WRE Is Too Comprehensive

Although the inclusiveness of WRE initially strikes us as a major advantage over foundationalist theories, it is also a source of pragmatic concerns about the method's practicability. Consider the length and breadth of WRE's welcome mat for the ingredients of moral reflection. Judgments about cases, moral principles, competing moral outlooks (i.e., moral theories), the accompanying philosophical arguments for those rival outlooks, theories of the role of morality in society, theories of moral personhood, notions of procedural justice, general social theories, and theories of moral development all have a role to play in the working out of RE. If we wish to know whether any particular proposition is (completely) morally justified, we have to subject it to the competing pushes and pulls of this entire network of beliefs.

The daunting nature of such a mission comes to light when we consider just one element of this overall process of justification—namely, those competing moral conceptions and their accompanying philosophical justifications. Suppose we wish to ascertain whether our views on cloning are morally justified. The method of WRE would demand, *inter alia*, that we at some point consider the rival claims of all the live options in moral theory—e.g., utilitarianism, Kantian theories of autonomy, Thomistic perfectionism, feminism, Aristotelian virtue theory, the capability theories of Martha Nussbaum and A. K. Sen, et al.—assess their competing arguments, and embrace the one moral conception that best coheres with the rest of our moral intuitions and background theories.

Such an agenda, of course, could well constitute the life's work of a professor of moral philosophy, but it is not all that would be required. We would then have to perform similar work on competing theories of the person, of social organization, and of the role of morality in society. Once all this work (and more) was done, we would need to see how all our disparate beliefs and theories fit together, making sure to nip and tuck those that conflicted with those beliefs and theories in which we had the greatest confidence. In contrast with casuistry, which views justification as a relatively simpler and more straightforward matter of bringing our judgments within the gravitational pull of competing paradigm cases, this picture of justification in WRE is daunting in the extreme. It truly seems like a job not for ordinary mortals but, rather, for Ronald Dworkin's legendary but fictional judge, Hercules.[30]

This problem of over-inclusiveness need not necessarily be a fatal problem for the moral theorist. Rawls, for example, concedes in *A Theory of Justice* (henceforth, TJ) that "it is doubtful whether one can ever reach this state,"[31] a position he later describes as "a point at infinity we can never reach."[32] Rawls consoles himself, however, with the thought that the theorist can at least canvass some of the most salient options in moral theory, if not all such options,[33] and still regard WRE as a *regulative ideal* toward which the theorist should strive.

It is less clear, however, whether the practical ethicist has this same luxury. Once we transcend narrow RE to encompass standard moral theories and their philosophical justifications—not to mention all the other background moral, political,

---

[30] Hercules is portrayed by Dworkin as an idealized omniscient judge who decides hard cases by forging legal principles that best "fit" all the legal precedents, best mesh with our legal history and institutions, and are most compellingly justified by our best moral/political theories of justice and equality. Dworkin realizes that fallible human judges cannot conceivably work their way through all these steps, but he asserts that this would be the ideal process of legal justification. See R. Dworkin, "Hard Cases," *Taking Rights Seriously* (Cambridge, MA: Harvard University Press, 1977), 81–130.

[31] Rawls, *A Theory of Justice* (1971) 49, (1999) 43.

[32] J. Rawls, *Political Liberalism* (New York: Columbia University Press, 2005), 385.

[33] As he does in *A Theory of Justice*, where he works out detailed critiques of both utilitarianism and perfectionism vis-à-vis his own preferred theory of justice as fairness.

and empirical theories—the ordinary working-stiff bioethicist is likely to find full-blown WRE to be a hopelessly cumbersome method of moral justification. If he is to make any progress at all, he will no doubt have to bracket many beliefs and theories that would normally play integral roles in an ideal process of RE. Indeed, it would not be surprising if *Reflective Equilibrium for Working Bioethicists, Version 2.0* were to bear a striking resemblance to narrow RE in many (but obviously not all) cases.

Bioethicists committed to the method of RE might not, however, view this as a fatal objection. Failure to reach a perpetually receding regulative ideal like WRE is to be expected, they might happily concede, while still contending that the wider our ambit of RE, the more justified our moral judgments will be. Justification, then, will be a matter of degree, with more grist channeled through RE generating a higher degree of confidence in our moral judgments, even if we'll never achieve complete justification that remains stable over time (i.e., in equilibrium).

Another factor potentially mitigating the problem of overwhelming comprehensiveness bears on the complexity of the context in which moral problems are encountered.[34] Many cases might require only the limited resources provided by NRE—e.g., the proper interpretation of the informed consent requirement in the context of a prosperous country with rigorous regulative oversight of biomedical research—while other cases, such as the problem of post-trial benefits in international drug trials, might require a searching examination of competing theories of global justice and human development. Partisans of RE in bioethics, then, might be at least partially successful in attenuating the problem of comprehensiveness by borrowing a page from J. S. Mill, who responded to similar criticisms of utilitarianism by emphasizing the availability of well-understood social rules of good behavior that can almost always relieve us of the burdens of painstakingly calculating all the possible consequences flowing from any given act or policy.[35] There is, however, a cost to this kind of response: if well understood social rules bequeathed by history are usually sufficient to get us through moral problems, who needs a special methodological technique like RE?

[34] Thanks to Tal Brewer, George Klosko, and Norman Daniels for these rejoinders to my initially harsher criticisms of WRE (personal communications).

[35] See J. S. Mill, "Utilitarianism," ch. 2, where he adds this delightful explanation, one of my all-time favorites in the history of philosophy: "Any ethical standard whatever can easily be 'shown' to work badly if we suppose universal idiocy to be conjoined with it! But on any hypothesis short of that, mankind must by this time have acquired positive beliefs as to the effects of some actions on their happiness; and the beliefs that have thus come down to us from the experience of mankind are the rules of morality for the people in general—and for the philosopher until he succeeds in finding something better."

WRE Is Too Indeterminate

A correlative problem concerns a disconcerting lack of precise guidance in coming to terms with all those competing moral outlooks and their corresponding supportive arguments. Exactly how is the process of analysis and comparison supposed to proceed? Rawls and Daniels say precious little about this. Even Rawls's attempt in *Theory of Justice* to vindicate his famous two principles of justice against the claims of various versions of utilitarianism and perfectionism has run into a barrage of cogent criticisms. The same worry obviously haunts the project of choosing among rival social theories or theories of the person. What criteria should we use to select one such theory over others? How exactly should the reasoning go? The problem here is that this openness to all rational conceptions of justice and their accompanying justifications threatens to purchase exemplary openness and flexibility at the cost of vacuity as a method that is supposed to direct our thinking on practical issues. As Scanlon observes, a conception of RE this wide might well devolve into the truism that the best method requires the careful rational assessment of all the relevant philosophical arguments bearing on a subject and assessing them on their merits.[36] Although such a daunting task might ultimately be necessary for complete and total justification at that ever-receding vanishing point, it can hardly be described as a *method* for proceeding in practical ethics.

Here again, WRE appears to be more a rather massive effort of hand waiving than a precise road map to moral justification.[37] Given the inherent vagueness in the charge to review all these various objects of belief, to vindicate some but not others, and to bring all the remaining beliefs into the broadest possible circle of coherence, it appears highly unlikely that WRE will eventually yield what method promises—*viz.*, definite action-guiding results.

The combined effect of these two related criticisms of WRE—i.e., that this method is both too comprehensive and too indeterminate—is to suggest a distinction between a theoretically ideal method of justification and a more rough-and-ready decision procedure that might helpfully guide our thinking in practical contexts.[38] WRE might well serve as a regulative ideal of moral justification for

[36] Scanlon, "Rawls on Justification," 151. Although Scanlon largely agrees that this is a big problem for Rawls, he insists that WRE isn't *completely* vacuous since it does exclude some potential sources of justification, such as various proposed foundationalist sources that would allegedly provide moral justification from outside the ambit of RE or, conversely, would exclude moral intuitions as bearing no weight at all.

[37] J. Raz, "The Claims of Reflective Equilibrium," *Inquiry* 25 (1982): 307–330.

[38] Alex London has cogently developed this theme in a series of articles on method in ethics. Rather than viewing the various proposed methods of bioethics as routes to justified true beliefs, he see them as helpful procedures for ensuring that non-ideal agents deliberating under real-world circumstances have the

theorists, especially if we were given more information about how the various moral conceptions and background theories should be evaluated and compared; but it is hard to imagine a more cumbersome or less action-guiding program for practical moral decision making. The omniscient but unfortunately fictional judge, Hercules, might be able to manage all those justificatory hoops, but ordinary mortals will have to settle for much less. As we've noted earlier, however, once we give up the expectation that justification must be an all-or-nothing affair, having to settle for less, getting whatever justification we can eke out, might be more a limitation built into the human condition than a disqualifying feature of a particular moral method.

WIDE REFLEXIVE EQUILIBRIUM AND THE LIMITS OF COHERENCE

As we have seen, WRE's rejection of foundationalism in ethics—the view that a certain favored set of beliefs, such as meta-ethical propositions, human nature, paradigm cases, moral theory, certain key intuitions, or the Bible—constitutes the incorrigible bedrock of moral reflection from which all other beliefs must flow. Within foundationalist moral systems, beliefs are justified by being "derived from" or "based upon" those more fundamental or foundational beliefs. Within WRE, by contrast, beliefs are justified—i.e., they acquire the greatest measure or warrant or support—by being brought into coherence with the widest possible set of other beliefs we hold. As Rawls puts it, the justification of moral principles "is a matter of the mutual support of many considerations, of everything fitting together into one coherent view."[39] RE is, thus, a particular version of the "coherence theory" of justification, which has applications not just in ethics but also in the theory of knowledge generally.[40] While much of the attraction of WRE derives from its repudiation of foundationalism, its embrace of coherence theory is viewed by some as deeply problematic. In this section I shall try to sketch, albeit all too briefly, the most salient of these doubts and worries, and assess their significance for the viability of WRE as a bioethical method.

---

best chance to decide an issue on the merits. See A. J. London, "Amenable to Reason: Aristotle's Rhetoric and the Moral Psychology of Practical Ethics," *Kennedy Institute of Ethics Journal* 10 (2000): 287–305.

[39] Rawls, *A Theory of Justice* (1971) 21, (1999) 19.

[40] J. L. Pollock, *Contemporary Theories of Knowledge* (Totowa, NJ: Rowman & Littlefield, 1986). Samuel Freeman, a faithful interpreter of the Rawlsian *oeuvre*, insists however that for Rawls, the Socratic and practical nature of the subject matter of ethics was particularly appropriate for a coherence theory of justification, and that he never intended his embrace of coherence in moral matters to extend to the broader frontiers of epistemology and science. See S. Freeman, *Rawls* (New York: Routledge, 2007), 41.

What Kind of Coherence Justifies?

If beliefs are justified by being brought into coherence with other beliefs, we first have to determine exactly what we mean by "coherence." There are several different interpretations of coherence, and it matters which one we select because they have very different implications for the project of moral justification. We might, for example, interpret coherence to mean the consistency of each element in the overall belief system, including both moral and empirical beliefs, vis-à-vis all the other elements. Although this gloss on coherence would no doubt be somewhat helpful, allowing us to ferret out contradictions among our various beliefs, it's hard to see how mere consistency with other beliefs can serve to justify any particular belief.

A more robust notion of coherence can be found in commentaries on the natural sciences, where the justificatory power of coherence is bolstered by two special features. First, coherence in the natural sciences is buttressed by observation statements that provide the data for theory building. True, even in the natural sciences some observations might be ignored if they happen to conflict with an especially powerful theory, so science, like RE, takes a holistic approach to justification. Still, most of us think that the observation statements in physics are on a much firmer epistemological footing than the considered moral judgments of various people, especially when we note that these sources of considered judgments may reflect major and irreconcilable cultural, religious, and class differences. Second, the kind of coherence available in science offers not just mutually consistent beliefs but also mutually supporting beliefs or "credibility transfers" that can reliably raise the level of the whole set of beliefs.[41] Assuming that the same natural world is the subject matter of all the sciences, beliefs developed in one zone of inquiry will have the effect of supporting similar beliefs developed in others. The upshot of this cross-cutting system of mutual support among scientific beliefs is that coherence in science exhibits a certain "boot strapping" effect that appears to be lacking in the moral domain.

We appear, then, to confront a dilemma: if we construe coherence weakly to signify consistency with our other moral beliefs and known facts, then just about any live option in moral philosophy will pass the test of coherence, and we won't have a test that will allow us to choose between such live options. Alternatively, if we construe coherence to entail the sort of boot strapping and credibility transfers that we encounter in scientific webs of belief, then we would indeed have a conception of coherence with legs—one that offered real justificatory power. Unfortunately,

[41] Griffin, *Value Judgement*, 16.

it is highly doubtful that the sort of relationships connecting our considered judgments, moral principles, and background theories can rise to this level. Certainly, various relationships can be discerned among these disparate elements of RE; but it is highly uncertain, to say the least, whether they can bestow the sort of heightened credibility on display in mutually supportive scientific beliefs.

Can Coherence Teach Us What and How to Prune?

According to Daniels, the method of WRE is an attempt to generate coherence in an ordered triple of sets of beliefs encompassing (a) considered moral judgments, (b) a set of moral principles, and (c) the set of relevant background theories.[42] We thus attempt to bring our beliefs at one distinct level (e.g., considered judgments) into harmony with our beliefs at the other levels (e.g., moral principles or background theories). If we encounter a disparity between any two of these disparate elements of our moral system, then RE calls for a movement to and fro, pruning a bit here, tucking a bit there, until the discrepancies are ironed out and harmony reigns among our beliefs.

But now a question arises: Assuming the appearance of a conflict between two different elements of our moral system—e.g., between a considered judgment and a given moral principle—*which one* should be pruned? As D. W. Haslett observes, coherence considerations by themselves are not enough to enable us to decide between any two conflicting elements within the ambit of RE.[43] While coherence can indeed direct us to prune either the judgment or the principle, it cannot tell us *which one* should be sacrificed in its name. Given any two sets of considered judgments and matching principles, there could, then, be *innumerable* different WREs corresponding to different (arbitrary) choices for nipping and tucking.

Haslett's objection gives us an additional reason to demand more from coherence than mere consistency. If that is all coherence means, then Haslett has indeed delivered a crushing blow to the claims of RE. The defenders of RE can respond, however, that coherence encompasses not just the bare-bones notion of consistency but also such important relations as providing the "best fit" or "strongest mutual support." While this gloss on coherence could be helpful in pointing our pruning shears in the right direction, it generates problems of its own. As Bo Petersson points out, the larger the network of intersecting elements in RE, and the more disparate their contents and varieties of interdependence, the more

[42] Daniels, "Wide Reflective Equilibrium and Theory Acceptance in Ethics," 258.

[43] D. W. Haslett, "What Is Wrong with Reflective Equilibria?" *Philosophical Quarterly* 37 (1987): 310.

difficult it will be to assign a definite meaning to such notions as "maximal coherence" and "strongest mutual support."[44]

In WRE we have a vast network of considered judgments, moral principles, and both moral and empirical background theories. The way in which empirical background theories may support various moral theories, for example, may differ significantly from the way in which considered judgments support moral principles. How are we to determine the relevance and strength of these different kinds of support in coming to an all-things-considered judgment about "maximal coherence"? For this purpose, should the number of supportive relations count for more than their "strength"? Since WRE contains such a huge mix of disparate elements and differing kinds of supporting relationships—e.g., exhibiting logical entailment, inductive support, or mere consistency—the notion of degrees of coherence implied by this alternative approach turns out to be yet another exercise in hand waving. If we cannot clearly ascertain which particular arrangement of all these disparate elements is the "most coherent," then the method of WRE, again in its more ambitious incarnations, will fail to provide a useful guide to either theory construction or practical ethics.[45]

Will the Coherence Approach Yield Interpersonal Convergence?

It's hard to think of a better method than RE to help each of us organize, systematize, and smooth out inconsistencies within our respective inventories of moral beliefs. Indeed, most discussions of RE stipulate that it is a method to be used by each individual inquirer to achieve moral justification of his or her own beliefs. What happens, however, when we abandon this first-person perspective and consider the reflective equilibria of other people in society? Will the widespread use of WRE tend to foster convergence of belief with regard to individual cases, moral principles, and background theories? Or, alternatively, will WRE be more likely to provide evidence of moral pluralism?

This is an important question because it goes to the heart of the whole rationale for employing a *method* of moral reasoning in the first place. In most fields of inquiry, the promise of method, as opposed to mere ad hoc, episodic ruminations,

[44] B. Petersson, "Wide Reflective Equilibrium and the Justification of Moral Theory," in *Reflective Equilibrium: Essays in Honour of Robert Heeger*, ed. Van der Burg and Van Willigenburg (Dordrecht: Kluwer Academic Publishers, 1998), 130–133.

[45] For an argument in favor of this pessimistic conclusion, see D. Bonevac, "Reflection Without Equilibrium," *Journal of Philosophy* 101 (2004): 363–388. Given the complexity of all the disparate elements that must be processed through RE, and given the highly disparate maneuvers we might make in adjusting and pruning, Bonevic goes so far as to claim that we have no reason to think, even in theory, that the process of RE will eventually terminate in a fixed point.

is that it will reliably guide us to discover "correct" results. As Scanlon observes in the context of a discussion of "considered judgments" as the starting point for theory construction, the whole idea of method would have us focus on moral principles that explain and render coherent our most confident judgments that are most likely to capture the truth of moral matters, if anything can.[46]

One indicator of intersubjective reliability is the ability of a method to produce a confluence of opinion or belief among those who use it. Although mere consensus is obviously no guarantee of moral truth—witness the Third Reich, which achieved consensus on utterly barbaric ends—it's hard to imagine a method of thought being reliable in the required sense unless it can produce convergence of belief among those who deploy it. It is thus an important question whether WRE can be counted on to deliver this sort of convergence with regard to moral beliefs.

Interestingly, Rawls never committed himself on this question,[47] and apparently for good reason. A moment's reflection on the matter should make it rather painfully obvious that in a liberal, pluralistic, democratic society, different groups of people will enter WRE with very different considered moral judgments. Although such judgments are not sacrosanct and incorrigible within WRE—they do not function as brute *data*—they do exert a significant influence on the moral principles we eventually embrace and the sorts of background theories we are willing to accept. Thus, we should expect fundamentalist Christians from the midwestern United States to start with dramatically different considered judgments from those of Jewish leftists living on the Upper West Side of Manhattan; and we should, moreover, expect both these types to differ fundamentally with the considered moral judgments of Shi'ite clerics in Bagdad or Shining Path Marxist revolutionaries in Peru. It is reasonable to expect, then, that the members of all four of these demographics will end up in very different *moral* places once they have gone through the required motions of WRE in their own heads. True, their considered judgments will not all be mutually exclusive; they will share a good deal with regard to nearly universal values bearing on truthfulness, respect for property (except those Marxists and anarchists who equate property with theft!), and the avoidance of gratuitous cruelty. They will, nevertheless, tend to differ on such key bioethical issues as the fair distribution of health care, the permissibility of artificial reproductive technologies, and the enhancement of human nature through biomedical technology.

In response to the charge of relativism, Scanlon notes that different results stemming from different practitioners of RE doesn't necessarily show that the

---

[46] Scanlon, "Rawls on Justification," 144–45.

[47] Rawls, *A Theory of Justice*, (1971) 50, (1999) 44.

method is prone to routinely generating incompatible principles. In any given case purporting to demonstrate a fundamental disparity between different sets of moral principles, Rawls would have the respective equilibrators interrogate the reasons behind the divergence and the soundness of all the steps taken throughout the exercise of RE. Surely, this kind of critical inventory of the processes through which we reach our respective equilibria would be a valuable exercise, providing us all with valuable insights into our own thinking and that of others, but it's highly unlikely to successfully deflect the charge of relativism. At best, this move would seem to function more as a temporizing tactic for Scanlon rather than an actual solution to the problem.

Why this should be so becomes especially clear when we take seriously two interrelated themes in Rawls's later work: *viz.*, the "burdens of judgment" and "reasonable pluralism."[48] Owing to the vagaries of our respective moral situations—including our geographic, socioeconomic and cultural location, our upbringing, the sheer complexity and difficulty of many moral problems, our finite and fallible powers of judgment, and our philosophical and religious differences about the nature of the good life—Rawls came to doubt the ability of citizens of a well-ordered liberal state to agree on a single philosophical rationale for the principles of justice that would bind them all together in one like-minded polity. They could ultimately each endorse the same set of overarching principles to govern their civic relationships in an "overlapping consensus," but they would each have to discover resources within their own comprehensive conceptions of the good in order to do so. In other words, given human beings as we find them, and given a liberal state that provides them with moral and political freedom, people will inevitably end up embracing a variety of comprehensive views of the meaning of life. Such differences are not to be denied, and uniformity should not be imposed via coercion. This state of affairs is what Rawls calls "reasonable pluralism," a defining characteristic of the liberal state in our time.

The relevance of this bit of Rawls exegesis is that, in his later period, Rawls views RE as operating between this variety of comprehensive views and his principles of justice. Those principles are pretty much the same as those worked out in Rawls's earlier theory of justice as fairness, but they now lack a univocal philosophical foundation in a Kantian theory of autonomy. Those principles are thus "freestanding," lacking a common philosophical grounding, but can still provide a unifying normative lattice for the liberal state. Most important for our purposes here, however, is that these principles are quite abstract and apply only to the

[48] Rawls, *Political Liberalism*.

basic structure (or constitutional essentials) of the liberal state. The key point is that these principles, reached through RE among the partisans of differing conceptions of the good, will be radically underdetermined with regard to most, if not all, of the major bioethical debates of our time.

Those debates will have to engage the comprehensive moral views of the participants, which will often lead to fundamental disagreements with regard to the morality of actions and policies. And this brings us back to the problem of relativism with regard to these substantive bioethical issues. Different people, operating according to different reasonable conceptions of the good, will likely start the process of RE with different considered judgments, and will most likely end up with different principles to explain and justify them. And this will, in turn, lead to different conclusions on many practical moral and political questions.

In sum, liberal societies characterized by reasonable pluralism will predictably exhibit a variety of different equilibria, hence the method of RE is highly unlikely to produce the sort of convergence we initially sought in a method of moral inquiry for bioethics. There may well be no other method of moral inquiry that could possibly achieve this kind of convergence and reliability; the moral world may simply be too fragmented for that. Even Rawls's staunchest defenders have admitted that WRE cannot achieve intersubjective consensus within the context of pluralistic societies, at least with regard to those controversies that implicate divergent visions of the good beyond the "overlapping consensus" on basic freestanding principles of justice. As Daniels now puts it, it was a "philosopher's dream" to imagine that the kind of philosophical reflection driving WRE could bring about convergence within pluralistic societies,[49] and he has therefore turned to other methods of justifying practical moral solutions within such societies, such as the political procedures of "deliberative democracy."[50] Along with Rawls, Daniels still believes that RE can generate an overlapping consensus on the core principles governing the basic structure of a liberal democratic society, but he now contends that we must seek the resolution of controversies arising beyond the basic structure, where most bioethical problems lurk, in a *political process* bounded by the norms of basic justice.

Tal Brewer has suggested to me that this turn toward a fair political process to adjudicate our often intractable moral disagreements on matters implicating our respective visions of the good need not be viewed as an abandonment of (or radical break with) RE, as Daniels implies. True to the colonizing spirit of RE, we could

---

[49] Daniels, *Justice and Justification*, 144–175.

[50] N. Daniels and J. E. Sabin, *Setting Limits Fairly: Can We Learn to Share Medical Resources?* (New York: Oxford University Press, 2002).

add to our inventory of beliefs the notion that political decisions made within a liberal social order should be regarded as *legitimate* by those subject to them. This demand for legitimacy could then quite naturally lead Rawls and us to embrace the sort of process Daniels has advocated under the heading of "accountability for reasonableness," a process that demands publicity with regard to decisions and their accompanying rationales, the adducing of rationales that all citizens can regard as "relevant," and procedures for amending decisions in light of challenges to them. Although this is a plausible extension of Rawls's method of RE, and although it may well generate legitimacy in decision making on many bioethical policy matters, it will clearly not generate convergence on the solutions reached.

Still, it may be unfair to harp on the inability of Rawlsian RE to achieve consensus. Notwithstanding Scanlon's claim, mentioned above, that one of the key objectives of any method of ethics should be to produce convergence on true or correct beliefs, we might have to face up to the possibility that, given the pluralism inherent in contemporary liberal societies, no proffered moral methodology is capable of achieving consensus. If this should end up being our considered judgment, then the very point and purpose of a concern for moral methodology will need further refinement.

Local vs. Global Coherence?

According to the partisans of WRE, we should seek coherence among the *widest possible* set of moral and non-moral beliefs. But how far and wide can we expect this set to extend into the entire domain of morality? What, in other words, is possible? On one view, morality can be properly regarded as a *unified system* of beliefs, principles, and theories. Any inconsistencies between disparate regions of the "moral world" should, from this angle, be ultimately remediable. On this reading, the sort of coherence we seek in moral reflection is ultimately *global*. This is a very ambitious thesis. Just how ambitious it is can be gauged by reflecting for a moment on the sort of phenomenon morality is. For those of us who don't believe that morality is given to us by God, helpfully inscribed on extremely durable and legible stone tablets, or by nature in such a way that the solutions to our disputes in practical ethics can be "read off" the nature of humans and society, morality will present itself to us as a historically and culturally conditioned achievement. Different considered judgments and moral principles developed in different historical settings exist side by side in contemporary cosmopolitan societies, and these differences may well prevent morality from being viewed as a coherent whole. If the domain of law can be aptly characterized by one of our most distinguished theorists as a "higgledy-piggledy assemblage of the remains of contradictory past political ambitions and beliefs,"[51] then, *a fortiori*, the same could be said of morality.[52]

This does not mean that achieving coherence isn't a desirable thing, for it clearly is. It does mean, however, that the sort of coherence that we can realistically seek among our moral beliefs is most likely local rather than global. As Raz nicely puts it, we should expect to find "pockets of coherence" rather than vast unified expanses of it.[53] Thus, the principles developed to govern the physician–patient relationship may be inadequate or counterproductive in other domains of the moral life, such as public health, environmental ethics, or assessing our obligations to the distant needy in other lands.[54]

What's So Great About Coherence?

I wrap up this excursion into coherence theory and RE with some remarks about the epistemological value of coherence. This topic runs very deep, so I can only scratch the surface here. This is the problem: Once we abandon foundationalist approaches to justification in ethics, we are apparently left with coherence as the only remaining source of justifiability. Yet coherence, on the face of it, may seem an unlikely candidate for this role.

The first thing to notice is that coherence is obviously not by itself a compelling virtue of moral outlooks. It's quite possible for someone to inhabit a seamlessly unified moral worldview and yet fail to be justified in her moral judgments.[55] Consider the case of Rush, a hypothetical teenager of middling intellectual gifts, subacute moral perception, and an embarrassingly bad complexion, who immerses himself in the world of right-wing politics in order to provide himself with "an identity." All day long, he listens to the rants of right-wing ideologues on talk radio, reads and rereads their screeds in pamphlets and books, and avidly participates in their website chat rooms. Rush emerges from this ideological bath feeling much better about himself as a committed Republican, free-marketeer, political libertarian, and sworn enemy of the welfare state, which he decries as a haven for losers and a drain on the energies of virtuous, wealthy entrepreneurs.

---

[51] J. Raz "The Relevance of Coherence," *Ethics in the Public Domain: Essays in the Morality of Law and Politics* (Oxford: Clarendon Press, 1994), 296.

[52] Scanlon, "The Aims and Authority of Moral Theory," 1–23; Brock, "Public Moral Discourse," 215–240.

[53] Raz, "The Relevance of Coherence," 317.

[54] S. Scheffler, "Individual Responsibility in a Global Age," *Boundaries and Allegiances: Problems of Justice and Responsibility in Liberal Thought* (New York: Oxford University Press, 2001), 32–47.

[55] The same reservations about coherence surface with regard to particular moral theories. One of the most coherent moral outlooks, by far, is the theory of act utilitarianism, yet this theory is regularly assailed by its many critics as overly simplistic and tolerant of immoral results.

What shall we say about Rush's worldview and his dismissal of the poor as a bunch of losers? Clearly, Rush's moral universe is exceedingly coherent. His moral, political, economic, and even artistic views all hang together quite nicely now, and his judgments about events and policy flow spontaneously from that coherent worldview. Still, many of us, even many conservatives, would probably say that Rush's moral and policy judgments are anything but morally justified. They would perhaps point to Rush's lack of intelligence, his lack of experience in the real world, and the urgency of his need for self-validation as factors vitiating the trustworthiness of his confident denunciations of the poor. Even if he has reached, within his own mind, a state of reflective equilibrium, most of us would deny that this equilibrium justifies anything about Rush's judgments. We would, for starters, recommend that he broaden his experience of the world, perhaps by joining Habitat for Humanity or the Peace Corps, and enlarge his reading list to include (at least) Charles Dickens, Victor Hugo, John Steinbeck, Frantz Fanon, and Martin Luther King Jr. Once he has exposed himself to such potentially transformative texts and experiences, he might well abandon his former beliefs; but even if he continues to embrace some version of political conservatism, his former beliefs will have been tested and transformed in the crucible of conflicting evidence. At least compared to his earlier beliefs, Rush's new beliefs will be more justified for having emerged from that crucible, even if his old web of beliefs was entirely coherent. This is where Daniels's exhortation for us to achieve coherence among the "widest possible" set of beliefs becomes absolutely crucial. Rush's judgments are not especially "considered" in the important Rawlsian sense.

But consider another case, that of Sophia, a hypothetical young woman—intelligent, well educated, widely read, well traveled, progressive, and deeply thoughtful early twentieth-century amateur eugenicist who advocates sterilization of the "unfit." Like Rush, Sophia inhabits an extremely coherent moral viewpoint. All the disparate elements of her inventory of belief—including the Bible, as she has learned to interpret it; "common sense"; the then-ascendant social Darwinist theory of political economy; and, of course, then-current theories of genetics—tell her the same thing: namely, that the white race is superior, that it is under siege, and that sterilizing the "unfit" represents the quintessence of social responsibility. In contrast to our response to Rush, it's harder to say that Sophia is intellectually dim, sheltered, badly educated, or psychologically deformed. She is, in the opinion of her contemporaries, a very serious, thoughtful, and politically progressive person. Still, most of us would now say that, in retrospect, her beliefs about sterilization were wrong and destructive, primarily because they were based upon background scientific and social theories that we now know to be empirically false. Were we to miraculously use time travel to inject our contemporary knowledge of genetics into her constellation of beliefs, Sophia would have to prune many of her considered judgments and background theories right down to their stumps.

Here we need to make an important distinction between justifying moral judgments, theories, or positions on controversial issues, on the one hand, and asking whether a given agent is justified in believing some proposition, on the other.[56] With regard to the former issue, we say that a particular judgment is justified if good and sufficient reasons can be adduced in its favor. With regard to the latter sense of justification, we can ask, as we did in Rush's case, whether a given agent is "justified" in making the claims that he does. The person needs to believe that he or she is making a judgment for good and sufficient reasons; but beyond that, he or she must engage in "due diligence" in coming to that judgment—i.e., the individual should not be guilty of negligence in his or her gathering of evidence, making inferences, and so on. Still, it's quite possible for someone to be personally justified in this way while the principle he or she advocates is (ultimately) not. For example, someone like Sophia might have applied herself assiduously to the formulation of her judgments, but factors beyond her ken—for example, subsequent progress in the science of genetics—might totally undermine her eugenic commitments.

The case of Sophia shows us, then, that even when we abstract from the question of whether *a particular agent* is epistemologically entitled to believe a proposition, we can still raise questions about the adequacy of beliefs that happen to meet the coherence criterion of justification. Thus, even supposing that Sophia had subjected her belief in eugenic sterilization to the test of maximal coherence, and even if that belief had passed the test in 1920, we would now say that it was wrong, both because it was based upon what we now know to be junk science and because we now place a much higher value on individual autonomy and bodily integrity than people did back then.

Our reflections on these two hypotheticals yield the following preliminary conclusions. First, any given agent's state of reflective equilibrium can fail to justify various elements of his moral outlook and practice if that agent is sufficiently obtuse, inexperienced, unimaginative, callous, or otherwise psychologically warped (i.e., Rush). Second, someone can possess all the requisite "epistemic virtues"—i.e., intelligence, open-mindedness, zeal in the pursuit of truth, etc.—and yet still be ultimately unjustified about some very important moral issues, such as eugenic sterilization. So even if we grant that, in cases like Sophia's, WRE can

[56] On this important distinction, see Scanlon, "Rawls on Justification," 140.

yield maximal coherence, we have to acknowledge that this is not the same thing as actually yielding ultimately justified claims.

Again, this does not amount to a refutation of WRE, just an acknowledgment of its limits. Indeed, such an acknowledgment of the finitude and provisional nature of moral judgments might well be regarded as a salutary feature of any moral methodology.

The Circularity Objection

Another major problem with coherence theories of moral justification is summed up in what I'll call the "circularity objection." According to this objection, RE yields results as reliable (or unreliable) as the considered moral judgments that get the ball rolling. As we have already seen, if we limit ourselves to the relatively narrow ambit of NRE, the problem is obvious: Considered moral judgments give rise to moral principles that "explicate" or "fit" them, yet why should we credit the moral bona fides of those considered judgments? If we cannot give a satisfactory answer to this question, we will be highly motivated to adopt WRE as our method, since it promises to advance both moral and empirical background theories to test the adequacy of our considered judgments and our principles derived from them.

Now, it won't do us much good at this juncture if the background theories deployed in WRE turn out to owe their credibility to the same considered moral sensibility that gave rise to our moral principles. That would obviously amount to question begging. So defenders of WRE must contend that the background theories they endorse, both moral and empirical, do not owe their existence or credibility to the same set of considered moral judgments as animate NRE. They must, that is, demonstrate that the considered moral judgments that ultimately give rise to various morally saturated background theories (e.g., theories of the person, of the role of morality in society, notions of procedural justice, etc.) are somehow independent of those that shaped the moral principles in NRE. Daniels calls this the "independence constraint."[57]

This is a plausible defense of WRE, and Daniels carefully works it out with his usual blend of scholarly and philosophical sophistication. There is, however, one remaining problem. Supposing that the background theories we use to discipline both our considered moral judgments and our principles all satisfy the independence constraint; suppose, in other words, that whatever moral judgments go into the development of those theories are drawn from a different set than go into the

[57] Daniels, "Wide Reflective Equilibrium and Theory Acceptance in Ethics," 260.

development of our moral principles. This would solve the circularity problem, but it remains something of a mystery how it is that the stock of our considered or "pre-theoretical" moral judgments could be compartmentalized in this way.[58] One would naturally think that *all* of our considered moral judgments would be pretty much cut from the same cloth of moral sensibility. If they are, then the circularity objection reemerges. But if they aren't, if some of our considered moral judgments can morph into background theories capable of criticizing the considered judgments that animate NRE, then we would have to explain how we are capable of generating two conflicting sets of considered moral judgments within the structure of the same moral personality, only one of which falls under the purview of NRE. It's unclear, to me at least, how this can be done. It's also unclear why this second set of considered judgments, lurking in the background until the stage of theory formation in RE, would have any greater degree of epistemic warrant than the first set that went into the formation of NRE. The fact that, as incorporated into morally informed background theories, this latter set of judgments might be used to criticize the first set does not establish that they actually provide firmer moral footing. The fact that they are different does not necessarily make them more morally trustworthy.

CONCLUSIONS

At the end of this long rumination on RE, we can draw together our conclusions. First, we can say that RE deserves its status as a *regulative ideal* for achieving ethical justification, but only on certain conditions. We are justified in our actions and beliefs to the extent that we have maximal confidence in them, and there appears to be no better way of achieving such confidence than by testing those beliefs against the widest possible set of other beliefs, including those that conflict with the belief in question. In this way, RE is clearly a powerful engine of rationality and consistency, which afford it a good measure of critical edge.

Second, we have seen, however, that even warranted confidence in a coherent system of beliefs, such as that possessed by our other hypothetical friend, Sophia—i.e., confidence *earned* through the diligent application of intelligence and moral perception to the thorough testing of all the various strata in our system of belief—we have seen that even this kind of moral justification is not enough to guarantee ultimate moral justification. Sophia was hypothetically well brought up, smart, and progressive, and she conscientiously tested her beliefs against the best

[58] Haslett, "What Is Wrong with Reflective Equilibria?," 310.

that contemporary religion, genetics, and social science had to offer. Although many of us might perhaps still fault her for a lack of empathy for the victims of involuntary sterilization, she could make a strong case that her belief system was justified (because maximally coherent) even though its scientific bases were later shown to be manifestly false. So even though the process of RE at its very best can promise ethical justification as a regulative ideal, we should not mistake this for a promise of ethical justification at any given moment, let alone for a promise of stable moral certitude.

Our third conclusion has been that *wide* RE is an unattainable ideal, especially in practical contexts, and that both its requirements (e.g., the critical evaluation of all live options in moral and social theory) and its putatively global scope will have to be significantly scaled back before this method can achieve traction in an area like bioethics. If we take seriously the suggestion developed earlier that the most we are likely to get is local, rather than global, coherence, then WRE, at least in its most ambitious global form, is not even a necessary condition for moral justification in the personal sense.

Finally, our fourth conclusion is that even if WRE, properly hedged, can serve as a regulative ideal of ethical justification, we should not expect it to deliver intersubjective convergence around particular moral judgments bearing on actions and policies. As we have seen, the fact of ethical, cultural, and religious pluralism within contemporary cosmopolitan societies will ensure a broad multiplicity of reflective equilibria bearing on bioethical questions. Each of these differing sets of belief in equilibrium will be shaped by differing respective visions of the good belonging to the agents in question. So even though we can reasonably expect WRE to have some salutary potential for rendering our beliefs more justifiable, and even though WRE practiced on the societal level might be helpful in bringing the disparate members of society together on some issues and reducing the differences among them, we should not expect this method to deliver intersubjective agreement on most bioethical controversies.

9

Concluding Reflections

METHOD IN BIOETHICS—THE VERY IDEA

WHERE WE'VE BEEN—PROS AND CONS

At the end of this long and winding road, mapping and critically ruminating on the ways we reason now, it's time to take stock and attempt to offer some general conclusions. Each preceding chapter can be summarized at the highest (and least helpful) level of abstraction as an exercise in dialectical thinking, always concluding "Yes, but. . . ." Before moving to deeper questions about the whole point of thinking about methods of ethics, it might be useful to review here some of the most significant "Yeses" and "Buts" we've encountered so far.

Principlism

The principlism of Beauchamp and Childress obviously has a lot going for it, both in terms of its formative influence on the developing field of bioethics and in terms of its substantive contributions to methodology. With regard to influence, principlism provided the field with an ethical framework suitable for public bioethics within a pluralistic, democratic society. This framework developed over time to incorporate the helpful criticisms of partisans of rival methodologies, resulting is a much richer synthesis encompassing contributions of feminists, narrativists, casuists, pragmatists, and many others. Interpreted (correctly) as a *framework* for moral deliberation and justification, as opposed to an algorithm susceptible to more or less mechanical application, principlism has made major contributions to the field. On the other hand, many enthusiasts of principlism did tend to naively apply the "Georgetown mantra" in an unreflective and ultimately indefensible manner.

On a more philosophical plane, principlism has provided a robust and highly plausible defense of the role of moral principles in ethics, providing a salutary corrective, in my view, to some versions of moral particularism. Beauchamp and Childress's eventual embrace of reflective equilibrium as *the* appropriate method of bioethics had the advantage of significantly expanding the inventory of sources of moral justification to include, *inter alia*, our most confidently held moral intuitions, principles, and background theories of morality, society, and personhood in a never-ending dialectic of justification. On the other hand, the inclusion of all these additional elements in their expansive account of reflective equilibrium signaled the end of principlism as we had heretofore known it—i.e., as a distinct method of moral thought that gave priority to principles over intuitions and moral–social theories.

The principlism of Beauchamp and Childress also advanced our thinking about the ultimate sources of moral justification. In earlier editions of their *Principles of Biomedical Ethics* (*PBE*), our authors located ultimate justification of our case judgments in high-level moral theory; in later editions they relocated the ultimate source of justification to their version of a "common morality." In view of seemingly intractable disagreements at the level of high theory, the grounding of bioethics in a pre-theoretical common morality was a good move. On the other hand, their claim that this common morality could serve as an ultimate foundation for all subsequent moral reasoning via reflective equilibrium appears, at least to me, as an ad hoc dispensation of common morality from the perpetual, foundationless dialectic of reflective equilibrium.

Casuistry and Narrative Ethics

As we have seen, the casuistry of Albert Jonsen and Stephen Toulmin provided a necessary corrective to the initially top-down direction of moral reasoning under early versions of *PBE*. They stressed the importance of paradigm cases and analogical reasoning in practical ethics, in contrast to the alleged deductivism and abstractness of early versions of principlism. Along with the contributions of "narrative ethics" and feminism, this kind of casuistry enriched bioethics with its emphasis on concrete detail—on the what, when, who, how, and how much—and its highly plausible account, both descriptive and normative, of how we actually reason our way through moral problems. Like Molière's M. Jourdain, who comically discovered with the help of a tutor that he'd been "speaking prose all his life," readers of Jonsen and Toulmin realized that they'd been casuists all along, thus breaking the spell of principlism and its early emphasis on top-down reasoning.

For their part, narrativists and feminists enriched a principle-driven bioethics by stressing the importance of concrete detail, relationships, the arc of each patient's (and family's) story, and the relevance of power relations to bioethics. To paraphrase Kant, these rival, more particularistic methodologies forcefully drove home the message that without principles ethics may indeed be blind, but without casuistical and narrative detail, ethics is empty.

The downside of these more particularistic methods has been their tendency to push their particularism too far. For example, in early statements of their casuistry, Jonsen and Toulmin appeared ready to do entirely without moral principles, which made it difficult for them to explain exactly what constituted a paradigm case. In later iterations, Jonsen stressed that he saw casuistry as an adjunct to principlism, and not as a replacement; and he defined paradigm cases as those that most powerfully embodied and expressed a moral principle.

Narrativists have faced similar problems. Although their emphasis on the narrative elements of case construction has been instructive and fruitful, their attempts to find ultimate normative significance in story telling—to base ethics on stories—have been less successful. The question that ultimately plagues such particularistic approaches remains: "nice story, but so what?"

Another problem with casuistry, as we've seen, is the tendency of a more or less exclusive focus on the analogical connections between the present case and past paradigm cases to ignore other important factors, such as the likely social consequences of norms that might make sense in theory but could lead to very unfortunate results when deployed in our fragmented and unjust society. The analogically driven case for a constitutional right to physician-assisted suicide is a telling example of this tendency to ignore the real-world policy implications of abstract rights.

Pragmatism

The above tripartite account of pragmatism, and especially the ethical reflections of James and Dewey, provides much food for methodological moral thought. In particular, there is much to admire in the pragmatist approach to moral principles, which views them as practical and flexible tools for resolving concrete moral problems. Instead of viewing moral principles as timeless norms stored in and retrieved from some celestial vault, the pragmatists view principles as finite, human creations designed to solve various ubiquitous problems in group living, such as violence, free riding, and inattention to the needs of others.

In my view, pragmatism is perhaps most instructive as an account of the origins and nature of ethics.[1] Instead of viewing ethics as necessarily tethered to some (illusory) transcendent realm of being and value, the pragmatists view ethics as an entirely natural phenomenon having no need whatever of religious or transcendent grounding. They've certainly gotten that right.

A pragmatist approach to morality also places a salutary emphasis on the consequences of adopting and deploying various moral norms. There has been a tendency within mainstream bioethics to spend most of our time trying to articulate and defend the right principles and their proper interpretation. A good example of this mindset is the vast literature on living wills and norms governing the foregoing of life-sustaining medical treatments. The rise of a pragmatically oriented empirical strain of bioethics has provided a salutary corrective to armchair speculations about death and dying. The take-home message of this literature has been that, in addition to theoretical inquiries into patients' rights and competing standards for foregoing life-sustaining treatments, we also need careful empirical studies that show whether such norms and the policies based upon them actually accomplish their objectives. Do such policies—such as an emphasis on living wills—actually work? And if not, what concrete approaches might stand a better chance of succeeding? At the end of the day, bioethical theorizing should lend itself to constructive professional behaviors and social policy through an iterative and self-correcting process of rational inquiry.

As a theory of substantive ethical norms, however, pragmatism suffers from a pervasive vagueness that makes it an unreliable guide to practical decision making. Whether we resort to Richard Rorty's postmodern advice to advance those ethical values and goals "that work for us," or the advice of John Dewey to pursue actions and policies that best promote individual and social "growth," providing action-guiding content to such notions of "working" and "growth" may well prove to be either too difficult, given the vagueness of such concepts, or too easy, in view of their ability to justify a broad range of mutually incompatible policies and behaviors.

Reflective Equilibrium

Finally, we come to the method of reflective equilibrium, which sprang from the pen of John Rawls in the early 1970s as a method of political theorizing, and was

[1] For an excellent recent pragmatic account of the origins and overall trajectory of ethics, see P. Kitcher, *The Ethical Project* (Cambridge, MA: Harvard University Press, 2014). See also his equally excellent, but shorter *Life After Faith: The Case for Secular Humanism* (New Haven, CT: Yale University Press, 2014).

popularized in the late 1980s via the embrace of Beauchamp and Childress as a method for bioethics, incorporating both their early and their abiding emphasis on principles and the insights of competing methodologies, such as casuistry, narrative, feminism, and pragmatism. Reflective equilibrium (RE) as a method of justification attempts to bring all relevant moral data into a relatively stable and coherent body of intuitions, principles, and background theories. Justification is achieved not by being grounded in some solid, unrevisable, foundational bedrock but, rather, through the harmonious meshing of all the disparate elements that constitute the flotsam and jetsam of our moral deliberations.

On the positive side of the methodological ledger, reflective equilibrium stands out as the most comprehensive and rational approach to moral justification that we can imagine. Suppose a moral reasoner discerns something missing from an assemblage of harmonious intuitions, principles, and background theories; this counts not as a strike against RE but, rather, as a reason to add that missing element to the mix. Doing so might mean that we will need to readjust some existing elements—deflate an intuition, trim a principle, etc.—but that's precisely how RE is supposed to work. Another way of putting this is to say that RE is quite simply the last method standing; it is the only fully reasonable alternative in the methodological toolkit. It owes this status to the fact that it has absorbed all the other methods we have canvassed into one massive network of interacting moral norms. "You gotta problem? Well, let's just add it to the mix."

On the negative side, we've seen that, in order to avoid the serious problems associated with narrow RE—i.e., an equilibrium narrowly focused on intuitions and their justifying principles—the advocates of RE dramatically broadened the purview of this approach by including background theories designed to guard against the potential bias and provincialism of theories consisting of merely refined moral intuitions. These background norms include not only various theories bearing on the nature of social institutions but also the full gamut of moral theories, such as utilitarianism, Kantian deontology, Aristotelian perfectionism, and virtue ethics. As I noted in chapter 8, sifting through and selecting favored theories from among this welter of possibilities might constitute a morning's work for a super-human theorist like Ronald Dworkin's fictional judge Hercules, but it would require a lifetime of hard work for any ordinary, genetically unmodified human. The result is that RE in its more ambitiously wide incarnation (WRE) begins to look more and more like an unattainable, perpetually receding ideal of reason rather than a method for bioethicists to practice in the clinic and corridors of policymaking. Not to put too fine a point on it, telling people to rationally assess all the live options in moral theory, moral principles, and moral intuitions prior to coming to judgment hardly looks like a *method* at all! And even if we grant this approach the honorific status of a method, it is wildly unrealistic to expect that in contemporary contexts of moral pluralism, it might someday yield sufficiently specific, action-guiding conclusions upon which all, or most, people of good will can agree. In other words, in its wide, hyper-ambitious incarnation, WRE is a method that fails to measure up to one putative goal of any self-respecting method: *viz.*, to bring its various practitioners into agreement.[2]

WHAT'S THE POINT?

At the end of this long and complicated rumination on the various "ways we reason now" in the field of bioethics and other ventures in practical ethics, we come to the ultimate question: What's the point of fretting over method?[3] As we have seen, many have conceived this debate as a contest for methodological supremacy. To paraphrase Tolkien, there must be one method to rule them all. I believe that some degree of methodological reflection is both unavoidable and salutary, but that the search for a single "best method" is a misguided enterprise. To my mind, the interesting question is not "Which method?" but, rather, "What does self-consciousness about method contribute to practical ethics?" Our analyses of these various methods have yielded many fruitful insights about their respective strengths, but also, importantly, about their respective weaknesses. The failure to discover or vindicate a single superior method for practical ethics, or a way to choose among alternative methods with reasonable certitude, might seem to suggest that it is not worth even thinking about methodology in this field of inquiry.

As we have seen, the unspoken assumption behind many appeals to method in various disciplines and practices is that following all the prescribed steps will at least make it more likely we will reach correct results. At its most daring, some might say presumptuous, this assumption amounts to the claim that just about anybody can reach the correct result, just so long as he or she adheres to the proper method. In the domain of morality this would mean that no matter who employs it, a method of ethical reflection can be counted upon to lead the inquirer to moral justification and truth.

---

[2] Of course, it might well be unrealistic to expect any method to be up to this challenge.

[3] This section is based on a paper co-written with Howard Brody, "Methods of Practical Ethics," in *International Encyclopedia of Ethics*, ed. Hugh LaFollette (New York: Wiley-Blackwell, 2013). Howard graciously stepped in to finish this article in time while I was recuperating from illness. If the reader notices a bump-up in quality, this is the reason.

The *locus classicus* of this traditional approach to method is Rene Descartes's *Discourse on Method*.[4] To simplify his thought greatly, Descartes sought to avoid the jumble of contradictory opinions he attributed to earlier philosophies by devising a method that could supposedly guarantee a path to truth and certainty—a path that he felt sure lay with reducing problems to their simplest elements, which then provided the raw material for a rational reconstruction. In the process of reduction and reconstruction, Descartes came to view most particular facts about the world as potential distractions, distortions, and snares rather than as sources of illumination.

If the project of thinking critically about method actually harbors the Cartesian assumption about the power and possibilities of method, then we should abandon that assumption. It is highly unlikely that method can live up to this billing anywhere other than in mathematics and the physical sciences, if even there.[5] If we continue to speak of *method* in the area of moral philosophy and practical ethics, we will have to considerably lower our expectations.

Philosophers like Richard Rorty suggest that in place of the Cartesian agenda, practical ethics would do best with a humble aim of muddling through as best as it can with the means at hand within our cultural and historical context, giving up any claims for universality in ethical judgment. It is false, Rorty would insist, to assume that the *only* way to avoid ad hoc and self-serving ethical solutions (a goal on which we can all agree) is to return to the Cartesian agenda. This plausible observation, unfortunately, tells us little about what means of muddling through are better than others, and what approaches best do justice to our cultural and historical context, given that both culture and history are moving targets.

To pursue the better rather than the worse ways to do practical ethics, even when the ideal way eludes us, seems to require some degree of reflection about methods. As tempting as it may be to say, "Why bother? Just do it," we actually have only two choices: to employ either examined or unexamined methods. If the unexamined life is not worth living, as Socrates famously declared, then guiding our thoughts by unexamined methods could be equally worthless, or at least highly problematic. Just as Thomas Kuhn noted long ago that the physical observations of scientists are shot through with theoretical presuppositions,[6] so too we can say that our day-to-day ruminations about bioethical problems are often heavily laden with methodological preconceptions. If we just plunge into the thicket of moral

---

[4] Réné Descartes, *Le Discours de la Méthode*, in *Oeuvres Philosophiques*, Tome I, ed. F. Alquié (Paris: Garnier, 1963). (Another tip of the hat to a former professor at the Sorbonne, Ferdinand Alquié—a small posthumous repayment of a big debt.)

[5] P. Feyerabend, *Against Method*, 4th ed. (London: Verso, 2010).

[6] T. Kuhn, *The Structure of Scientific Revolutions* (Chicago: University of Chicago Press, 1962).

deliberation without giving any thought to the tools we are using, we are unlikely to be aware of their respective advantages and disadvantages. Given the ubiquity of principlist and narrative forms of reasoning in the literature, for example, unreflective commentators might be unaware that principlism and stories can seem to be as natural as the air we breathe while at the same time harboring some serious drawbacks and limitations in certain contexts.

Given the above alternatives, examined methods seem preferable. Practical ethicists can make many highly pertinent distinctions and propose a variety of systematic ways to approach cases, even without relying exclusively on mid-level principles and general theories. The development of stakeholder theory in business ethics might serve as one example of a helpful methodological advance of this sort.[7]

Appropriate humility about what method can accomplish for us aids this practical level of inquiry. Instead of imagining that method can provide some sort of foolproof algorithm by means of which anyone who studies it can arrive at moral truth, we should instead see method as something that can help to launch us in promising directions for thinking about practical moral problems in better ways and with improved insight. If we set out in search of the Holy Grail of method in the former sense, we will probably reject out of hand modest methodological advances that bring incremental improvements in our ethical discernment, only to discover at the end of the trail that the Grail is unattainable.

The earlier discussion listing the pros and cons attributed to the various possible methods of practical ethics suggests a way forward toward this more humble but ultimately more practical and helpful way of thinking about method. To return to the metaphor of tools in the workshop, we have now seen both a list of available tools and a set of detailed arguments as to what each might be good and not good for. Imagine that we were to follow up this exercise by compiling a detailed typology of case studies in any given field of practical ethics, trying to match the strengths and weaknesses of each tool with the features of that case which might help determine whether that tool would or would not be useful in understanding the case's ethical intricacies. Ultimately, again without any assurances of truth or infallibility, one might achieve a much better idea of how to think about a new case that presents itself in the future. I hereby bequeath this daunting methodological inquiry to those who might follow in my faint footsteps before they disappear in the sand.

---

[7] E. Freeman, *Strategic Management: A Stakeholder Approach* (Boston: Pitman, 1984).

Modesty about what method can and cannot achieve is also helpful in discerning important constituents of moral thought that have little to do with method. As I noted in my discussion of RE, it is certainly important to try to get the various sectors of our moral world to fit together into as coherent a whole as possible, but it is equally if not more important to try to improve our capacity for making sensitive and discriminating moral judgments. As philosopher Michael De Paul puts it, tweaking what he takes to be the intellectualist-scientistic pretensions of RE, we need to spend equal if not more time attempting to refine the measuring instrument itself—i.e., our own sensibility as moral agents.[8] Thus, he suggests that we need to focus more on developing the inquirer's capacity for making discriminating moral judgments, rather than merely tidying up and systematizing whatever judgments this capacity happens to turn out.

If De Paul is right about this, then our efforts to formulate the best method would need to be supplemented by traditional Aristotelian concerns about character formation and training in virtue. Were we to go this route, then the cultivation of good judgment would share center stage with the cultivation of consistency and coherence; and formative works of art, such as novels and films, would assume much greater importance both in moral education and in our quest to improve the output and reliability of our ethical methods.[9]

A final reason for practical ethics to be reflective about its own methods lies in its contributions to the larger enterprise of philosophical ethics. Toulmin, in a classic paper in bioethics, ruminated on "How Medicine Saved the Life of Ethics."[10] He claimed that philosophical ethics, by focusing exclusively on metatheory, had in the middle of the twentieth century become increasingly irrelevant to practical affairs and, as a result, intellectually sterile. The renewed interest in practical ethics came at exactly the right time to inject a much-needed dose of practical concerns into ethics, enriching and enlivening the entire field, even for those philosophers interested primarily in ethical theory. On this account, if practical ethics fails to think carefully about its methods, it will miss major opportunities to contribute to the larger ethical enterprise, as well as compromising its own effectiveness.

[8] M. De Paul, *Balance and Refinement: Beyond Coherence Methods of Moral Inquiry* (New York: Routledge, 1993).

[9] See also M. Nussbaum, *Love's Knowledge: Essays on Philosophy and Literature* (New York: Oxford University Press, 1992).

[10] S. Toulmin, "How Medicine Saved the Life of Ethics," *Perspectives in Biology and Medicine* 25, no. 4 (1982): 736–750.

INDEX